Politics and Public Debt

The Dominion, the Banks and Alberta's Social Credit

The Bank of Canada's first governor, Graham Ford Towers, 1935.
Photograph by Yousef Karsh. National Archives of Canada,
Yousef Karsh collection, Acc. No. 1987–054, Item 2126–1.

POLITICS AND PUBLIC DEBT

THE DOMINION, THE BANKS AND ALBERTA'S SOCIAL CREDIT

Robert L. Ascah

The University of Alberta Press

Published by

The University of Alberta Press
Athabasca Hall
Edmonton, Alberta, Canada T6G 2E8

Copyright © Robert L. Ascah 1999

ISBN 0-88864-306-3

Canadian Cataloguing in Publication Data

Ascah, Robert L. (Robert Laurence), 1954–
  Politics and public debt

Includes bibliographical references and index.
ISBN 0-88864-306-3

  1. Debts, Public—Canada. 2. Canada—Economic conditions—1918–1945. 3. Canada—Economic conditions—1945–1971.* 4. Canada—Politics and government—1930–1935.* 5. Canada—Politics and government—1935–1957.* 6. Alberta—Economic conditions—1905–1945.* I. Title.
    HJ8513.A82 1998   336.3'6'0971   C98-910779-5

All rights reserved.

No part of this publication may be produced, stored in a retrieval system, or transmitted in any forms or by any means, electronic, mechanical, photocopying, recording, or otherwise, without the prior permission of the copyright owner.

Printed on acid-free paper. ∞

Printed and bound in Canada.

Printed by Hignell Book Printing Ltd., Winnipeg, Manitoba, Canada.

The University of Alberta Press gratefully acknowledges the support received for its publishing program from The Canada Council for the Arts. In addition, we also gratefully acknowledge the financial support of the Government of Canada through the Book Publishing Industry Development Program for our publishing activities.

The Canada Council | Le Conseil des Arts
for the Arts | du Canada
since 1957 | depuis 1957

Canadä

Contents

Charts and Tables — vi
Acknowledgements — vii
Foreword by Paul Boothe — ix
Preface — xi

1. Public Debt and Debt Management — 1
2. Capital Markets and the Players — 13
3. Political Uncertainty and New Institutional Arrangements, 1930–1939 — 31
4. The Alberta Default and Its Impact on the Dominion's Credit — 53
5. Broadening the Ownership of the Debt and Bank Resistance, 1935–1939 — 81
6. Wartime: Conscription of Capital If Necessary, But Not Necessarily Conscription, 1940–1945 — 95
7. Attempts to Keep Faith with Bondholders, 1945–1952 — 117
8. Politics, Public Debt and Debt Management — 133

Appendices

Appendix A	Synopsis of Major Domestic Borrowing, 1930–1952	146
Appendix B	Synopsis of Dominion Loans Issued Abroad, 1930–1950	148
Appendix C	Credit Rating of the Dominion of Canada and Selected Provincial Governments: Moody's Investors Service, 1930 through to 1953	149
Appendix D	Government of Canada Bond Yields, 1930–1939	150
Appendix E	Government of Canada Bond Yields, 1940–1945	151
Appendix F	Government of Canada Bond Yields, 1946–1952	152

Notes — 153
Bibliography — 185
Index — 199

Charts and Tables

Chart 1.1	Distribution of debt by currency of issue: 1900–1952	5
Table 1.1	Dominion of Canada funded direct and guaranteed debt at March 31, 1930	7
Chart 1.2	Direct funded debt and average interest rate: 1930–1952	8
Chart 1.3	Term to maturity of funded debt at March 31, 1930	9
Chart 1.4	Distribution of public debt: 1938–1950	10
Chart 2.1	Sale of Canadian bonds by issuer: 1928–1952	27
Chart 3.1	GDP and unemployment rate: 1930–1939	35
Table 3.1	Provincial government debt, January 1, 1938 by currency of issue	37
Table 3.2	Provincial governments—Gross Debt Charges	38
Table 3.3	May 1931 conversion loan	44
Chart 4.1	Farm receipts and provincial income—Alberta	55
Chart 4.2	Alberta's public finances, 1926–1937	57
Table 4.1	Province of Alberta public debt as at March 31, 1936	59
Chart 6.1	Victory loan campaigns	107
Chart 7.1	Canadian/U.S. exchange rate, 1939–1951	125

Acknowledgements

Without the Encouragement of Professor Paul Boothe of the Department of Economics at the University of Alberta my study on politics, public debt and debt management in Canada would not have been developed into this book. His research on the early fiscal history of the Province of Alberta brought him to read much of what follows.

I have fond memories of my research time at both The Bank of Nova Scotia Archives in Toronto and the Bank of Canada Archives in Ottawa. Jane Nokes at ScotiaBank and Jane Witty of "The Bank" were always courteous and supportive in locating material and reviewing the appropriate references and text of the quotations used. In revising my dissertation for publication, I have also had the assistance of Corrine Millar of the Bank of Canada Archives and Matt Szybalski of the Bank of Nova Scotia Archives.

During my time in Ottawa, I had the great pleasure to meet the late Ralph McKibben who served as deputy governor of the Bank of Canada. Mr. McKibben was an invaluable source of information and perspective in giving context to the period under consideration. The late George Watts, also a former senior officer with the Bank of Canada, was extremely helpful in discussing some of the files routed out of the Public Archives (now the National Archives of Canada) and the Bank of Canada. Alec Keith, who was the Bank of Canada's senior representative in Edmonton during the time I embarked on my research, was generous in arranging interviews and explaining the nuances of central bank's cash management to an uninitiated political scientist. I would also like to thank Nigil Gunn of Bell Gouinlock whose sense of humour and remarkable recall of events in the 1930s gave this fascinating period in Canada's financial history excitement and life.

I would also like to acknowledge the assistance of the anonymous reviewers whose suggestions on organization have been invaluable in clarifying the intent and themes of the book. In addition the professional editorial and production support of Mary Mahoney-Robson at the University of Alberta Press was critical in the final stages of this project.

This book has been published with the help of a grant from the Humanities and Social Sciences Federation of Canada, using funds provided by the Social Sciences and Humanities Research Council of Canada. The support of the Aid to Scholarly Publications Programme is gratefully acknowledged especially the encouragement of Dr. Michael Carley, the program's former director.

The Institute for Public Economics at the University of Alberta also provided additional funding and resources toward the publication of this study. The Institute's mission is to, through research and teaching, create and disseminate knowledge of the public sector and its influence on the economy and society.

It is somewhat difficult to understand why writing a book based on a completed dissertation would be more difficult and time consuming than completing the doctoral requirement. My usual approach to these things is to throw as much energy into the project and then, hopefully, to glide it to a "perfect" landing. As my wife, Linda, kept reminding me, perfectibility and writing books are *not* compatible. Consistent with that wisdom, the loss of my full text in the computer was one of the several setbacks that forcibly revealed this truth. Linda's willingness to give me time to plug away at the book, while she looked after our daughter Rachel, was critical to the completion of this book and is deeply appreciated.

Foreword

In 1992, I attended a lecture by Professor John McCallum at the C.D. Howe Institute. McCallum was talking about the economic consequences of Quebec separation and the audience included a number of Canada's captains of industry. In the question period following the lecture, the discussion touched on the issue of government debt default and I was astonished to hear a leading member of Canada's financial community boldly assert that no province had ever defaulted on its debt.

Two thoughts immediately sprang to mind. The first was the famous quotation by Spanish philosopher George Santayana: "Those who cannot remember the past are condemned to repeat it." The second was the pressing need for someone to set down on paper the story of government debt in Canada, and, in particular, the amazing events surrounding the default of the Government of Alberta under Premier Aberhart.

Robert Ascah's book fills that need admirably. Through a tremendous effort of scholarship, the author takes us beyond the facts and figures into the paneled board rooms to meet Bill Aberhart, R.B. Bennett, Graham Towers and Clifford Clark. One can almost imagine the smell of cigar smoke and the taste of after-dinner port as bankers denounce the cancer of Social Credit and describe how it imperils the very foundations of western civilization, not to mention the dividends of their shareholders. In the hours before the default, the clock can be heard ticking and one can almost feel the nervous tension as Aberhart and his officials wait for the federal reprieve that never comes.

This is a story that cries out to be told, and Robert Ascah has done us a great service in bringing alive this little-known, but critical chapter of our history. His account of this period helps us to see how the economics and politics of government debt shaped the development of our country and brought us to where we are today. Throughout the 1990s, issues of government debt—both federal and provincial—have dominated Canada's political agenda. Reading this book gives us a new perspective with which to understand the events of the last decade, as well as some valuable lessons about the interface between politics and finance. With these lessons in mind, perhaps we will be able to avoid the fate of those who forget their history. I hope so.

PAUL BOOTHE

Preface

My interest in the study of public finance began in the mid-1970s while I was a junior auditor with the Office of the Auditor General of Canada. It was during this period that the beginning of the public debt build-up began. Between 1945 and 1975, federal public debt had grown negligibly, and, as a percentage of gross domestic product, the public debt was a mere blip on the radar scene of Canadian public finance. This would soon change and with it the character of the debate on public debt. But this debate did not really commence for another decade. What tweaked my intellectual interest in the subject was the near religious views of economists that the public debt was *not* an issue. In fact, in those days there seemed to be a view that public debts hardly mattered at all.

When I began my research on politics, public debt and debt management in the early 1980s, I found a general indifference or bemusement about the subject of public debt and a lack of questioning as to the implications of growing debt on the political system. The issue was, and remains today, largely a nonissue for political scientists, with certain exceptions.[1] With the stratospheric interest rates witnessed in the early 1980s and stratospheric deficits arising from the "Volcker induced" recession, seminars on government deficits and debts became fashionable. During the early to mid 1980s academic opinion tended to be divided whereas the opinion of the financial press and most business economists was almost universal in condemning the continuing failure of the federal government to rein in their deficits.[2]

By the early 1990s, the issue of public debts and deficits was no longer a matter for government technicians and investment bankers, the subject was now on the top of every government's agenda in this country.

By 1994, Canadian taxpayers and Canadian and foreign financial communities had finally discovered the magnitude and policy implications of the federal and provincial governments' deficits and accumulated debts. At that time, one frequently heard utterances from "think tanks," provincial politicians and officials that federal and provincial deficits were reaching "crisis" proportions.[3] In March, 1993 Premier Clyde Wells of Newfoundland spoke of the need for managing provincial finances "in a manner *that will not jeopardize our credit rating.*"[4] That April the International Monetary Fund warned that Canadian governments' deficits will push Canada's external debts "to levels that could have increasingly negative effects on market conditions."[5] In the fall of 1993, it was also reported that federal officials were quietly canvassing the country's financial community about contingency plans for provinces in the event that they could no longer refinance their maturing debt.[6]

In December 1993, comments attributed to a senior official of Standard & Poor's suggested that "tough measures" by the provinces were needed to avoid a downgrading.[7] In February 1995, a few weeks before the federal government's budget was to be introduced, Moody's Investors Services announced that it had put the Government of Canada's debt on review for a possible downgrade, a downgrade which was confirmed that April.[8] During that 1994–95 period, similar reports, which would have been unthinkable a decade before, discussed openly stories about foreign investment counsel recommending to their well-heeled clients reductions in their "exposure" to Canada.

During the period from 1982 to May 1998, credit rating agencies (Moody's, Standard & Poor's, Canadian Bond Rating Service, and Dominion Bond Rating Service) downgraded the provinces' ratings 65 times with upgrades occurring 14 times. From 1993 until 1998, the Government of Canada had been downgraded at least once by major agencies and twice in the case of Moody's. At present, there are no provincial credits that enjoy the coveted triple "A" rating and the federal government's foreign debt is not rated "AAA" by *any* major Canadian and U.S. rating agencies. Clearly government policy-makers are coming under increasing pressure from the media and financial community to do something about the rising public debt.

The emergence of deficit reduction and debt repayment in the mid to late 1990s illustrates the impact of capital markets on government policies. The resistance of finance capital to the financing of ever-expanding public debt by raising the cost of borrowing to governments accounts in significant measure for the emergence of the "neo-conservative," market-based fiscal and economic policies.

Most recently, a "consensus" has emerged amongst Canada's economists to the effect that the "debt crisis" is over and a "virtuous cycle" of debt repayment is about to occur at the federal level. This optimism is in my view is premature for several reasons. Firstly, only recently has the debt as a percentage of Gross

Domestic Product (GDP) begun to fall. Secondly, in 1998, Canada is experiencing its sixth year of economic expansion—a recession is likely to occur in the next two or three years that will negatively affect expected government surpluses. Thirdly, economists often fail to account for the impact of political expediency that tends to limit a government's opportunities to significantly reduce debt. Related to this is the absence of any meaningful statutory limitations federally that require balanced budgets and debt repayment. It is this author's contention that when the next recession hits there will be another crisis over public debt and interest rates that will bring to the fore the tension between democratic control over the banking system and finance capital's influence upon democratically elected governments.[9]

The deficit and debt reduction that has been achieved over the past three years at the federal and provincial levels (with the arguable exception of British Columbia, Ontario and Quebec) illustrate the influence of finance capital over fiscal and economic policy-making. The federal cutbacks to provincial transfer payments and provincial cutbacks to municipalities, schools, hospitals and social assistance recipients, as well as the ideological drive to lower taxes, are all a testament to the serious consequences of high levels of indebtedness. Indeed, in Alberta, the crusade of Ralph Klein's government was very much premised on the notion that government, like a household, had to keep its deficit and debt under control or it too would go bankrupt. This fundamental issue is central to the book's exploration of the financial crisis arising from the election of the Social Credit Party in 1935.

One of the most interesting observations arising from research into Alberta's fiscal history is an astounding absence of knowledge about the 1936 default. Indeed, during my employment with the Treasury Department in the mid 1980s, when the Province began to borrow abroad, the fact of the default required disclosure and very few Treasury managers were aware of this episode. It is as if this failure to honour obligations has either been lost or selectively forgotten in Alberta's history.

Politics and Public Debt attempts, through the window of history, to examine the interaction of politics and capital markets from the perspective of the debt management function. Why should political scientists be interested in public debt and debt management? This book answers that question by asking a series of questions such as "who holds the debt?" If holdings of public debt are concentrated, do these holders have influence over a government's financial and economic policy-making? While this book addresses these "political" questions, it is also hoped that this historical account will be of interest to economists, political scientists, bankers, investment dealers, credit analysts, institutional investors and historians.

Structure of the Study

The book is based on my Ph.D. dissertation completed at the University of Alberta in the fall of 1983 under the direction of Professor Garth Stevenson. In light of current events, the dissertation has been considerably rewritten with a focus on the critical debt management issues for the Dominion government during the 1930–1952 period. Given the significance of Canada's debt situation today, the concluding chapter comments on some of the important lessons to be drawn from the study that may be relevant for contemporary policy-makers and capital markets participants.

This book asks "do public debts, particularly rising public debts, matter?" by examining the interaction between politics and financial markets through the debt management function. It covers two periods of acute social, political and economic turmoil, the Depression and World War II (1930-1945) and a period of relative economic and political stability, the post-war years (1946-1952).

My study begins with a definition of debt management, objectives and constraints guiding the debt manager, and a summary of the changing character of the Dominion's debt immediately before and during the period under study. To frame the discussion of the debt management process the key figures involved in the debt management function are described in the second chapter, "Capital Markets and the Players." In the chapters following, key issues, objectives and constraints relating to the debt management process are examined. As will be shown, each subperiod is unique insofar as the issues facing the debt manager.

The time period selected—1930 to 1952—was chosen for specific reasons. Firstly, fuller access to archival records is an essential source in comprehending the actions of the players. Secondly, this period is a time of remarkable change (depression, war and reconstruction) and one of severe financial challenges to governments. Thus, this period offers an interesting precedent as Canadian governments face significant fiscal challenges today.

Finally, any "facts required to be stated or any facts omitted that are necessary to make the statements and analysis herein not materially misleading" are those of the author's alone. For those with comments on the book, please write me on INTERNET— rlascah@planet.eon.net.

1 | Public Debt and Debt Management

According to J.M. Keynes, the "permanent relations between debtors and creditors...form the ultimate foundation of capitalism."[1] Exploring the central factors that influence the prices for government bonds and deviations from this relatively stable set of "permanent relations between debtors and creditors" makes these "permanent relations" more intelligible.

To understand the nature of debt management, its legal aspects must be understood. Debts are legal obligations between a debtor and a creditor. Debts imply that a *trust* has been bestowed by the creditor upon the debtor, that is, the borrower will repay interest and principal in a timely fashion. Viewed in these terms, debts of the state are conceptually no different from debts of an ordinary individual. Nevertheless financial arrangements between the Dominion government as borrower and public creditors, such as banks and insurers, are more complicated due to the government power to legislate, to tax, to create legal tender, regulate banking and to expropriate property. Still, a creditor holds a promise to repay and by threatening to withhold further loans, that may influence the actions of debtors. Heavy indebtedness, the enforcement of security arrangements, and the withholding of new credit may all give creditors the opportunity to exert influence on the policies of the Dominion government.

Canada's early economic development and its evolution from a colony to an independent Dominion depended on the provision of loans by London. Indeed, Canada's greatest economic historian, Harold Innis regarded Confederation as a "credit instrument."[2] The *British North America Act, 1867*, devoted considerable attention to the disposition of public debts of the former colonies.[3] Tom Naylor in his colourful history of Canadian business claimed that the only thing that the Canadian colonies had in common were their debts to the Baring Brothers.[4]

United Kingdom investors and institutions loaned heavily to colonial and provincial administrations and to the Dominion government and private corporations (often with a governmental guarantee) to finance canal and railroad construction. This debtor-creditor relationship was vitally important and its modalities depended largely upon Canada's population growth, its economic development, and the export price of raw materials with which it earned foreign exchange to pay interest and retire principal.

Debt Management

Debt management is a complex governmental function possessing its own vocabulary, culture and community. Sound debt management depends upon an intelligent reading of capital and money market movements, an extensive network of contacts on the "street" (a street which is increasingly international in scope) and that elusive and priceless asset, "good judgment." Debt management is a decision-making process based on policies (e.g., borrow "long" or "short") and on judgments. Debt management includes the following functions: (1) advising the borrower (the minister of Finance) on the terms, conditions, timing and size of a new offering; (2) changing the term structure of the debt outstanding in the hands of the public by buying and selling securities on the government's own account (e.g., as "principal"); (3) maintaining data on outstanding direct and guaranteed debt; and (4) carrying out related administrative tasks (e.g., legal documentation, fiscal and paying agency arrangements, securities registers, cancellation and destruction of securities).[5] In Canada, the Bank of Canada advises the Department of Finance whose minister then recommends to the governor-in-Council the terms and conditions of a new issue. It is the minister of Finance who is ultimately responsible and accountable to Parliament for the conduct of debt management.

Objectives[6]

The main objectives of debt management are:

- To minimize interest and borrowing costs to the issuer. To accomplish this proper pricing was critical. To pay three or four basis points more than market rates was seen as poor debt management. Selling bonds with a shorter term to maturity during periods of falling interest rates was another method to reduce costs as borrowers waited to borrow "long" as long-term rates reached a trough.

- To ensure that an issue brought to market is absorbed with a minimum of disturbance to the prices of outstanding issues traded in the secondary market.

- To broaden the market in government securities by selling to as wide a group of investors as possible and into different capital markets. A wide placement of debt implies less fluctuations in price should any group of institutional investors be forced to, or decided to, liquidate their holdings.

- To maintain a balanced spread of maturities in order to avoid an extremely heavy refinancing operation at one point in time. This goal necessitates periodic "funding" operations.

- To provide flexibility in operations by not adhering in a doctrinaire way to a set formula on debt management. Flexibility can be achieved by a variety of means including improved spacing of maturities, and the use of "call" features.

Constraints

The main constraints facing debt managers include:

- *Form of the Debt.* Call features, two or three pay bonds (optional-pay bonds), tax-exempt features, nonmarketable debt instruments which can be cashed at any time (e.g., savings bonds), are all examples of important variables that reduce, or provide, flexibility to the debt manager.

- *Market Conditions.* Canada's relatively underdeveloped capital market took its direction from London and New York. Hence, international developments such as key elections or defaults had a crucial influence in setting the "market tone" and thereby the course of Canadian interest rates.

- *Investor Resistance.* As one life insurance executive stated before the Porter Royal Commission on Banking and Finance: "the only way you can influence the rate of the next one is not to take this one."[7] Resistance by chartered banks in the early 1930s took place over the roll-over of maturing issues. The banks as a collective unit were in a particularly strong position to influence the outcome of the negotiating process.

- *Inflation, Bank Borrowing and Monetary Policy.* This issue was crucial during and after the war. Sales of debt to the banking system (including the central bank) leading to a rapid growth in the money supply would have inflationary consequences *if* production did not correspondingly increase. Borrowing from the banking system could eventually lead to lower bond prices as investors' real returns were diminished through the inflationary process. As finance capital's [see definition below] expectations adjusted to inflation investors in Canadian dollar securities would exchange their Canadian dollar securities for other securities that investors believed would better hold their value. This decrease in the demand for Canadian securities would reduce the price and hence Canadian interest rates would rise to compensate finance capital for the greater risk. This in turn added to the government's debt servicing costs.

- *Political Factors.* Political instability, especially at the time of elections consistently causes finance capital to delay decisions as to investing in certain securities for fear in the fall of prices. The greater the uncertainty as to a break in government policy would cause capital markets to sell off or "stay on the sidelines" until a clearer policy direction was evident. Between elections unexpected calls for changes in policy also disrupted capital markets. For instance, calls by Social Credit for more central bank financing and the Co-operative Commonwealth Federation's (CCF) demands that interest rates be brought down significantly did give Dominion officials some ability to use these demands as a lever against the chartered banks. At the same time, the central bank had to be cognizant of the fact that should a widespread perception grow that the central bank was at all sympathetic to the inflationary calls of Social Credit, a crisis of confidence might arise forcing interest rates to rise.

THE DOMINION'S PUBLIC DEBT: EVOLUTION 1900–1952

Students of Canadian political economy are familiar with Canada's dependence upon British finance capital that purchased bonds of Canadian governments and railway syndicates to finance railroad and canal construction. The initial *raison d'être* for borrowing abroad was for economic development, to foster territorial expansion and consolidation through railway and canal building. Between 1896 and 1913, a huge investment boom took place in Canada with $1.4 billion invested in transportation infrastructure; between 1900 and 1910 $1 billion was invested in agriculture and $800 million in manufacturing. Reliance on London's capital markets was necessary given these huge requirements and the relatively unsophisticated nature of Canada's bond markets prior to 1914.[8] One important assist in facilitating the raising of these enormous sums was the placement, in 1900, of the Dominion of Canada on Great Britain's "trustee list."

The Great War changed forever Canada's reliance on the United Kingdom for finance. War financing arrangements saw the Dominion advancing funds to the United Kingdom for its purchases in Canada with Canada paying for its war expenditures incurred in Canada. By 1915, London was no longer a source of funds save for financing Canada's overseas war effort. By 1917, Canada's advances exceeded those from the "mother country,"[9] which meant, for the first time, Canada was exporting capital to the United Kingdom.

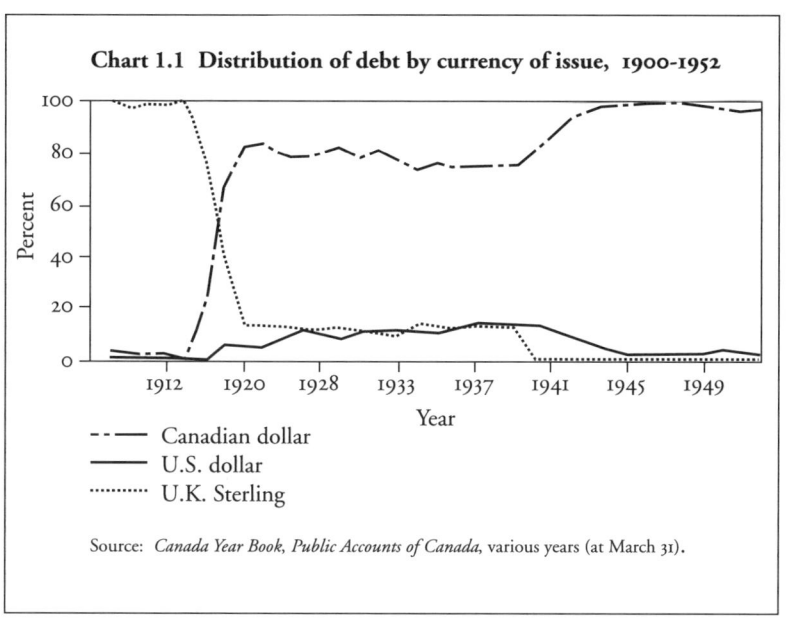

Source: *Canada Year Book, Public Accounts of Canada*, various years (at March 31).

Distribution of Debt by Currency

During the Great War, the Canadian Government was compelled to rely on Canada's ill-developed capital market to raise the necessary funds required for Canada's contribution to the war effort. The Dominion's domestically issued debt, which stood at only 0.2 percent of total debt in 1914 mushroomed to 67 percent in 1918 reaching 81 percent in 1920. The portion of Dominion debt payable in sterling dropped from 98 percent in 1914 to 13 percent by 1920 (excluding the Canadian Northern Railway's debt assumed in 1919), a rather astounding change (Chart 1.1).[10] Thus, the Great War necessitated a re-evaluation of the role of London in meeting the Dominion's borrowing requirements.

Towards the end of the Great War, the first attempts were made at tapping funds in New York. From 1920 onwards foreign borrowing was, in the main, refunding of maturing loans although there is some evidence that during 1931, the Dominion sought to borrow in New York to protect Canada's "gold reputation."[11]

During the R.B. Bennett's primeministership (1930–1935), there does not seem to have been any concerted effort to reduce Canada's foreign indebtedness. However, with the Bank of Canada's establishment, the understanding that principal and interest denominated in foreign currencies were less controllable and therefore less desirable than domestic placements, due to foreign exchange risk, was articulated in the Bank's third *Annual Report*.

> Any considerable reduction of our foreign debt must, in any case, take many years, in view of the magnitude of the task. Considering only Dominion and Provincial Governments' direct and guaranteed debt, and that of the Canadian National Railways, there is still about $1,307 millions payable abroad, and not only that, but an even larger total of debt—$1,379 millions to be exact—carries the option of payment in one or more foreign markets as well as in Canada. Our efforts should, of course, be directed first towards a reduction in such optional payment bonds. Certainly it is undesirable that any additions to this class of indebtedness should be made from the point of view of the Canadian economy as a whole.[12]

The Second World War not only cut off England's financial resources but led to the repatriation of some $300 million of Dominion and Canadian National Railway (CNR) securities held by U.K. citizens and institutions. On top of that transfer was a billion dollar contribution in the form of a gift to enable England to meet part of her foreign currency shortfall.[13] Canada's role in aiding England to purchase supplies in the United States was made more difficult by the invocation of the *Neutrality Act* sanctions that prevented Canada from raising new funds in New York until the U.S. entered the war in December 1941 after Pearl Harbor.

The huge domestic borrowing operations combined with repatriation, left most of the debt domiciled in Canada at war's end. After 1945, new foreign borrowings were initiated by a concern for the value of the Canadian dollar, the latter day equivalent to protecting one's "gold reputation," and not by the Dominion's inability to borrow domestically. The small percentage rise after 1945 in foreign-pay debt is a reflection of the large retirement of domestically held debt, not the growth of foreign loans except during the 1948–1949 drawing on Eximbank's credit facilities and the 1949 U.K. borrowing.

Quantum of Debt and Interest Rates

At March 31, 1930, a little over 10 percent of the Dominion's direct and guaranteed debt was payable in the United Kingdom as Table 1.1 illustrates. This table also shows interest on the debt (direct and guaranteed) ranged from 2.5 percent to 7.0 percent. Much of the debt issued during World War I

Table 1.1
Dominion of Canada Funded Direct and Guaranteed Debt

March 31, 1930

Direct

Payable in Canada Variable (4.5–6%)	$1,804,977,029
Payable in London Variable (2.5–4%)	257,185,700
Payable in New York Variable (4.5–5.5%)	165,965,900

Guaranteed

Railways, principal and interest Variable (3.5–7%) including gold bonds	677,154,484
Railways, interest only	216,207,142
Other, e.g., harbors	32,335,118
Total	**3,153,825,369**

Source: *Public Accounts of Canada,* pp. 14–16.

was tax exempt in the hands of holders. In addition, a number of guaranteed railway issues were "gold" bonds meaning that holders were entitled to receive payment in gold.

Direct funded debt (i.e., excluding short-term treasury bills or notes) rose quickly from $2.2 billion in March 1930 to $3 billion in March 1935 as a result of the Depression. With modest economic recovery and fiscal restraint direct funded debt stood at $3.4 billion by March 1939.

From 1940 to 1945, funded debt rose nearly fourfold to $15.7 billion in order to finance the war effort. Thereafter the debt declined modestly to $15.2 billion by March 1950. At the same time, while the debt rose exponentially, the average interest rate declined to its lowest level in this century (Chart 1.2). As a result, interest payments on the debt as a percentage of Gross National Expenditure (GNE) only rose from 3.2 percent to 4 percent between 1939 and 1945 although the funded debt rose fourfold during the war. After the war, large surpluses resulting from an unexpected postwar boom allowed the Dominion to retire some of the outstanding debt.

Average interest rates on the Dominion's direct funded debt began a slow secular descent commencing in 1934 (Chart 1.2). This decline reflected

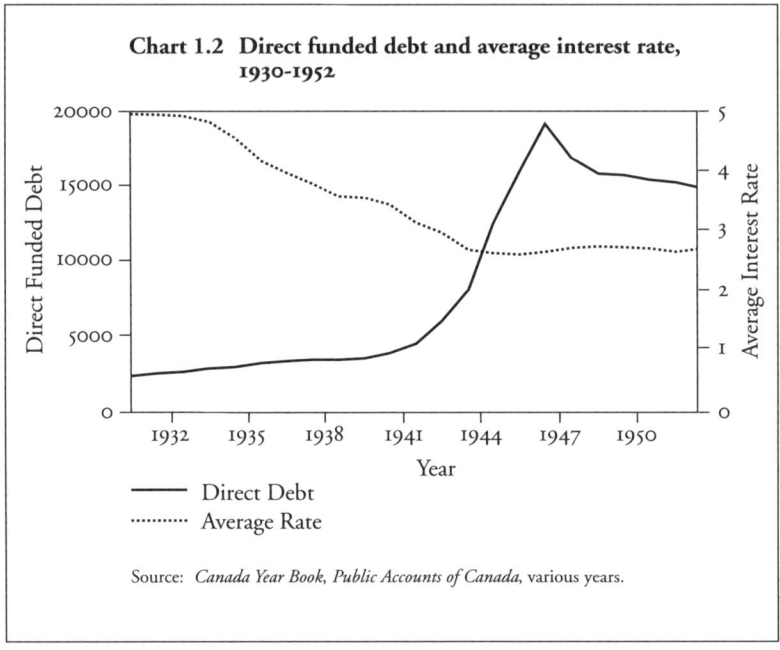

Chart 1.2 Direct funded debt and average interest rate, 1930-1952

Source: *Canada Year Book, Public Accounts of Canada,* various years.

the secular decline in worldwide interest rates as a response by central banks to the chronic unemployment and unused industrial capacity experienced. For Dominion debt managers, the refunding of large maturities beginning in 1934 allowed interest cost to decline despite continuing large government deficits. The average interest rate continued to drift lower throughout the Depression providing welcome relief to governments seeking to balance their budgets as well as to cope with swelling relief costs.

With the war effort underway, rates dropped sharply as governments recognized the importance of financing the war at rates significantly lower than during the Great War. Thus rates drifted to levels not seen since in this century. This deliberate policy was emphasized in 1944 when rates were lowered again in anticipation of higher unemployment associated with reconstruction. Dominion policy-makers were taking no chances of a return to prewar unemployment levels.

Term to Maturity of the Debt

Another important characteristic of the debt at this time was the large volume of debt maturing between 1933 and 1937 (Chart 1.3).[14] This had important implications for debt management in the first half of the 1930s.

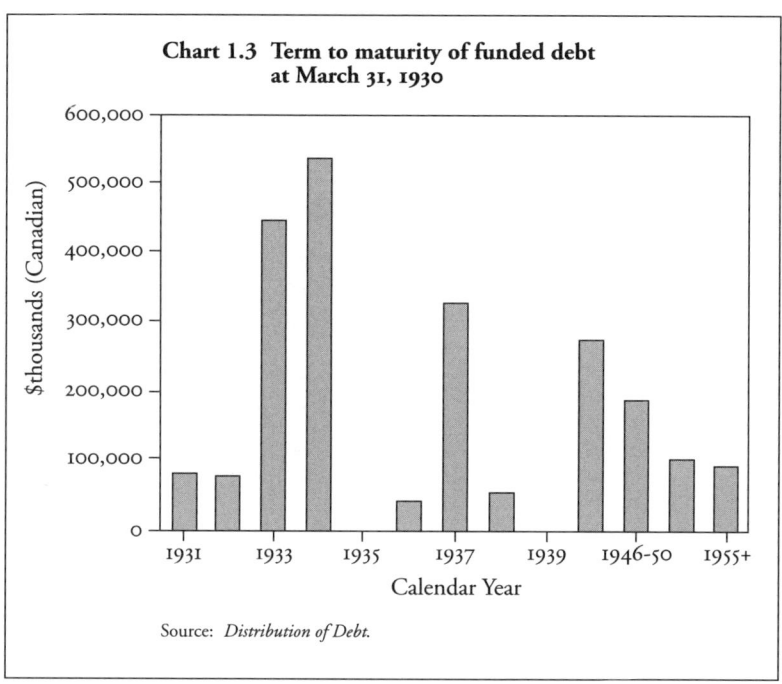

Distribution of Debt

Before the Second World War commenced 30 percent of the Dominion's debt was held by nonresidents (as distinct from currency of issue), 20 percent by Canada's chartered banks, ten percent by insurers, five percent by the Bank of Canada and the remainder held with the general public (Chart 1.4). By 1946, this changed dramatically with nonresidents holding only six percent, the central bank 11 percent, chartered banks with 19 percent, insurers 11 percent and the general public 45 percent (including Canada Savings Bonds (CSB)). This development ran parallel to the Dominion's policy of tapping the domestic market for funds and broadening the distribution of the public debt.

The key trends through this period were the relative stability of the holdings of the banking system (including the central bank) and the insurance sector. After the war, the government's holdings increased reflecting their large fiscal surpluses that were employed to soak up sales by the general public of Victory bonds. The key change however was the decline in nonresident holdings that were made up by the rise of holdings by the general public and the central bank.

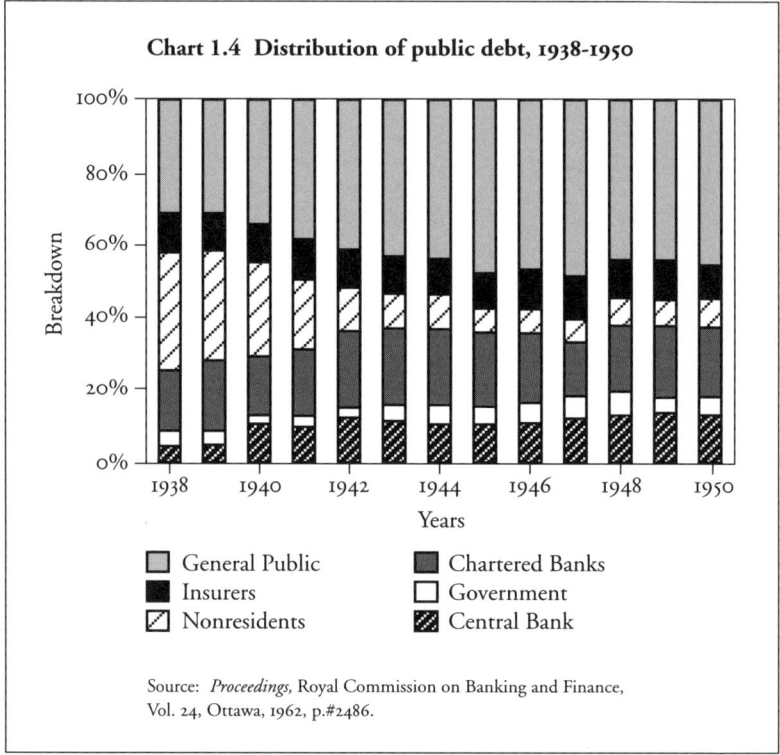

Chart 1.4 Distribution of public debt, 1938-1950

- General Public
- Insurers
- Nonresidents
- Chartered Banks
- Government
- Central Bank

Source: *Proceedings,* Royal Commission on Banking and Finance, Vol. 24, Ottawa, 1962, p.#2486.

In setting the context for examining the interplay of Canadian politics and debt management, the key themes that reoccur throughout are: (1) who holds the debt (the suppliers of capital (e.g., domestic, foreign, banks, the general public), the structure of the debt (e.g., term to maturity) and the financing requirements of the Dominion.

An examination of the evolution of the Dominion's public debt structure shows that it was the external shock of the United Kingdom's inability to export capital and the Dominion's needs for funds that dramatically changed the character of Canada's public debt by 1918. By closing off its capital markets to the world, the United Kingdom assisted in the development of Canada's capital markets. The large Victory war loan issues formed the basis of a nascent government bond market and led to the growth of the securities industry. For the very first time, the Dominion Government had a direct interest in the level of domestic interest rates as the pre-eminent borrower. Previously, interest rates set in the City of London affected the Dominion's timing in its borrowings but over which it had no influence. Another important consequence of domesticating the public debt was the distribution of the debt-holders and the timing of maturities. As will be shown in the following chapters, both the distribution of the debt and its maturity structure had significant implications for the Dominion's politics and debt management.

2 | Capital Markets and the Players

> It is not from the benevolence of the butcher, the brewer, or the baker that we expect our dinner, but from their regard to their own interest. We address ourselves, not to their humanity but to their self-love, and never talk to them of our own necessities but of their advantages.
>
> Adam Smith[1]

Capital Markets

In *Financing of Economic Activity in Canada,* William C. Hood defined the capital market "as the set of contacts between buyers and sellers who effect exchanges involving *non-monetary financial assets.* Considering that all exchanges are effected 'in markets,' we shall say that exchanges involving non-monetary assets take place 'in the capital market'."[2]

In Canada the capital and money markets are contiguous as there are no legal impediments segregating these financial markets. A key subset of the capital market are equity or "stock exchanges" where shares, representing ownership interests in companies are traded. Unlike stock exchanges where the visitor can watch transactions consummated at the various "trading posts" on the exchange's floor, capital markets are not located in one central place. Instead debt instruments, representing rights to fixed periodic payments, are traded in an "over-the-counter" or "between-dealer" market. Thus the capital market consists of a system of telephone and telex interconnections between the "bond desks" of the central bank, the chartered banks and investment dealers. Those telephone connections were used by traders to determine the availability, price and denominations of specific bonds. After making inquiries on "the street," a bond trader will then make a bid (purchase) or offering (sale) "firm." Importantly, as Adam Smith states, the behaviour of individual actors in the capital markets tend to be predictable, in the sense that they act out of necessity, and expect to make gains from their transactions.

The origins of Canada's capital market may be traced to the emergence of brokers (market intermediaries) in Montreal and Toronto in the 1840s. In 1863 a Board of Brokers was formed in Montreal. However, the main impetus for a domestic capital market came during World War I. The heavy wartime financial requirements of the Dominion government, which had previously done virtually all of its borrowing on the London market, necessitated the intensive mobilization of domestic savings.[3]

Money Markets

The money market is a structured set of financial relationships between buyers and sellers of debt instruments with a term to maturity of less than three years. More specifically:

> the money market embraces the various arrangements by which (1) most non-equity fixed income securities maturing within three years are issued, traded and redeemed, (2) short-term funds are borrowed and lent on the security of these obligations *on an impersonal basis*.[4]

Money markets are a crucial component for a developed banking system because it provides accommodation for banks who need to borrow money immediately and usually for a short time. Access to funds on a same day or next-day basis allows banks to meet large commercial borrowers' needs whose demands could be unpredictable and sometimes large. Interest rates determined in the money markets also determined short-term borrowing rates as banks price their loan rates above their borrowing costs on the money market, in order to earn a spread or profit.

The initial impetus for a sensitive, broadly based, money market came with the creation of the Bank of Canada in 1935. Prior to the establishment of the Bank of Canada, the chartered banks' money market activities were confined to New York's call loan market. The establishment of an efficient money market was essential from the perspective of the central bank because it meant a more rigorous and optimal employment of capital, and the setting of interest rates with more precision. The absence of an active money market in the 1930s was one of the criticisms that the Canadian Bankers' Association (CBA) made in opposing a central bank.[5] Professor Sayers states:

> The growing doubt that eventually checked the multiplication of central banks was, however, not the basic questioning of the theory but rather reflection upon the experience of some of the infants. In one country after another open-market operations were just a dream;

because there was no market in which to operate. The member banks were powerful institutions; many of them free to draw upon their own offices in the world's leading financial centres and never needed to go near the central bank, whose rediscount rate remained completely inoperative, published in the pious hope that someone would notice what it was.[6]

In reviewing postwar monetary policy before a House of Commons Committee, the Bank of Canada's first governor, Graham Towers remarked:

> A broad and responsive market in Government of Canada securities and the existence of the machinery which makes such a market possible helps to develop a better market for other securities and to channel funds where they are needed for the development of the country.[7]

To paraphrase Towers, capital markets bring savers and borrowers together and, secondly, establish a mechanism for, in effect, the pricing of credit. From a debt management perspective, the absence of a fully functioning money market, *including players outside the banking system*, limited the Dominion's flexibility in choosing the timing of long-term issues. The banks' dominance of the short-term, immature, Canadian money market, posed serious challenges to the debt manager.

Before the introduction of a formal money market in 1953 the principal instrument for trading, the treasury bill, was held primarily by the banking system. At the end of 1952 only $30 million of $450 million in outstanding bills was held *outside* the banking system. During the period under study, trading in treasury bills was confined to trades between the central bank and chartered banks. This method of trading allowed the chartered banks to hide their liquidity desires from their competitors. The Bank's entry into purchase and resale agreements with the largest investment dealers in 1953 enabled the latter to take into inventory (a "long position") large holdings of government bills.[8] Shortly after these arrangements were instituted the chartered banks began to make day-to-day loans to dealers under which securities held under purchase and resale agreements were pledged as collateral.

Three other terms frequently used are "primary distribution," "after-market" and the "secondary market." A primary distribution occurs when an issuer of a security (e.g., government, corporation) sells new securities to the public. The after-market is the trading in those securities between third parties (i.e., not the issuer) after the issue is priced but before the securities are delivered to the buyer.[9] Finally the secondary market is that portion of the capital markets that engages in the trade of securities that have previously been distributed.

FINANCE CAPITAL

In the first comprehensive study of public debt in the English language American Henry Adams noted there was a specific class interest associated with public borrowing.[10] Referring to the situation in France during the Napoleonic Wars, he notes that the borrower (the state) and the lenders (the banks) "were separate only as legal personages."[11] State indebtedness then becomes a political instrument.[12] This bond holding class is not the group of hypothetical young orphans and older widows, an argument often used to justify public debts as a sort of charitable undertaking. Instead, Adams found the bond holding class was relatively small and geographically concentrated in New York and New England. Adams argued that while

> we may not say public debts bear with them a distinct and independent social tendency, it is yet true that they exert a social influence in *rendering permanent such class relations as spring from disparity of possessions, and that they introduce conflicting interests between citizens.*[13]

Professor Donald MacGregor, a University of Toronto economics professor, also posited the view of distinct and conflicting economic interests when examining the relations between the class of creditors and debtors.[14]

Finance capital is defined broadly here to include (1) debt and equity securities traded in the capital markets; (2) the issuers of such securities; (3) the set of institutions (e.g., the central bank, banks, dealers, institutional investors, credit rating agencies, stock exchanges) and relations among these institutions that hold or trade such securities; (4) that segment of the legal community that defends the contractual rights represented by security documentation and includes the judiciary, which represents and adjudicates between security holders and security issuers; and (5) the assumptions and values shared by issuers and the holders of securities about sanctity of market forces in determining the value of securities. A fundamental tenet in the dynamic between issuers and purchasers of securities is the desire of issuers to pay as low a rate of interest as possible and for purchasers to receive as high an interest rate for the perceived risks of default, a lowered credit rating or inflation.

International finance capital is distinguished from finance capital in that it includes a selected subset of finance capital. These players include the central banks of industrialized countries, the departments of finance of these countries, the Bank of International Settlements, the International Monetary Fund, the major stock exchanges in the capital exporting countries (e.g.,

United Kingdom and United States), securities regulators in these portfolio exporting centres, and the largest financial institutions in the industrialized countries whose operations are international in nature and depend upon the stability of and interdependence of capital markets. The objectives shared by these players include: (1) a stable international financial system (e.g., banks); (2) the enforceability of contracts; and (3) the increased mobility of finance capital, or conversely, the elimination of barriers to the import and export of finance capital.

DOMINION GOVERNMENT: LEGAL AND ADMINISTRATIVE PROCESSES

Department of Finance

Under subhead 91(4) of the *British North American Act, 1867*, (*BNA*) Parliament is authorized to borrow "Money on the Public Credit." Subhead 91(1A) makes Parliament responsible for the "Public Debt." This Act of Westminster also granted the Dominion Parliament explicit and *exclusive* authority with respect to the chartering of banks and savings banks, currency and coinage, interest and legal tender. In short, the BNA accorded the federal Parliament pre-eminence in the banking sector while the capital markets fell under the jurisdiction of the provinces.[15]

The *Exchequer and Audit Act*[6] and its successor Act, the *Consolidated Revenue and Audit Act, 1931*,[17] deal directly with the debt management function. The 1931 Act fell under the administration of the minister of Finance who was directly accountable to Parliament for the debt management function. Section 6 authorized the governor-in-Council (federal Cabinet) to appoint a fiscal agent to negotiate loans on the Dominion's behalf, to pay interest on the public debt, to manage sinking funds and to perform other duties normally associated with the fiscal agency function. The Act permitted the Cabinet, subject to the terms of the enabling Loan Act, to issue a variety of securities—debentures, stock, "terminable annuities," exchequer bills or bonds at rates *not* exceeding six percent per annum. The interest ceiling stipulation accords with provisions of the *Interest Act* and *Bank Act* that set limits on the rate of interest to be legally charged on loans. Section 7(a) authorized payment of interest from the Consolidated Revenue Fund, the Dominion Government's bank account. Section 13 permitted the Cabinet to change the form of the funded debt so long as the principal and annual interest thereon remained the same or were reduced. This allowed refunding at lower rates without recourse to Parliament.

The Act also contained a provision authorizing the Cabinet to borrow sums for periods not exceeding six months at rates of interest not to exceed seven percent. The amount so raised could not exceed the deficiencies in the Consolidated Revenue Fund. The Cabinet was required to present the details of the borrowing to Parliament within 15 days of the opening of the new session.

The borrowing procedure under this statutory framework begins with passage of a Loan Act authorizing a maximum sum to be borrowed. After negotiations between the government's fiscal agent and a banking syndicate or group of primary distributors was completed, a recommendation to the Cabinet by the Finance minister was drawn up. This Order-in-Council specified the Loan Act under which funds were to be borrowed and the terms, conditions and amount of the loan. Usually the price was not entered until the last moment as "breaks" in the market could jeopardize the marketing of the issue, leaving dealers holding large amounts of unsold bonds.

Bank of Canada

The creation of a central bank in Canada was a controversial political issue. Prime Minister Bennett was initially cool to the idea, but because he was frustrated in getting the private chartered banks to increase credit, he came to appreciate its political and economic merits. In meeting with the banks' general managers in October 1932, Bennett indicated he had circulated a memorandum prepared by J.A. McLeod, general manager of the Canadian Bank of Commerce, to his Cabinet colleagues, that proposed that a committee of financial and banking experts be appointed to control the volume of credit.[18] However, the failure of the banks to extend credit, coupled with the appointment of W. Clifford Clark as deputy minister of Finance, set the stage for a central bank.[19] On July 31, 1933, Bennett announced the creation of a Royal Commission on Banking and Currency, chaired by Scottish jurist, Lord Macmillan, who would study, among other things, the need for and structure for a central bank.

Predictably, the commission recommended the establishment of a central bank, but there were several political issues that, in effect, assisted Liberal opposition leader Mackenzie King in the 1935 election. Firstly, Bennett decided to establish a central bank that was *privately* owned. King framed his attack against the government by positing a potential conflict between the directors of a privately owned bank and the sponsor government.

> In the world of finance, the money power as it is termed, is of course the all-important factor that many people believe is greater than the power of the government itself. What I am anxious to be perfectly sure of is that the government of the day, in parting with

some of the ownership of the money power to a privately owned and controlled institution which will be allied to all of the banks of the country and through them to all the financial interests of the country, is not bringing about a situation in which at some critical time should a question arise as between the financial interests in a large way, the two might clash, and the government find itself powerless, at least until parliament should be called together, to deal with the situation. In the meantime, in such a case, the financial interests may have had their way in furthering their interests, albeit their action might be against the public interest.[20]

Further King manipulated the widespread phobia of the Bank of England in certain quarters to gain voter support. During final reading of the Bank of Canada Bill, King claimed: "the present legislation establishing the Bank of Canada, is a definite step in the establishment of an imperial policy of finance, under which the financial destiny of Canada is placed under persons independent of parliament, who can maintain, through the Bank of England and other central banks of empire nations, a definite and positive control of the empire, currency, credit and trade."[21]

With this backdrop, the search for the Bank's first governor began. Given the strong nationalism, that individual must be a Canadian, who was knowledgeable about banking, economics and international trade. The individual selected, Graham Ford Towers, turned out to be an exceptional choice. Only 37 years old when he was appointed, Towers was born in Montreal of "Scotch and U.E.L. stock"[22] and educated at St. Andrew's College in Toronto and at McGill University. After returning from the First World War, Towers joined the Royal Bank of Canada and quickly rose through its ranks to become chief inspector in 1929 and assistant general manager in 1931. His salary, $30,000, higher than the prime minister's, drew some criticism, but otherwise his appointment was universally endorsed.[23] Towers was known for his cool cerebral nature but closer confidants referred to his wit, compassion and storytelling ability.[24] Towers was appointed in September 1934 and set off to travel around the globe to study the operations of other central banks. Interestingly, the Bank's first deputy governor, J.A.C. Osborne, was a citizen of the United Kingdom.

On March 10, 1935 the Bank of Canada commenced business taking over the role of fiscal agent and functioning in this capacity without remuneration. Section 23 of the *Bank of Canada Act*[25] named the central bank as "manager of the public debt." Before 1935 the Government dealt directly with a banking syndicate put together by the Bank of Montreal;

after 1935 the Government worked through its own creation, the Bank of Canada. In 1937, the venerable investment firm Morgan Stanley was appointed lead manager and fiscal advisor to the Dominion of Canada in the United States. In London, the Bank of Montreal remained the Dominion's "paying agent."

Under Section 21 of the *Bank of Canada Act* the Bank's investment powers were specified. While the Bank's investment powers were considerable, in practice, the Bank held and traded Dominion government securities primarily. It was the daily market contact that also enabled the Government, through the Bank, to gather for the first time relevant and independent market information directly from its own fiscal agent. As an active participant in the market, the Bank was able to provide the Government with vital market information. To paraphrase a former Finance Department official, "in order to know the market one must be actively in the market."[26] The Bank also provided the Dominion with vastly improved statistical information on bond prices, new issues and exchange rates.

Relations between the central bank and the dealers can sometimes be strained when the latter attempt to read trends into the Bank's open market operations or are frustrated by the Bank's secrecy.[27] In the words of the 1964 Porter Commission:

> Some frustration is inevitable in any relationship between the central bank and securities markets, especially since the monetary authorities cannot always disclose their hand, even when they are certain of their future policy. In fact central bankers are often not exactly certain about underlying economic forces or what state of credit conditions is appropriate to them. Moreover, they must frequently use trial and error methods— known in central banking as "successive approximation"—until financial markets give them more guidance or the results of their previous policies become somewhat clearer. However, we believe that secrecy can be overdone, and the benefits of frank and full information are sometimes not fully appreciated by Canadian authorities.[28]

Relations with commercial banks and investment dealers also had to be handled in a delicate fashion. According to Governor Graham Towers in a 1936 briefing to a Dominion-Provincial conference:

> …our position versus the commercial banks and the security market is a very special one. For example, we can never obtain opinions from any outside source when we are formulating our advice to the

> Government regarding new issues. Thus we never enquire the views of anyone outside the bank. A central bank must be independent and impartial, which means that on most occasions it must play a lone hand.[29]

The relationship between the Dominion government and the central bank was also a delicate one and particularly the distinction between the locus of advice and the locus of decision-making. Again Governor Towers in a response to comments made by the Honourable C.D. Howe on the Bank's involvement in the May 1938 refunding operations.

> I mentioned also that the relation of Central Bank to Government was a very special one, and that the name of the former should not be mentioned by Government as a source of advice. If it was only mentioned as the source when the Government is being criticized, the Bank would get into bad repute. But it would not be sensible for the Government to mention that they had received our advice on every occasion when they took action of a financial character. In any event, *we were not the makers of policy in relation to Government finances.*[30]

MARKETING THE PUBLIC DEBT

Before the Bank of Canada was created, domestic issues were arranged by a banking syndicate put together and, usually, led by the Bank of Montreal. The banking syndicate would normally be composed of the major banks and investment houses who would advance funds to the Government when the securities were delivered for distribution. This function is known as underwriting. Advertising of the issue was usually the responsibility of the distribution group, although beginning with the 1931 Conversion Loan the minister of Finance took some initiative in advertising. Gradually there evolved more government sponsorship of advertising these issues, especially for the conversion of Victory Loans. The banking syndicate would then sell to a distributing or selling group—dealers, banks and brokers—the securities at a price slightly above that paid to the government. Dealers, banks and brokers would then sell bonds to their clients and take some of the bonds into their own inventory. The allotment by the banking group was a matter of intense debate for dealers and brokers who, if they could not satisfy their initial orders were forced to purchase bonds in the after-market, often at a premium, while being committed to deliver these bonds to the investor at a stipulated price.

The entrance of the Bank of Canada in 1935 changed the relationship between the Dominion as borrower and the banking syndicate. No "negotiations" took place although informal consultations between the Governor, his officials and the financial community were frequent and ongoing. One of the very first tasks of the new central bank was to reorganize the procedures for Dominion offerings. What evolved was the selling of a certain amount of the bonds "firm" to primary distributors on the Bank's list of authorized distributors. Applications accepting the bonds "firm" and requests for additional bonds were to be accompanied by a 5 percent margin deposit. The final allotment was done on a pro-rata basis and was influenced by the "placing power" or distribution record of the distributors. Commissions were established by the Bank and price restrictions placed on the bonds during the primary distribution phase.

It is also important to distinguish between a public offering or public placement and a private offering or private placement. The former involves an offering through an underwriting group of bonds to the public. This procedure ensures as wide as distribution as possible. In New York, for instance, Morgan Stanley as the lead underwriter was capable of involving well over 400 insurance companies, investment banks and commercial banks in the distribution of a Dominion of Canada issue. This procedure, while requiring a considerable expenditure of marketing energies, meant the bonds would be widely held. The second procedure, the private placement, involves a smaller group of institutional investors negotiating directly with the borrower or agent over terms of the loan. The advantages for the borrower were: (1) the preparation of a formal prospectus[31] was not required; and (2) the negotiations could be finalized relatively quickly. However the lenders, in expediting the loan, usually demanded a rate of interest slightly above that prevailing in the secondary market since there was not the same ability to resell private placement issues that were not traded in the markets making price determination more difficult, and hence, more uncertain.

CHARTERED BANKS

Nature of Commercial Banking

A particular banker lends among his customers his own promissory notes, to the extent, we shall suppose, of a hundred thousand pounds. As those notes serve all the purposes of money, his debtors pay him the same interest as if he had lent them so much money. This interest is the source of his gain. Though some of these notes are continually coming back upon him for payment, part of them continue to circulate for months and years together. Though he has generally in circulation, therefore, notes to the extent of several hundred thousand pounds, twenty thousand pounds in gold and silver may, frequently, be a sufficient provision for answering occasional demands. By this operation, therefore, twenty thousand pounds in gold and silver perform all the functions which a hundred thousand could otherwise have performed.[32]

In a certain sense, banking may be regarded as a social function, that is, of mobilizing idle money balances and transferring the funds to individuals and businesses requiring these moneys. According to the Marxist economist Ernest Mandel:

> Contrary to the industrialist and trader, the banker has in fact to play a *social role directly*. He is useful to the capitalist mode of production only to the extent that he can overcome the fragmentation of social capital into the multitude of individual properties. It is in this function of *mobiliser* and centraliser of social capital that his whole importance to society consists. This function goes beyond the class limits of the bourgeoisie in the strict sense and embraces the centralisation of funds saved by landowners, rich and middle peasants, craftsmen, civil servants, technicians, and even skilled workers in prosperous periods.[33]

The business of banking involves the accepting of deposits, on which interest may be paid and the lending or investing of deposits and shareholders' equity to borrowers at a higher rate of interest. The "spread" between banks' deposit rates or expenses and their investment earnings from security holdings and loans constitutes the main source of bank profits. Profits on foreign exchange transactions were also a source of earnings and of losses.

The *Bank Act* goes into minute detail specifying the type of security or collateral that banks may acquire when lending and their powers as secured creditors. Unlike life insurance and trust companies, banks primarily lend for a short term, that is less than two years. Banks therefore held shorter term government paper that could be liquidated to provide funds to "write" new loans.

Liabilities

Before the creation of the Bank of Canada, Canadian banks issued their own bank notes whose circulation was limited to the shareholders' paid-in capital and bank reserves. Prior to the establishment of a central bank, chartered banks paid a one percent tax per year on their outstanding note issue.

The largest liability of a chartered bank was the "notice deposit." Thousands of individual savings deposits, earning from 2 to 3 percent (1.5 percent during the Second World War), provided banks with approximately 50 percent of their funds while demand or chequable deposits (mostly for businesses) represented almost 30 percent of a bank's liabilities.[34] Demand deposits were essentially drafts against a bank account payable to a third party through the banks' cheque clearing system. The level of demand deposits was very sensitive to business conditions and the level of available credit. Notice deposits, on the other hand, remained relatively stable during the Depression. While demand deposits dropped 30 percent and note circulation 27 percent between 1929 and 1933, notice deposits fell by a more modest 7 percent.

Assets

After 1929 a sudden contraction in commercial lending took place. This shift was caused primarily by the serious loss of faith resulting from the deflation experienced during 1930–1931. Banks shifted their investment portfolios from more lucrative, but riskier, commercial lending, to gilt-edged government securities carrying virtually no risk of default. During the 1930s, this tendency to become more risk averse quadrupled bank holdings of government paper while commercial loans were cut nearly in half. This development gave rise to the often heard charge that banks were not fulfilling their obligations to agriculture and industry.[35] According to one student of Canadian banking though, the increase in securities holdings was "well advanced" before the Great Crash—the crash simply accelerated this trend.[36] Furthermore, as the banks often claimed, they had too much cash in their tills with too few credit-worthy customers who would borrow. While there is little doubt that the economics of banking gave banks an incentive to lend to industry and commerce there remained a widespread fear that losses would easily erase earnings from good loans that led to a systemic contraction of credit.[37]

During the Second World War, the banks' securities holdings trebled as the Dominion's financing requirements grew rapidly. Commercial lending, which saw a small increase early in the war, was effectively frozen as the Dominion, through the deposit certificate mechanism, monopolized the supply of credit made available through increases in bank deposits. From 1946 to 1950 total lending doubled, prompting utterances from the central bank that capital projects should be financed without short-term bank credits.[38]

In spite of this expansion of credit, it was not until 1952 that commercial lending replaced security holdings as the largest asset of the chartered banks.

Liquidity

A very important aspect of banking deals with liquidity management. Prior to 1935 this requirement was satisfied, in large measure, in New York's call loan market. Banks could access "call loans" quickly by calling their loans one day and receiving cash on the next banking day. After the Bank of Canada was established, it became for all intents and purposes, the sole "jobber" of Canada bonds and bills by quoting firm prices for standard lots (normally $25,000) on all outstanding issues. Bills could be sold to the Bank for settlement in Bank of Canada funds the very same day.[39] This enabled the banks to acquire ready cash resources in much the same fashion as in New York, but without the export of funds.

Industry Structure

Chartered banks are regulated under the *Bank Act*, which historically was revised, according to statute, every ten years. The Act provides the legislative framework for a "branch," as opposed to a "unit" banking system, as in the United States. A branch banking system is seen as superior to a unit banking system due to its capacity to draw upon a wide base of deposits. A wide deposit base provides essential stability to a banking system by reducing the fear that one or two major deposit withdrawals, for instance a major corporate client, could precipitate a calling of loans and a run on the bank by depositors wishing to withdraw their gold or deposits. This type of fear was particularly acute in the last century when banks were much smaller and regionally concentrated and bank notes were redeemable in specie. These factors made a bank especially vulnerable to periodic depressions and the loss of faith of depositors and note holders.[40] It is generally believed that cyclical downturns in the auto or pulp and paper industry, for example, can be offset by gains in the clothing or agricultural sectors thus obviating the problems of a narrow depositor and loan base. During the Great Depression, criticism of Canadian banks was somewhat muted because no bank failed, in contrast with the United States, which saw thousands of bank insolvencies.

In 1900, the Canadian Bankers' Association was formally recognized in *An Act to incorporate the Canadian Bankers' Association*.[41] In the 1901 revisions to the *Bank Act*, the Association was given authority to supervise the issue and destruction of bank notes, certain powers of inspection and supervision, and to act as "curator" and, where possible, to arrange the sale of the assets to another bank.⁴² These changes sanctioned for the first time an institutional framework to resolve the recurring problems of bank insolvencies by making the industry itself responsible for seeking out ways to prevent losses to depositors, noteholders and shareholders. The amendments were associated with a wave of takeovers and mergers in the banking industry during the first two decades of the twentieth century.⁴³ In the decade preceding the 1901 revision, there were no bank mergers or takeovers with five bank failures; between 1900 and 1910 ten banks merged while only three failed.⁴⁴ This merger movement made it in turn more difficult for regional banks to get off the ground. Of the 11 charters issued and banks opening for business between 1900 and 1920, three banks failed while the remainder were absorbed by larger institutions, several of which were ultimately taken over.⁴⁵ By 1930, all banks still operating had received their charters before 1900.

The two leading banks, the Royal Bank and the Bank of Montreal controlled nearly $2 billion in assets, or roughly 55 percent of all banking system assets. The Big Four, including the Canadian Bank of Commerce and the Bank of Nova Scotia, controlled $2.9 billion in assets, or nearly 65 percent of total banking assets in Canada. Proposed bank mergers (Royal Bank of Canada and Bank of Montreal; and the Canadian Imperial Bank of Commerce and Toronto-Dominion Bank) in 1998, if they had been approved, would have resulted in the top two banks controlling approximately 70 percent of total banking assets. One key implication of this structure would have been the relative ease by which government direction could have been communicated to the banking system—direction could be achieved by placing three or four phone calls to the CEOs or arranging a meeting through the auspices of the CBA.

INVESTMENT DEALERS

Activities

Investment dealers, known as "investment bankers" before the 1934 *Bank Act* revision, earn their livelihood from: (1) commissions on the sale and purchase of debt obligations (bonds, debentures) and equity capital (common and preferred shares); (2) capital gains on inventory dispositions; and (3) underwriting new stock and bond issues.⁴⁶ An investment dealer buys and sells securities either as an agent, for clients, or as a principal, for the firm.

Underwriting, which is core function of investment dealers, involves the formation of an underwriting syndicate whose task is to bid on bonds at a set price or make an offer to an issuer to buy the bonds at a negotiated price, and undertake the distribution of the bonds to clients. The underwriting group would require the financial assistance of a bank(s) (banking syndicate) to line up the funds to advance to the borrower or issuer after their tender was accepted, but before they sold the bonds to their clients, usually wealthy individuals or institutional investors. Prices were normally established at the last possible moment before "coming to market" as a safeguard against a sharp break in the market.[47] As so much of a firm's revenues derived from the new issuance of bonds, a sudden drop in prices could leave the dealers exposed to heavy losses. As one dealer put it "the money (is) made in underwriting (the) last million."[48] When a dealer cannot sell all their bonds, they usually go into their inventory—for to unload the bonds immediately into a declining after-market would usually drive prices down further. Being left with the bonds often meant paying substantial interest charges to the bank that arranged the initial financing. During the Depression, as a result of the deterioration of provincial credit ratings and their own capital base, to minimize the risk in underwriting new bond issues, dealers formed in 1932 a central co-operative of dealers that would handle the more risky, western issues.[49]

Profitability was affected by the volume of new issues and conversion offers, the amount of secondary trading, the spread between the prices paid for the bonds from the borrower and that received for the bonds from the investor. Dealers were constantly on the watch in their position as fiscal agent or advisor to a municipality or province to recommend the best time to come to market. It was in the interest of the dealer to encourage new borrowing or refinancing because new issues produced underwriting profits and commissions for new secondary market trading.

Another parameter affecting profitability was the allotment received under a syndicate agreement. If a dealer received fewer bonds than it was committed to sell, it would then be forced to purchase the bonds on the after-market, often at a premium to fill the order. Rising bond prices in the after-market provided an inducement for dealers to "pad" their orders to assure themselves that they would receive sufficient bonds to meet clients' needs.

Finally, investment dealers have an important economic stake in the active trading of these bonds as they generate significant commissions primarily from the life insurance and trust industry. The dealer also acted as a jobber, by taking "a position in securities that are being traded, reduces short-term price fluctuations in that way and thereby improves the functioning of the market, an improvement based on his superior knowledge of market values."[50] In this function as a jobber dealers are constantly in the market buying and selling securities.

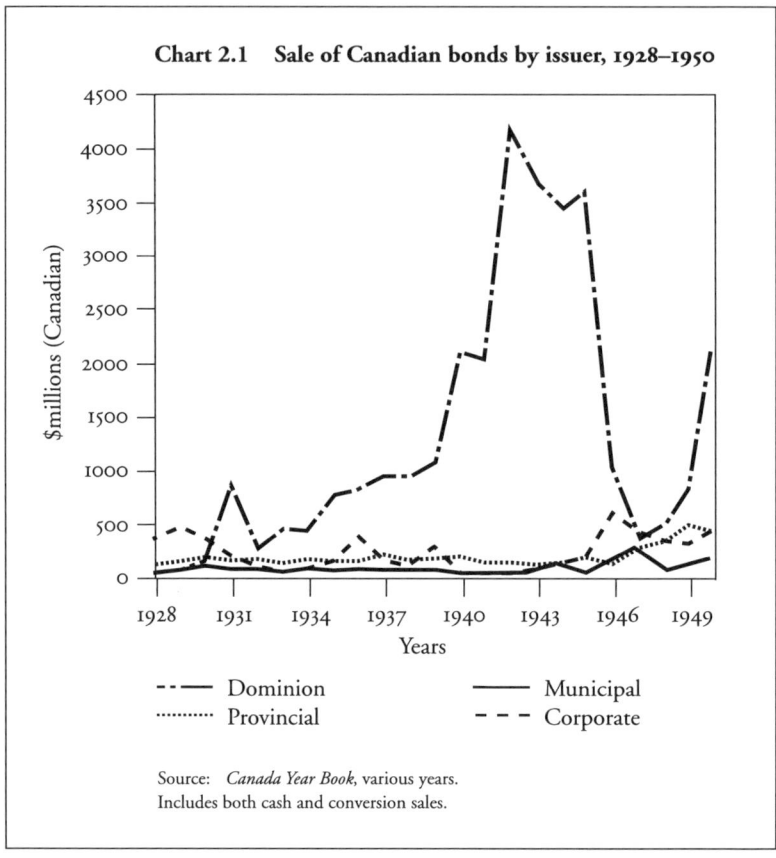

Chart 2.1 Sale of Canadian bonds by issuer, 1928–1950

Source: *Canada Year Book*, various years.
Includes both cash and conversion sales.

In the 1930s the securities industry was in very poor financial shape because of the virtual extinction of new corporate bond and stock issues.[51] The stock market collapse caused a severe erosion of the earnings and the capital base of most firms by reducing the value and volume of the underlying stock traded which served as the basis for calculating commissions. Chart 2.1 shows that the market for new municipal, railway and corporate issues dried up dramatically after 1930. Throughout the decade government business became the dealers' main activity.

Dealers, unlike the banks, were more receptive to the creation of a central bank. Besides being a new player in the market, it was expected that the Bank of Canada would exert a steadying influence, smoothing price drops and rises. The Bank's desire to see a broader and deeper market in debt instruments seemed to guarantee the dealers some prospect for a larger role in the sale and distribution of government debt, which eventually came about with the creation of a money market in the early 1950s.

Industry Structure

The structure of the investment business was, and remains quite decentralized in comparison with Canada's concentrated banking system. The investment industry was comprised of many small firms specializing in certain types of equities or municipal, provincial or corporate bonds. The larger, more established firms such as Wood, Gundy and A.E. Ames became "integrated" with research, government finance, corporate finance and securities trading departments. Most firms were either partnerships or privately held (often in a family), where the chief executive officer had their own capital at risk and these firms therefore tended to be more aggressive in promoting underwritings, secondary market trading and seeking representation on underwriting syndicates.

Capital markets depend on financial assets to trade. Absent the effects of inflation, the more assets traded on a daily basis, the more accurate becomes the pricing of these financial assets. Government debt, as a financial asset, forms a basis or foundation of developed capital markets because these assets are essentially free of default risk; that is to say, principal and interest will be repaid. With government debt trading in significant volumes, it is then possible to create markets in other financial assets by pricing off the "risk free" rate of the national government's bonds. Thus there developed markets for Dominion government guaranteed bonds (e.g., Canadian National Railways), provincial and municipal bonds, and corporate bonds. Each of these financial instruments were priced above Dominion bonds and traded according to their coupon rate (interest payable) and their term to maturity. The larger the volume of national government issues, the easier it would become to buy or sell these securities and this in turn allowed the capital markets to respond to the chartered banks' demands for cash in order to fund commercial loans. Moreover, the larger the volume of trading the smaller the spread between the price a bond was offered and the spread the bond was bid. However, most importantly, the rate at which the Dominion government borrowed set the benchmark for borrowers by farmers and those purchasing homes. When the Dominion government's borrowing rate was increased through market forces so too were the rates for the general public.

The establishment of the Bank of Canada was an important development for Canada's small capital market because the central bank became the largest holder of the Dominion's debt. Also the central bank had a mandate to ensure price stability of bonds or interest rate stability while acting in the best interest of the economic life of the nation. This broader mandate meant the Bank would act to minimize economic dislocation and act to eliminate "speculative excesses" in various markets (e.g., capital, real estate, and commodities). To accomplish this objective, the Bank acted in the capital markets to adjust, over time, the prices of government bonds, and hence interest rates, to conform to its statutory goals of price stability and economic welfare.

3. Political Uncertainty and New Institutional Arrangements, 1930–1939

International Markets and Canada's Financial System

Prelude to Depression

By many indicators the 1923 to 1929 period was a prosperous era for Canadians. Exports expanded by one-third, real income grew by 25 percent, and immigration during the decade exceeded one million.[1] Sectors experiencing the most rapid growth were wheat and pulp and paper, buoyed by rising commodity prices. Fixed capital formation and provincial public works also expanded rapidly, especially due to hydro-electric developments and road building.[2]

The Great War left the United States in the position of the world's largest creditor. According to one analyst, there were three basic reasons why America's new-found hegemony tended to destabilize the world's financial system. Firstly, the operation of the gold standard was most successful when London was the unchallenged centre of international finance.[3] After the War, with both Paris and New York competing as world financial centres, the probability of complications arising multiplied. Secondly, New York was "inexperienced" as a world trade centre and this weakness was magnified by its lack of dependence on foreign trade. Unlike England, which would immediately suffer from a drying up of world trade and credit, American financiers and legislators tended to see more benefits flowing from a policy of autarky than the dangers inherent in trade protectionism. The conflict between domestic and foreign economic policy was sufficient to produce Smoot-Hawley and other tariff barriers; measures which would have been suicidal for the United Kingdom's economy. And thirdly, the New York capital market was largely, although not exclusively, a money market.[4] Therefore, it was capable of disbursing only short-term credit to debtor countries when long-term assistance was required.[5] Compounding these problems of international financial realignment was the intractable question of Germany's reparations payments, French insistence on seeking damages and American demands for repayment in full.

The New York money market played a crucial role in the years immediately preceding the Great Crash when vast sums poured in from abroad to speculate on a rising New York Stock Exchange. As stock prices escalated more money was demanded by investors and loaned through the short-term, "call loan" market. During 1929, the call loan rate peaked at 20 percent on March 26th and remained between 10 and 15 percent during the summer of 1929. Despite these rates, The Bank of Nova Scotia commented "the demand for funds at call was insistent, and it seemed as though the market could not secure enough at that figure."[6] Yet one year after this speculative binge, call loan rates stood at two percent but demand had dried up.

During the speculative boom some Canadian bankers, to their credit, cautioned against speculative excesses. Sir John Aird of the Canadian Bank of Commerce, speaking before the Bank's 1928 Annual Shareholders meeting, noted:

> In view of the widespread prevalence of speculation it is well to remember that a rise in prices in the stock markets does not in itself increase the wealth of a country. In so far as it is due to inflation of credit it amounts to a revaluation on paper mainly made in anticipation of what the future may bring. If these anticipations are realized all goes well, but, too often, the reverse is the case. The supply of credit from the banks should be based, not on mere anticipations of future wealth, but on that which is actually in existence, and which can be utilized for the increase of bank reserves. On this basis alone can a sound expansion of bank credit take place.[7]

Onset of Depression: Impact on Capital Markets

Following the Great Crash in October 1929, during the wave of credit contraction that spread through Canada between 1930 and 1935, banks liquidated industrial and farm loans, purchasing government bonds instead. The conservatism of bankers preserved the integrity of Canada's financial system; a fact emphasized time and time again by government ministers and bankers alike. This desire to keep safe and sound, which was essential for maintaining a functioning financial system, led to a broader economic contraction than expected. According to Professor R. Craig McIvor, bankers were incapable, and perhaps unwilling, to recognize the interrelationship between individual bank action and the operations of the banking system on the economy as a whole.

The point at which the banks may be criticized is not that they were wrong in keeping safe and sound, or even that in the process of doing so they effected a highly undesirable contraction of the country's means of payment. The ultimate responsibility for this contraction must rest not with the banks but with the government which failed to assume any responsibility for control of the total means of payment in the economy. The basic criticism of the bankers is rather that they neither understood nor were willing to learn the economic consequences of their own actions, and they consequently provided a great deal of ill-informed opposition to the subsequent formation of a central bank. It should of course be emphasized that the failure to recognize the connection between monetary contraction and the aggravation of the Canadian depression was no means confined to the bankers. It was almost universal in those early days.[8]

In September 1930, a sharp break in the bond market occurred as a consequence of investors' fears that negotiations then underway between international creditors and national debtors would break down leading to default. Even before England's flight from the gold standard, Acting Deputy Finance Minister Watson Sellar termed the New York market "disorganized" in face of fears that the U.S. savings bank system was ready to collapse.[9]

The collapse of commodity prices brought into question the large debts owed by staple exporting nations, Australia, Latin America and Canada. In 1931, Australia reduced all interest payments on internal public debts and some private debts by 20 percent. In March 1931, when Watson Sellar advanced proposals for a New York issue of $100,000,000 "to safeguard our gold exchange position," he noted that Canada was suffering from a "bad reputation" on Wall Street. This bad reputation was not based on politics, but on the dreary economic news emanating from the Dominion Bureau of Statistics. Sellar, knowing the market's reaction to poor economic news, recommended that we "feed out short items every two or three days dealing with our financial position, and arrange with some of the press boys that they put the stuff on the wires in their own names. *I would also urge that a censor be placed on the release of the stuff by the Bureau of Statistics.*"[10] The implications for Canada's credit rating and borrowing costs were abundantly clear—bad news meant falling bond prices and higher interest rates.

The withholding of financial reports by the Government was the subject of a lengthy tirade by Canada's most astute observer of public finance, University of Toronto economics professor Donald MacGregor. In an article published in *The Canadian Forum* in 1933, MacGregor charged:

It is not easy to follow the changing position of Canadian finance as long as the federal authorities continue to suppress the usual monthly figures of revenue, expenditure and debt. Suppression of financial returns began last spring, and continued until August when quarterly figures of revenues and expenses (but not of debt) for the first quarter of the fiscal year were published. Early in January the accounts for the three months ending December were released, but no figures whatever of the net debt have been published since March 31, 1932. It is a sad reflection upon the alertness and courage of whatever financial critics there are in the opposition, and in the press of the country that Ottawa has been able to suppress the usual publication of such important statistics for nearly a year without being exposed. If the weekly returns of the British exchequer were delayed as much as a fortnight, the whole Empire would know about it. But the Canadian figures are delayed six months and nothing is said.[11]

In March 1931, Peru suspended payments, extending its moratorium the following January. In January 1932, Mexico formally revoked its previous undertakings of July 1930 and July 1931 to maintain a new schedule of debt repayments. Similar rescheduling occurred with Portugal, Greece, Turkey and Bulgaria. In May 1931, the giant Austrian bank, *Kreditanstalt* collapsed sending a wave of panic north through central Europe. Increasingly, pressure was placed on the United Kingdom as many institutions were preoccupied with England's loans to Germany. This led to a heavy redemption of gold against the United Kingdom's reserves during the summer of 1931 and eventually to the decision on September 21, 1931 to abandon the gold standard.[12] Canadian bond prices fell three and four points during the next few days as did the Canadian dollar in New York. After the British announcement, a "drastic drop in the price of U.S. securities" took place in which the yield of 90-day treasury bills rose more than 110 basis points (one basis point is one one-hundredth of one percent) between the end of September and the third week in October.[13] As deflation accompanied a devaluation of currencies against the U.S. dollar, many debtor countries had very little choice except to default to, primarily, American bondholders. As one investment dealer said, "this (abandonment of the gold standard) led to a distrust of everything."[14]

Soon afterwards pressure was applied to Canada as markets believed Canada would also be forced to abandon gold. Prime Minister Bennett vacillated for several weeks calling for Canadians to conserve gold, and during that time the dollar plunged in value against the United States dollar. When

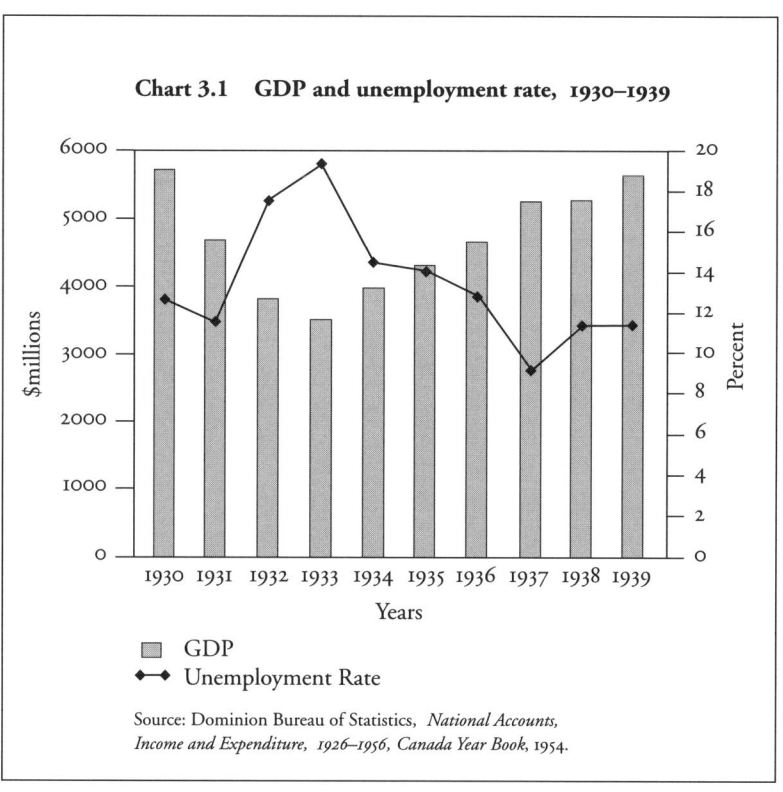

Chart 3.1 GDP and unemployment rate, 1930–1939

Source: Dominion Bureau of Statistics, *National Accounts, Income and Expenditure, 1926–1956, Canada Year Book*, 1954.

Canada did abandon gold on October 19, 1931, the dollar eventually dropped to a low of 80.36 cents in December 1931 recovering to around 90 cents the following spring. This devaluation had an immediate effect on increasing dramatically debt servicing costs for the federal government and, in particular, provincial governments (see Table 3.2).

The unsettled nature of capital markets at this time made the timing of trips to the markets exceptionally tricky. For example, in the fall of 1932 refinancing in New York had to be completed well before the Presidential elections to avoid the possibility of a decline in bond prices.[15] The unsettled character of the markets was highlighted by testimony presented before the Royal Commission on Banking and Currency by the Investment Bankers Association of Canada (IBAC) in September 1933. Ward Pitfield, President of the IBAC, noted that bond dealers could no longer offer firm bids for bonds "for fear that government policies changing overnight."[16]

Municipal defaults in the early 1930s and rumours of impending defaults also had a negative psychological impact on capital markets. As a consequence, there was a movement away from corporate and railway bonds into the debentures of the most credit-worthy governments, specifically the Dominion and the Province of Ontario. In October 1932 Vancouver defaulted and the City of Windsor called for a five-year halt on bond repayments. That December, Calgary refused to pay a $300,000 exchange premium on funds destined for the United States. By 1934, the total defaults of Ontario municipalities reached $84,000,000 with Quebec municipal defaults of $15,000,000.[17]

Amidst, and due to these financial convulsions, the Canadian economy experienced the worst downturn of this century. Gross Domestic Product (GDP) fell by nearly one-half between 1930 and 1933. Concomitant with falling output, the official unemployment rate doubled from 10 to 20 percent in these three years. As a consequence, government revenue fell dramatically, especially in the commodity producing prairie provinces. Aggravating the problem was the fact that even though interest rates began to fall from late 1931 onwards, governments faced higher costs due to the depreciating currency and the fact that most long-term issues were not callable.

The Political Context and the Government's Response

One of the very first indications that Bennett and his party would meet the expectations of finance capital came in the wake of Britain's abandonment of the gold standard. With the rapid fall in bond prices in September and October 1931, Bennett's cabinet quietly passed an Order-in-Council making unnecessary a write-down of security values on banks' balance sheets.[18]

In April 1932, as the Depression deepened, the first concerted attack against the federal government's interest rate "policy" was initiated by Progressive Member of Parliament G.G. Coote (MacLeod). Jumping on the Conservatives' quiet passage of the Order-in-Council, Coote attacked high interest rates. Exorbitant rates were, in Coote's opinion, harming provincial and municipal finance and ruining the national economy.[19] At the same time M.N. Campbell, another Progressive member, proposed lowering the maximum rate charged borrowers, thus forcing the banks in turn to "reimburse themselves by reducing the rate of interest paid on deposits." By lowering these savings rates to one and a half or two percent, depositors would possibly place their funds instead at the disposal of the Dominion and the provincial governments by purchasing bonds.[20] Further attacks on the level of interest rates came from A.A. Heaps, Labour member from Winnipeg who criticized the Government for selling bonds at 5.25 percent which "meant the adding of millions upon millions of dollars to public debts in this dominion; because

Table 3.1
Provincial Government Debt, January 1, 1938 by currency of issue ($millions Canadian)

Borrower	Canada	New York	Canada or New York	Canada, New York or London	Canada or London	London	London or Paris
Prince Edward Island	5.6	–	–	–	0.5	–	–
Nova Scotia	52.3	–	40.6	–	–	5.7	–
New Brunswick	41.8	–	34.6	0.3	3.8	4.0	–
Quebec	179.1	–	39.0	16.8	–	5.7	4.7
Ontario	410.0	8.9	57.6	247.4	–	5.9	–
Manitoba	32.9	0.2	42.9	3.5	11.2	8.2	–
Saskatchewan	56.4	–	52.6	4.7	10.9	–	–
Alberta	29.8		65.8	19.9	4.0	15.3	–
British Columbia	34.1		66.5	5.7	20.2	26.9	
Total	**842.0**	**9.1**	**399.6**	**298.3**	**50.6**	**71.7**	**4.7**

Source: Bank of Canada, *Statistical Summary*, January 1938, Table IV.

Table 3.2
Provincial Governments—Gross Debt Charges ($thousands)

Borrowers	1913	1921	1926	1930	1933	1937*
All provinces	11,531	28,287	48,035	58,038	80,084	80,011
Prince Edward Island	42	61	114	148	214	296
Nova Scotia	456	862	1,871	2,672	3,318	3,828
New Brunswick	447	1,251	1,913	2,600	3,473	3,624
Quebec	1,214	2,997	4,886	4,336	7,223	8,890
Ontario	1,722	8,593	20,369	25,119	34,145	33,230
Manitoba	1,731	3,418	4,488	5,020	6,901	6,060
Saskatchewan	1,539	2,691	2,982	4,500	7,451	10,222
Alberta	2,326	4,005	6,498	7,185	9,027	5,300
British Columbia	2,054	4,409	4,914	6,458	8,332	8,661

*Excluding unpaid interest, Province of Alberta, estimated at $3.4 million.

Source: Royal Commission on Dominion-Provincial Relations, *Book III, Documentation*, table 46, p. 121.

the moment the federal government issued bonds at 5 1/4 percent our provincial government had to pay 6 and 6 1/2 percent on money it wished to borrow."[21] Thus, the apparent inability of the Dominion to control the rate of interest, which it supposedly was constitutionally entrusted to do, was highlighted by western-based politicians.

Table 3.1 illustrates the provinces' borrowing structure by currency at January 1, 1938. This shows that all provinces, but particularly Ontario and the western provinces, were especially exposed to a decline in value of the Canadian dollar relative to the United States dollar.

Table 3.2 shows the rise in debt servicing costs facing provincial governments in the 1930s stemming in large part to the depreciation of the Canadian dollar. It was not so much the rate of interest that had weakened provincial finances but rather the debt management program adopted generally by provincial governments through the 1920s. For example the amount of public debt issued by the Dominion, Canadian National Railways and the provinces in Canada and New York rose from $343 million in 1921 to $660 million in 1930. Similarly triple pay optional bonds rose from $187 million in 1921 to $705 million in 1930.[22] Between 1930 and 1933, after the Canadian dollar depreciated against the U.S. currency, gross debt charges rose by $21 million although gross debt had increased only marginally.

The Liberal Party also included in its ranks a number of monetary reformers, principally from Western Canada. Gerry McGeer, the colourful former mayor of Vancouver, was another Liberal monetary reformer who shared with members of the Social Credit party a distaste for the "debt creating system."

> We borrowed to build roads, to build railways, and to build bridges across the St. Lawrence believing that posterity was to carry the load. But, unfortunately, for this generation we have caught up with posterity, and the load which we thought posterity was going to bear we cannot carry ourselves. *A debt claim system, under which men interested in interest bearing bonds control the issue of currency and credit, is not a safe system.* If we are going to have progress financed and democracy maintained we must do what has been done with the post office, administer it as a public utility largely free from partisan influence.[23]

It was important for Mackenzie King, in opposition, to strike a balance between showing some support for debtors (since debtors outnumbered creditors by a wide margin, especially in western Canada) while at the same time not alienating finance capital, an important source of election funding. Mackenzie King and the Liberals' sporadic attacks against the "money power," which began early in 1933, were carefully tailored to meet the mood of an increasingly desperate population and to capitalize on Bennett's decision to create a privately owned central bank along the lines of the Bank of England.[24]

Another quotation illustrative of the attractiveness of simplistic solutions came from Liberal Senator Lynch-Staunton of Hamilton who urged an immediate lowering of the rate of interest.

> I believe that arbitrary legislation with some feature of compulsion may be necessary to bring about such a reduction. Certainly our credit will have to be much higher than it is to-day if such a campaign is to succeed. If arbitrary legislation is enacted, is it not repudiation? Is there any difference between the confiscation of principal and the confiscation of interest? That some readjustment in the bonded indebtedness of this country is essential is apparent to all. How to bring it about is the question. That there must be a readjustment

with the debtor class in this country if we are to have a return to prosperity is as clear as day. There can be no prosperity when our farmers are "broke". How is this readjustment to be made? At the expense of the creditor class, of course.[25]

As 1934 and 1935 brought little improvement to Canada's economy, politicians from debtor regions began to moot the idea of a general reduction in debts. The beneficiaries of deflation, besides those with a job, were individuals receiving income under fixed contracts who increased their share of national income in the early years of the decade.[26] Progressive Member of Parliament William Irvine was categorical in his demand for a general reduction of debts, a reduction which he imagined would benefit creditors as much as debtors "for with their power of controlling money they can make more money in a year under prosperity than they are going to lose by the cut in debts which will have to be made." [27] In Irvine's view, debt reduction was legitimate, necessary, and inevitable in restoring the balance between debtors and creditors in the wake of the disastrous fall of commodity prices.

One of the earliest problems that disturbed capital markets in Canada and abroad was the premier of Ontario's revocation of hydro contracts to four privately-owned, Quebec based power companies. This move drew the ire of the prime minister who calculated the annual loss to the treasury, necessitated by the sudden withdrawal of its London conversion loan, at $700,000 for 20 years.[28] The response of Canada's financial community to Hepburn's action was swift and categorical. That June, when Ontario requested bids for a new bond issue, no bids were received. "So far as official records show," reported *The Monetary Times*, "this is the first time that any Ontario government which called for public tenders, has failed to receive a single bid."[29] Hepburn concluded a conspiracy had taken place and he used this boycott to announce the opening of 30 branches of the Province's new savings and loan offices fuelling wild speculation that he was working on some Social Credit scheme.[30] Other observers believed that dealers simply did not bid because they were afraid of being left with their hands full of unmarketable Ontario bonds.[31]

In apparent response to rising sentiments of repudiation, especially in the West, which would render new borrowing by the Dominion more difficult, the following comments of Prime Minister Bennett are noteworthy.

> We have been responsible for the effort which has been made to maintain the financial integrity of Canada. I have heard jeers that we should care more for our people than for our credit, but I wonder if there is an hon. member familiar with business who does not

> know that the salvation of the people depends upon the credit *which is maintained for them.* How are we to secure the very things which we need in this country if we destroy our character? *Our character is our credit and our credit is our character.*[32]

In developing this theme, R.B. Bennett acknowledged that Canada's thirst for new capital imports could only be quenched if default and repudiation were spurned. In keeping trust with foreign creditors, in preserving Canada's credit rating, the public interest would be served.

Similar views were also expressed by Bennett's successor in the Finance portfolio, Edgar Rhodes who, when assessing the interest rate situation in 1935, opined:

> It appeared that the time was fast approaching where practically all public bodies could secure the advantages of refunding outstanding issues at substantially lower interest rates, but a temporary clogging of the market and certain unfortunate, widely heralded statements have clouded the outlook for the time being. It is to be hoped that this situation is only a temporary one, *but it behooves all debtors to remember that credit is a tender plant and must be carefully cultivated.*[33]

This sentiment was endorsed a few years later by Manitoba Conservative Senator McMeans who allocated blame for the financial crisis on the respective western provincial legislatures. Noting that "no financial institution which has a board of directors in Montreal or Toronto will lend a dollar in the West," McMeans chastised the western provinces for "the awful legislation" they are passing,[34] adding:

> How can they expect to get along after they drive every financial institution outside of their borders? They come to the Dominion Government and say: "We are hard up. We have no money and we cannot collect what is owing to us." But, I repeat, they are in this condition because of their own laws. *It seems to me that unless there is some control over the legislation of these provinces we must expect the present condition will continue to exist.*[35]

After the 1935 federal election, new Social Credit M.P.s advocated easier money, which worried Canadian and international finance capital anxious not to see returns threatened by central bank monetary expansion.[36] The chief spokesmen on the subject of interest rates, usury and the burden of the debt were Joesph Needham (The Battlefords) and J.C. Landeryou (Calgary East). Needham and Landeryou pointed out that high interest rates, when compounded over the years, exceeded the Dominion's principal indebtedness.[37] Needham and his colleagues queried the need to pay interest on money borrowed, or "debt money" advocating the issue of "debt-free money" through the central bank.

> We heard a good deal this afternoon about loans and bonds. I say with all seriousness that if the credit of this country is good for a dollar bond, it is just as good for a dollar bill. If the credit of the country is good to float a loan of $100,000,000 through financial institutions, it should be just as good to float that loan by the government itself.[38]

Debt Operations

Refunding

The first major discussion about refinancing and commissions in the 1930s took place between J.H. Gundy, president of Wood Gundy (representing a syndicate comprised of A.E. Ames, Wood Gundy, Dominion Securities, the Bank of Montreal, the Canadian Bank of Commerce and the Royal Bank), and Liberal Finance Minister Charles Dunning in March 1930. Gundy was anxious to take advantage of the Dominion's desire to advance refund the huge volume of maturing issues at a time of relatively low interest rates. This proposal was made at a time of severe strain on the dealers who sought an operation that promised both success and large volumes, and thereby, handsome commissions.

Gundy, in the capacity of an unofficial financial advisor, prepared a lengthy memorandum for Charles Dunning, in which he noted:

> The amount of re-financing to be done in 1933, 1934 and 1937, aggregating approximately One Billion Two Hundred Million dollars, constitutes *a problem that will be too heavy if left to the time of maturity*. There is no doubt in my mind it should be dealt with without any further delay, as the first maturity of $447,000,000 is only three years from next November followed by a maturity of $512,000,000 one year later.[39]

This proposal was put on hold until after the June 1930 election, but the question of an early refunding scheme was actively pursued by the Toronto investment dealer and officials of the Department of Finance. It was evident that the new Conservative administration was in fundamental agreement with the thrust of the Gundy memorandum and the urgency of the refunding operation.

In an interesting "counter-proposal," put forward by a group of smaller dealers, it was suggested that the Dominion pay advertising costs, that banks receive a negotiated commission, and dealers receive a 1/2 percent commission and sub-agents, 1/4 percent.[40] This proposal was not taken up although the suggestion that the Dominion assume the advertising costs was adopted for the Conversion Loan of May 1931 and subsequently became standard operating procedure.[41]

In September 1930, Watson Sellar, acting deputy finance minister, noted that the refunding of large maturities was "made somewhat acute," by the "absence of callable features which might expedite refunding" and the "presence of tax exemption features."[42] The absence of callable features forced the Dominion, as borrower, to offer a substantial inducement to holders to convert their debentures before maturity dates (advance refunding). Early refunding, in the mind of Sellar, would alleviate undue pressures on the domestic capital market, improve the term to maturity structure and avoid "last minute reliance" on New York.[43]

Documents relating to the resumption of talks with Gundy in the Autumn of 1930 show official reticence to the prices offered and the commissions requested. Commenting on the Gundy proposal,[44] the chief of the Public Debt Division found the charges asked to extinguish the tax-exempt feature too high and the price to the public too low compared with outstanding issues then traded.[45] In a follow-up memorandum for the minister prepared by Sellar the offer was allowed to lapse as the spread of $1.75 was "too large in favour of the Syndicate." "I am satisfied," added Sellar, "that the Canadian banks will hold on to theirs, and I cannot see any hope of getting 1933 tax-exempts from rich men who are paying in excess of 25% income tax, therefore, I do not think the Government should be penalized in interest rates in testing out a hypothetical project."[46]

1931 Conversion Loan

The solution arrived at in early 1931 was rather elegant as it balanced the difficulties in obtaining the surrender of tax-advantaged securities with the need to remove uncertainty about refunding the large maturities in a depressed economy. As Prime Minister Bennett, who was also finance minister at the time, stated the May 1931 conversion loan was designed "to do something to remove the dark cloud" of heavy financing from the horizon.[47] As there was no question that the Dominion would arbitrarily abrogate its contract with respect to call and tax-exempt features, especially in these uncertain times, the May 1931 Conversion loan offer to holders of bonds included extra "talons" attached to the bonds that carried the tax free privilege for the 1931, 1933 and

Table 3.3
May 1931 Conversion Loan

Maturity Date	Outstanding ($millions)	Converted	Percentage Converted	Annual Savings
5's of Oct. 1, 1931	$53,000,000	$38,400,000	72.45	$ 197,000
5.5's of Nov. 1, 1932	73,000,000	37,000,000	50.68	370,000
5.5's of Nov. 1, 1933	446,000,000	273,200,000	61.26	2,732,000
5.5's of Nov. 1, 1934	511,000,000	278,200,000	54.44	2,782,000
Totals	**$1,083,000,000**	**$626,900,000**	**57.89**	**6,071,000**

Source: House of Commons, *Debates*, 17th Parliament, 3rd Session, April 6, 1932, p. 1756.

1934 maturities. All holders would receive the rate of interest originally contracted for until the date of maturity after which the interest rate dropped from 5.5 percent or 5 percent to 4.5 percent.

The Dominion decided against buying out the holders of these bonds by offering a bonus payment. This undertaking might have been politically damaging since it was believed most bonds were closely held by estates, banks and corporations. Instead the Government opted for a program to refund in advance of maturity to minimize the potential for troubles with such large maturing issues hanging over the markets. The loan aimed at the conversion of only $250,000,000 of four World War I issues maturing between October 1931 and November 1934.

Table 3.3 illustrates what issues were converted and the percentage of each issue converted. The table also shows that the investors' response to the offer was extremely good for the Dominion received conversion requests for nearly 60 percent of the maturities while only aiming for 25 percent. The issue was unique in the sense that all tranches were callable ten years before the final maturity date with 60 days' notice. Bennett estimated the annual savings from this operation to be approximately $6 million per annum.[48] This highly successful conversion loan was subsequently followed by Refunding Loans in 1933 and 1934 which converted a further $475 million.

The conversion rates for the earliest maturities were greater than for later maturities, which reflects the greater uncertainty in the minds of holders of locking in rates farther into the future. As it turned out, the Dominion gained an advantage from fewer conversions since rates fell between May 1931 and November 1933 and 1934.

The Drive for Lower Interest Rates

The main push for lower interest rates came during the summer of 1932 after the crisis in Europe stemming from Britain's departure from the gold standard. With continuing deflation and low demand for industrial credit, the United Kingdom government during 1932 floated a very successful conversion loan. This operation set the tone for the Canadian domestic market.[49] Adding support to this direction were Canadian pronouncements at the World Monetary and Economic Conference in 1932 promising Canadian co-operation in bringing the rate of interest down further. Intense pressure was being exerted by western opposition M.P.s to lower interest rates.

At a meeting in September 1932, an effort to expand credit through a "rediscounting" operation was attempted. Edgar Rhodes arranged an increase in advances to the banks under the *Finance Act*. Under the agreement, the Dominion sold the banks $35 million in 4 percent Treasury notes that the banks then pledged for Dominion Notes (e.g., currency) at 2.5 percent. This rediscounting proposal was reluctantly accepted by the bankers who objected "on the ground that they had more money in their tills now than they could find good risks for, Leman expressing the view, which was concurred in by the others, that the ratio of depositors to borrowers at the present time was about five to one."[50] Rhodes evidently was worried about financing "as cheaply as possible, *and with as little embarrassment as was inevitable* in connection with a large transaction."[51] This effort was greeted with some skepticism in social democratic quarters as inflationary along with similar doubts in the halls of financial institutions.[52]

At the same meeting, Watson Sellar reiterated the Dominion's desire for lower rates and credit expansion by introducing the possibility of a political backlash should the banks not fall into line. According to the Canadian Bankers' Association record:

> The Comptroller of Finance suggested the original proposal for three-year treasury bills would enable the banks to borrow on them under the *Finance Act*, thus providing a showing of increased advances which would *be some answer to the demands in the west and elsewhere,* particularly since the publication of the report of the

Monetary Committee of the Imperial Conference recommending an increased supply of cheap money as a means of raising commodity prices. *Otherwise at the forthcoming revision of the Bank Act there would most certainly be a controversy over the utilization of the Finance Act.*[53]

Unfortunately, for the Dominion, the banks interpreted advances as a sign of weakness and consequently other outstanding advances were drawn down making the effect on credit expansion negligible. Between December 1932 and April 1933 advances declined from $59 million to $39 million. Some analysts, including S.R. Noble, assistant general manager of the Royal Bank, believed this action put a halt to further loan liquidation, but the lack of satisfactory loan demand still did not encourage the expansion of loans and investments as loan liquidation proceeded until 1936.[54] It is true however that the banks' note supply did not decline after 1932 and by 1934 total bank assets began to grow slowly again.

In reviewing the Government's abortive attempts to compel the banks to increase their cash reserves and their lending, Governor Towers later observed:

If it seemed desirable to encourage expansion there was no way for the Government to take the initiative. It is true that an exception to this rule is found in Mr. Bennett's action in November of 1932 when he persuaded the banks to borrow $35 millions under the *Finance Act.* No more satisfactory way of accomplishing his purpose was open to him. But the very fact that such a transaction had to take place made it obvious that a central bank must be organized in Canada.[55]

Tied to the question of interest rates was the issue of rates paid depositors— the banks' major liability. Given a clear desire on the part of the Government to force interest rates down and thus lower its own financing costs, plans were laid to reduce interest paid to depositors. In the Spring of 1933, a statement was made to the House of Commons by Finance Minister Rhodes detailing the Government's reasons for lowering deposit rates on Post Office Savings Bank accounts.

However, believing that it was of the utmost importance to business and trade generally that interest rates should be lowered, the government has reduced the interest rate paid on post office savings bank deposits by one-half of one percent effective May 1, thereby *co-operating* in the general program to lower interest rates paid on savings deposits by the chartered banks and other depositories in Canada. The government participated in this matter to lay the ground for an effective reduction in the cost of money to all classes of borrowers and to promote the stimulus to business recovery which would result therefrom.[56]

In announcing a reduction in the rates paid on post office savings bank accounts, Rhodes was careful to state "the Dominion government is not charged with the duty of determining the rates of interest allowed by chartered banks on deposits nor with the rate of interest charged their customers for banking accommodation."[57] This was a curious admission for section 91 of the *Bank Act* set the maximum legal rate of interest charged by a bank at 7 percent and the *BNA Act* granted Parliament exclusive jurisdiction over banking, interest, currency and credit.[58]

The importance of reducing interest rates was also shared by the recently appointed deputy minister of Finance, W.C. Clark.

> Absolute necessity for gradually effecting a lowering of interest rates in this country. If this cannot be achieved *by normal processes, we will probably face irresistible pressure for compulsory conversion of outstanding debts on an arbitrary basis. We believe it to be very much in the interest of the banks themselves* to co-operate wholeheartedly with the Government in the attempt to effect a reduction in the interest burden by normal economic processes.[59]

At this time several parliamentarians pressed the Government to commit itself to a cheap money policy. For instance, cheap money meant a "good deal below 4 per cent" for H.E. Spencer.[60] During the Autumn 1933 financing discussions, Government officials sounded out the banks on the conversion of maturing obligations. Questions were raised by the banks about the 4 percent coupon rate which might be discounted to yield 4.5 percent, the market rate.[61] From the standpoint of public psychology and public relations, only a 4 percent coupon rate was acceptable to Dominion officials.

In return for this 4 percent concession, Bennett agreed that all conversions would be effected through the banks and for new cash sales "the general presumption would be that the bond dealers were to deal through the banks."[62]

In July 1934, Edgar Rhodes and W.C. Clark met again with CBA representatives to discuss interest rates. Clark put forward the Government's position that unless interest rates were brought down immediately, "there would develop a strong public attitude in favour of repudiation and scaling down of debts." In response, CBA President Jackson Dodds held that interest rate sensitive money would leave the country adding that, in his opinion, "there was a still greater necessity for the balancing of budgets and in the case of the Dominion the real problem was the railway problem which Mr. Rhodes readily admitted."[63] In order to resolve the impasse, it was arranged to have the banks lower their savings deposit rates further to 2 percent from 2 1/2 percent. The Government also agreed to "use their best endeavours to induce trust and loan companies to reduce their rate."[64]

Several months later as the Autumn financing approached, the minister requested a meeting with the CBA to confirm this understanding. This meeting followed discussions between bankers and trust company officials on September 21 at which time an agreement was struck to reduce trust company savings rates effective February 1, 1935. This arrangement however was not entirely satisfactory to the banks. According to the CBA record of the meeting:

> The President felt that it was possible (reduction of rates) and stated that while the banks did not desire to take any drastic action, *they would try to get all organizations in line*. He felt that the trust companies should be *asked to undertake to accept no new deposits at the present rates*, and that such deposits should only be accorded the rates which would be generally effective in January next. Mr. Clark felt there would be no difficulty about this. The President asked Mr. Clark to telephone to representatives of the trust companies after two days. After further discussion it was agreed that Mr. Clark should ring Mr. Watson of the Toronto General Trusts Corporation about 11 a.m. on September 25th. The President also asked Mr. Clark to telephone the Montreal City and District Savings Bank.[65]

By this nonmarket arrangement, the lowering of financing costs to the Government was transmitted through the banking and financial system reducing markedly the interest paid depositors. The Government's desire to reduce its borrowing costs therefore placed it in the position of acting as an intermediary to bring other financial institutions "into line."

This *in camera*, personal, non-arms-length financial relationship was again apparent during negotiations surrounding the refunding operations in the fall of 1934. At the end of July the president of the CBA, Jackson Dodds, and the prime minister debated interest rates over the phone. Bennett insisted the Government could not afford 3 percent, anything in that range would have an adverse effect on the Government's Autumn financing plans. In a revealing exchange:

Mr Bennett reiterated this over and over, and said *the country and the banks must swim or sink together*. Mr. Dodds pointed out the danger of bringing down the interest structure too fast and while admitting this Mr. Bennett still said that the Government could not pay 3% in this instance.[66]

Dodds then went on to point out that the 2.75 percent rate would be unprofitable to the banks and lead in turn to a reduction in bank dividends, to a further undermining in confidence and to a weakening of the country's credit standing.

The foregoing exchanges demonstrate the positional power of the banks in effecting the lowering of rates, and the shared values of Conservative politicians and bankers. Finally, the influence of parliamentary demands can be seen as an offsetting factor to the shared beliefs of Dominion officials and bankers.

FOREIGN BORROWING

New York

In September 1931, Bennett was apprised by his acting deputy of the "disorganized" state of New York's bond market fearful of a collapse of American savings banks. Given this situation, Sellar thought it was an opportune time to come to market for the view was widely held that Canadian credit was excellent. It was certainly excellent when compared with Latin American nations which were defaulting about this time. However, when England went off the gold standard in September 1931, foreign borrowing operations were cancelled in light of the sharp rise in short-term rates in New York during October.[67]

In 1932, assessments of the New York market took into account the November presidential elections. In order to avoid unsettled market conditions, it was suggested that the refunding of November and December maturities be settled before mid-October.[68] It was believed that the uncertainty of the election result would unsettle the markets for the two or three weeks leading up to the election and, depending on the outcome, for several weeks thereafter. Subsequently, U.S. $60,000,000 in one-year treasury notes were sold on October first, well before the U.S. presidential election.

London

In London, after the success of the huge United Kingdom refunding loan in the summer of 1932 signalled a return to lower, long-term rates, the Canadian High Commissioner was advised that the time was now right to come to market.

> ...if carried through at once, would meet with a favourable reception in the City of London, which point we feel to be of tremendous consequence inasmuch as it entails Canada's first entry into the London market as a borrower since pre-war days, and therefore, the success is of utmost importance.... We trust that you and your Government will appreciate the fact that only an extraordinary abundance of idle funds in London, enable us to put up such advantageous terms, and we take this opportunity of stressing the fact that absolute secrecy on this matter is essential to its successful conclusion.[69]

What was secret about this operation seemed to be the rather peculiar recommendation from Messrs. Rowe, Swann and Co. that "an understanding that a substantial portion of the proceeds would be devoted to the purchasing of British Rolling Stock for use on the State Railways" would be of considerable assistance in making the issue a success.[70] High Commissioner Ferguson's diplomatic reply read, in part, "I am quite sure, however that the desire of the Canadian Government will be to buy here anything they cannot procure at home."[71] This exchange can be considered the only blatant *quid pro quo* demanded in the documents on foreign borrowing examined during the period under study.

Another instance of market advice from London came from Nivisons and Company in regard to the possible conversion of the 3 1/2 percent stock of 1930–1950. Nivisons advised:

> The market is at present in position to deal with further large loans and we expect that there will now be a pause and that the Bank of England will not favour any more issues for the moment. *Recent events in the Dominion do not make the present moment any more opportune.* At the same time the British Government remains firm and money cheap and it is confidently expected that after a rest from new loans the way will be open again when we will immediately advise you.[72]

The preceding advice incorporated what Nivisons believed to be the stance of the central monetary authority, the Bank of England. Naturally, one of the most important variables in timing an issue was to avoid conflict of dates with an expected treasury financing. As the market could absorb only so much financing each day, it was essential for the borrower to know the dates that were relatively free of major corporate and governmental bond issues. Also critical was the merchant bank's attention to "recent events in the

Dominion." This was an allusion to the spread of social credit ideas in the west and to continuing depressed economic conditions that did little to support the Dominion's reputation.

After-tax Rates of Return

American and British investors, like their Canadian counterparts, sought as high a return on invested capital as possible, taking into account foreign withholding taxes. The existence of withholding taxes led necessarily to a discounting of the bonds by foreign investors. Undertakings by the Government or corporations that bond issues would be free of tax were and still are an integral part of foreign borrowing. Canadian governments and companies borrowing abroad frequently covenant to reimburse lenders up to a specified amount if taxes were imposed during the term of the financial contract.[73]

In June 1931, Finance Minister R.B. Bennett introduced a two percent withholding tax on interest and dividends payable to nonresidents. The rationale or justification for the proposal was that holders in the United Kingdom, France and the U.S. could use the tax payable as a credit against their own taxes payable. Nevertheless in the face of strong opposition from international finance capital, Bennett withdrew the proposal on July 16th, commenting that the move was inopportune in view of "European repercussions."[74]

During the Depression, worries of foreign investors surfaced several times that the cash-poor Dominion and provincial governments might impose special withholding taxes. For example, in March 1933, Edgar Rhodes proposed a 5 percent tax on all dividend and interest payable in Canadian dollars (with the exception of the Government of Canada) to all nonresidents. This tax also applied to interest payable under optional pay securities in foreign currencies trading at a premium to the Canadian dollar.[75] Predictably objections were heard from the financial press as well as from Quebec Premier Taschereau that this measure would harm Canada's and Quebec's credit.[76] On the London exchange, Canadian securities trading was suspended. At home Bennett and Rhodes were attacked for violating "sanctity of contract" on the basis that once a contract was signed then the holder had a right to be free of taxes for the duration of the contract.[77] Anxiety concerning the levy of the withholding tax prompted R. Nivison and Company, the London investment house, to write the Bank of Montreal. Nivisons stressed the vexatious uncertainty surrounding Dominion, provincial and municipal bond taxation and called for a Dominion:

> …understanding with the Provinces that no Dominion taxation of any kind will be levied on holders of Provincial Stock and Bonds

who are not resident in Canada. As soon as the policy of the authorities here permits of Provincial and Municipal borrowing, it must surely be in the interests of the Dominion of Canada to afford every facility for these operations in London, and to do this it is essential that the Provinces should be able to give the same undertaking to the investors as the Dominion itself...English investors have become insistent on adequate protection, from such taxation, *and there is little prospect of their being induced to invest their money in stocks which are not safeguarded in the manner suggested above.*[78]

Nivisons strongly intimated that Dominion bond prices would be discounted should the Dominion or provincial governments make moves to penalize foreign investors. This request also suggests that, in the eyes of the foreign creditor, Dominion, provincial and municipal credit were virtually synonymous, at least as far as "market psychology" was concerned. After several weeks of intense pressure, Rhodes and Bennett amended the proposal and instead imposed a 5 percent tax on all dividends and interest received from Canadian debtors (except the Dominion of Canada) by nonresidents. In addition, a withholding tax of 5 percent was made payable for Canadian residents holding optional pay bonds that were at a premium to the Canadian dollar.[79]

Canada's dependence on the goodwill of foreign bondholders also made the Dominion vulnerable to provincial politicians' proclamations about finance capital in general. The Dominion's vulnerability in this matter was painfully apparent during the Spring of 1935 when Premier Mitchell Hepburn of Ontario abruptly cancelled hydro purchase contracts with several major private Quebec power companies.[80]

The depression years reinforced the importance of government policies in Canada that were hospitable to the claims of finance capital. Politicians were under enormous pressure to revise the rights of debtors and often were obliged to pronounce directly on the centrality of credit-worthiness for the nation. This allegiance was a necessary corollary to the huge refunding and ongoing borrowing operations which, in order to be a success, required favourable capital markets. Favourable markets in turn meant government policies that maintain stability in the relationship between debtors and creditors.

4 | The Alberta Default and Its Impact on the Dominion's Credit

> The Province has the power to make it impossible for any bank to operate within its borders, to prevent it enforcing its claims for debt, to make the business of money-lending illegal and impossible, to publicise banking practice, and in many ways to inflict severe penalties upon the financial interests. I do not suggest that the financial interests in their turn have not the power to inflict damage upon Alberta but I do not believe that that power, if seriously challenged, is anything like so great as it is popularly supposed to be. Nor do I think that the condition of affairs in Alberta would be very much worse, except possibly for a very short time, if such very ill-advised action upon the part of the financial authorities were put to the test. The financial system is essentially a system of black magic and one of the best protections against black magic is not to believe in it.
>
> Major C.H. Douglas[1]

Alberta's Default

On April 1, 1936, Alberta was Canada's first, and only, province to default on a principal debt payment. In this unusual case of a default, the interests of a governmental debtor and institutional creditors clashed. The Dominion government recognized the importance of meeting the expectations of finance capital but Alberta's provincial government was committed to thwarting the claims of finance capital. The reaction of the Dominion government, the Bank of Canada, the chartered banks and international finance capital to the default is well documented. The inter-relationship of these various players illustrated the importance of government's maintaining "credibility" when borrowing in the capital markets.

Prelude to Default
Economic Backdrop

Before the Leduc oil discovery and the OPEC oil embargo, the economy of Alberta was heavily dependent on the production and marketing of grains. In 1929, nearly 40 percent of provincial income was derived from the activities of the independent commodity producer and wage labour hired by the farmer.[2] Deflationary pressures, which commenced on grain exchanges in 1929, reduced the average price per bushel of wheat from $1.14 in that year to a low of 32 cents for 1932.[3] The heavy reliance on grains, seeds and hay for income resulted in a staggering drop in farmers' income (Chart 4.1). Farm receipts were cut to one quarter the level of 1928 by 1933 even though total production was cut by only one-third. While other agricultural sectors, including livestock and fruit and vegetables, also suffered heavy declines these losses were not as extensive nor as consequential to this recently-settled, heavily indebted, grain exporting region. Falling export prices, combined with agricultural protectionism on the continent and the heavy devaluation of the Argentinian and Australian currencies, left the western producer with greatly reduced marketing opportunities, forcing the Conservative government into a band-aid program of stock-piling wheat.[4]

The lack of markets, low prices and high, fixed charges for transportation and debt service rendered wheat production virtually uneconomical by 1932. For 1932 in Alberta, Professor D.C. MacGregor estimated that of a total of $67 million in farm receipts, interest consumed one quarter of the farmers' estimated expenses of $68 million. Debts contracted when wheat sold for $1.25 per bushel became financially impossible at 40 cents a bushel. On top on this difficulty, charges were made by farmers, and substantiated by politicians and bankers, that the legal maximum rate of interest (7 percent) was exceeded by the practice of discounting the farmers' promissory notes.[5] The cost of transportation and threshing charges, which at one point constituted more than one half of the total value received by farmers, also cut into their net income.[6] And finally, the tariff, which protected the manufacturing industries primarily located in central Canada, tended to reduce the downward movement of prices of semi-processed and finished goods that were key inputs for production. The Rowell-Sirois study calculated that by 1931, the cost of tariff-protected manufactured goods to the wheat producer had doubled.[7]

Causes of the Crisis in Alberta's Public Finance

There are several related factors that account for the widening of Alberta's deficit in the early 1930s. In the first instance, the Liberal government left a

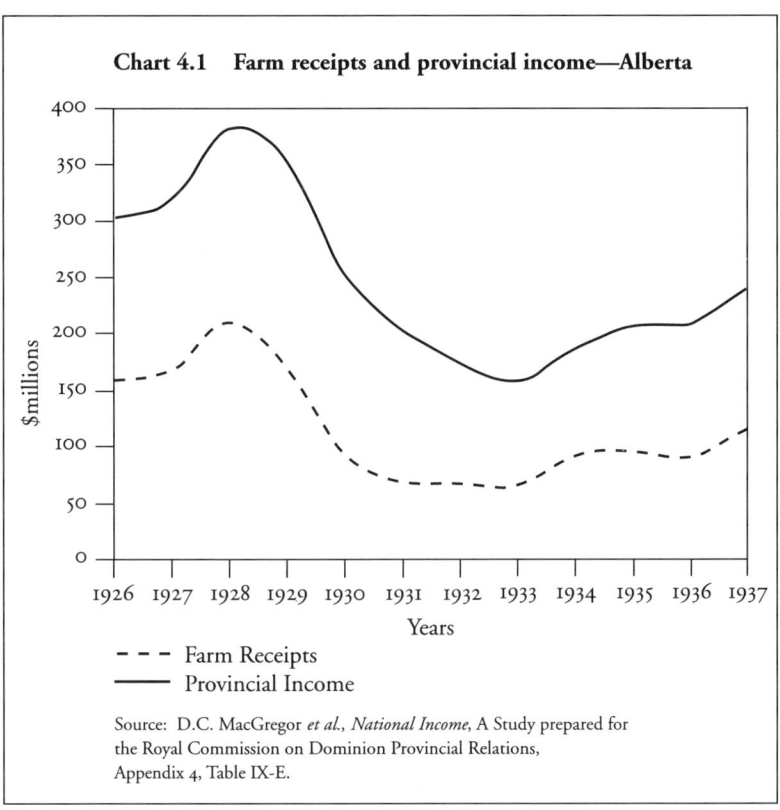

legacy of large, unproductive debts for the United Farmers of Alberta. According to the Bank of Canada's 1937 survey of the Province's finances:

> By the end of 1922, Alberta had direct and guaranteed debt (on which it was paying interest or for which it was later to become liable) which was some 50 per cent larger than in the much older province of Manitoba and more than twice as large as that of Saskatchewan though Saskatchewan had a 30 per cent larger population. Substantially more than half the Alberta total represented accumulated losses and deficits, or so-called assets which were proving a constant drain.[8]

Among those assets "proving a constant drain" were included $20,000,000 which had to be written off because the Province was unable to maintain its telephone system.[9] Another source of the acute financial embarrassment were guarantees provided to several railway and irrigation projects in Southern Alberta.[10] Thus, loose financial management, wildly over-optimistic capital expansion projects and poor judgment left the Farmers' government with a heavy burden of debt on their hands when it took office in 1921.

The second principle source of Alberta's public indebtedness and revenue deficiency stemmed from the United Farmers of Alberta (UFA) policy of not raising taxes to cover the growing demands for roads, schools, public works and all the operational costs associated with these capital projects. Indeed, per capita taxes in 1929 were lower than the 1921 level.[11] According to the central bank's analysis, "the province could scarcely have expected a more favourable opportunity than that presented in the years 1925–1929 to recoup itself from the rural areas for some of the large expenditures made on them. The opportunity was allowed to pass, and no reduction in the dead weight debt took place."[12]

When the Depression struck the "dead-weight" nature of the debt involving fixed interest charges and an insufficient revenue base, prompted a thorough examination of Alberta's provincial and municipal taxation system. The Alberta Taxation Inquiry Board, appointed in December 1933, took evidence from business, labour, citizens groups and manufacturers. The principal conclusion of the inquiry was a recommendation to boost taxation to the level of other provinces.[13] This report, along with the recommendations of R.J. Magor, "orthodox financier" and J.C. Thompson, provincial auditor, figured prominently in the production of the Social Credit Government's March 1936 budget that raised tax rates and imposed a two percent retail sales tax.

A third reason for the Government of Alberta's financial predicament was the heavy burden of relief charges especially in the cities of Edmonton and Calgary. Costs for relief and other forms of public assistance soared with the onset of the Depression, more than doubling between 1929 and 1936. Other efforts to reduce costs were made during the 1930s including a 10 percent cut in the salaries of civil servants and reduction in teachers' salaries.

Character of Alberta's Public Debt

By 1932, after racking up official deficits of $2.3 million and $5.3 million, the credit of the province was virtually exhausted. The province was unable to borrow abroad and could only borrow in Canada from the Dominion or from domestic sources at punitive rates. Between January 1933 and the April 1, 1936 default the Province was able to borrow only $7.6 million from domestic sources while borrowing $26 million from Ottawa during the same

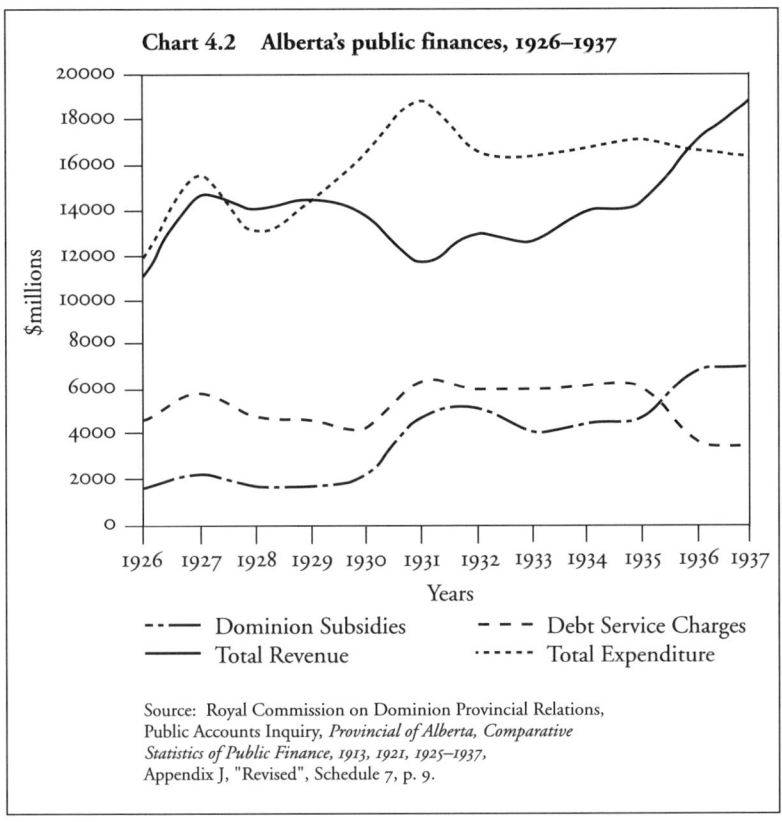

Chart 4.2 Alberta's public finances, 1926–1937

Source: Royal Commission on Dominion Provincial Relations, Public Accounts Inquiry, *Provincial of Alberta, Comparative Statistics of Public Finance, 1913, 1921, 1925–1937,* Appendix J, "Revised", Schedule 7, p. 9.

period at rates between 3 and 6 percent. This series of short-term treasury bill financings allowed the Province to avoid default by borrowing from the Dominion at one-half point above federal long-term rates but about 200 basis points higher than the prevailing treasury bill rates.[14]

The most damaging aspect of the structure of Alberta's public debt was the existence of optional-payment bonds and the absence of call features (Table 4.1). The optional-payment bond insulated the holder from foreign exchange risk while the issuer's position could be seriously jeopardized if one currency fell significantly in relation to another. This happened in the wake of England's flight from gold when the Canadian dollar, though trading at a premium in relation to the pound sterling, fell to a 10 to 20 percent discount in New York. As a result, between March 1932 and March 1934, nearly $2 million was expended on unanticipated, extraordinary charges associated with the payment of interest and principal to holders in U.S. funds. Had a larger proportion of these optional payment bonds been "London or Canada," these unexpected charges would not have been incurred. It was not surprising therefore for the provincial treasurer to request a fixed exchange rate and a return to the gold standard as a remedy for the problems associated with exchange rate fluctuations.[15] However, it should be remembered that these bonds were issued at a time when fixed exchange rates under the gold standard were the rule of thumb and there was no apparent reason to believe that such dramatic shifts in currency alignments would occur.

A second problem associated with Alberta's large per capita debt was the absence of call features. With a call feature, in a period of falling interest rates, the issuer will normally sell new bonds at lower rates, retire the higher coupon bonds and, in the process, realise substantial interest savings. Of the three series of debentures subject to a call provision, one was callable in 1949 and another in 1962. A third issue of $7,400,000 payable in sterling was callable at any time but at a large premium to be paid the holder, making the provision uneconomic until rates dropped to very low levels. For all intents and purposes then, Alberta's debt could not be called and this inflexibility made bondholders most unwilling to renegotiate and to return their relatively high yielding stock in exchange for lower yielding securities without any premium paid.

Another factor, which made the default situation more complicated was the debt's international character. Default of Canadian-pay debts was one thing, but default to foreign holders of the optional-pay instruments would, undoubtedly, lead to a general distrust of *all* Canadian obligations.

The extent of the fiscal crisis faced by Alberta in the months leading up to the August 22, 1935 Alberta election is captured in the following correspondence between Towers, Deputy Provincial Treasurer J.F. Percival, and George Hoadley, minister of Trade and Industry and Railways and Telephones. At the end of March 1935, Percival tested out the waters to see if the Bank of Canada would be willing to advance a loan to prevent default on an April first maturity, payable in U.S. funds. In a revealing letter to Thomas Bradshaw, Toronto financier and a member of the Bank's Executive Committee, Towers mooted the idea of becoming the Province's financial advisor.

> Profits,[16] of course, do not enter into it, and there would therefore be no object in our treating this as an isolated transaction to help Alberta over their present difficulty. From that point of view it would be better to leave them in the hands of the Dominion Government. *If, however, we assume that it is possible to make general arrangements*

Table 4.1
Province of Alberta public debt as at March 31, 1936

Classification	Amount ($thousands Canadian)	% of Total
Total Outstanding	$160,831.0	100.0
Direct Issues	154,016.5	95.8
Guaranteed Issues	6,814.5	4.2
Treasury Bills outstanding	25,427.0	15.8
T-bills held by Dominion	25,218.0	15.7
Amount of debt callable	15,267.0	9.4
Tax Free	134,149.5	83.4
Canada	55,804.0	34.7
Canada or New York	65,843.0	40.9
Canada, New York or London	19,915.0	12.4
Canada or London	4,000.0	2.5
London	15,269.0	9.5
Coupon Rates		
4.0	33,331.0	20.7
4.5	51,756.0	32.2
5.0	45,773.0	28.5
5.5	8,632.0	5.4
6.0	20,890.0	13.0
6.5	450.0	0.3
Maturing in:		
2–5 years	750.0	0.6
5–12 years	1,650.0	1.3
over 12 years	125,599.0	98.1
(excluding treasury bills)		

Source: Province of Alberta, *Comparative Statistics of Public Finance, 1913, 1921, 1925 to 1937*, Schedules 10, 11, 13, 14.

> with them whereby we would become their financial advisors, with the authority to speak on budgetary matters and general financial policy, including the time and terms of public issues the matter deserves careful study. Clark feels that if we can approve the risk we should not overlook an opportunity to start the ball rolling by consummating an arrangement of this kind. Alberta's financial position is not good, but they have made serious efforts to do their best. *As you know, the Province may now be considered one of the strongholds of monetary cranks, and some offsetting influence is highly desirable.*[17]

In exchange for providing advice to Alberta from Towers (Canada's "Prime Minister ex officio," according to Major Douglas), Alberta was to become the initial proving grounds for what was essentially a loan council coordinating provincial debt management and budgetary policies. Moreover, Towers foresaw a "partnership" of the province, the provincial government's banker (Imperial Bank of Canada), and the Dominion.

Later that month, Percival informed Towers that a $2 million loan would not cure the situation "except by prevention of default."[18] Two weeks later, Percival wrote to Towers giving his analysis of the financial and political situation of Alberta.

> Present bond prices indicate a wave of non-confidence throughout Canada; and in the face of a decided improvement of our revenues and in practically all lines of commercial business and that of agriculture, it is, to say the least, discouraging to find that pending elections and Government action should destroy what appeared to be a very strong and stable bond market. However, I am not altogether surprised that this should take place. Most of us here are suffering from what might be called a Social Credit headache, and during the next three months anything may happen.[19]

Percival's comments were prescient. They also reflect the shared perceptions and assumptions of bankers and treasury department officials of the natural and negative reaction of bond markets to political events which would reduce the price of outstanding issues. Falling prices, in turn determined what it would cost for new money.

That June, George Hoadley, the minister of Trade and Industry called Towers outlining his province's frustrations in attempting to raise $2,000,000 for an election road-building program. "In stressing the Province's need for the additional money," wrote Towers later, "Mr. Hoadley said that if they had to confess their inability to proceed with the road program, *Aberhart's campaign would be greatly assisted.*" It appeared the Bank of Montreal and the Royal Bank of Canada would no longer lend to the Province, at least on the terms the government desired. The Alberta's Government's banker, the Imperial Bank of Canada, was prepared to advance $2,000,000 *if* the Province was willing "to hypothecate the amount due the Province by Canadian Pacific and Canadian National Railways"— approximately $5,500,000 payable in 1939. This hypothecation would also cover existing "IBC" advances to the Province of $4.2 million.[20] Later that afternoon, Towers advised the Alberta minister against accepting the bank's terms.

> It had not been the practice in Canada for Provinces or the Dominion to pledge specific assets as security for borrowings and in this case it might be thought *that one creditor was obtaining an unfair advantage* in view of the fact that the security represented a value of at least $3,500,000 in excess of the new money being obtained; and this excess would be applied as security for existing indebtedness. I suggested that he should obtain Mr. Bennett's opinion in view of the fact that the Dominion Government is an important creditor and may be called upon for additional assistance.[21]

However, this time the Dominion did not come to the rescue but the Imperial Bank did.

Social Credit in Office

In August 1935, newly elected Premier Aberhart did not anticipate that the provincial treasury was so empty that the regular civil service payroll was imperilled. A temporary loan from the Dominion for $2.2 million was soon arranged with the Bennett government. One active observer of these events, A.J. Hooke, has claimed that conditions were attached to the Bennett loan, namely that Robert Magor, a financial advisor and formerly the "trustee in bankruptcy" of the Dominion of Newfoundland be appointed Alberta's financial advisor.[22] However, another participant who was also close to these negotiations denied there ever was an understanding between Bennett and Premier Aberhart on this matter.[23] Nevertheless it would appear from a pragmatic point of view, the hiring of Magor and requesting funds from the Dominion were a necessary accommodation in order to meet the payroll and to avoid the prospect of losing credibility in the early part of its mandate.[24] Moreover Aberhart and his colleagues believed that the issue of straightening out the public finances was a completely separate question from establishing the basic dividend and that Major Douglas need not be offended by the presence of Magor.[25]

While correspondence between Premier Aberhart and Major Douglas topped the news in January and February 1936, provincial treasurers were meeting in Ottawa to give initial approval to an amendment to the *BNA Act* creating a Loan Council.[26] The day following this historic agreement, Charles Dunning announced the provision of a $2,000,000 loan to the Government of Alberta in order to meet bond maturities. According to press reports "no strings were attached," nevertheless as events transpired strings were indeed attached.[27]

Less than one month later, controversy erupted over publication of a letter from Major Douglas condemning the Loan Council proposal that would "filch away" the Province's financial autonomy and that predicted Alberta would break away from the stranglehold of "orthodox finance."[28] As the due date of April first drew closer for the repayment of a direct debenture obligation of $3,200,000 (Canadian), it was learned that the prospect for further Dominion aid was in fact *conditional* on Alberta's acceptance of the proposal.[29] Ten days after this disclosure, rumours abounded that the provincial government was about to legislate a compulsory refunding scheme "with teeth in it."[30] This rumour led Charles Dunning to remind his provincial counterpart that much damage had already been done to prices of Western Canadian bonds from the March 15th announcement of a 3 percent refunding scheme.

The flurry of activity in March 1936 prior to the April 1, 1936 default is indicative of the fear that western provincial defaults would spread and therefore a coordinating mechanism was needed to prevent the floodgates of repudiation and default from bursting open. As the date of the April 1st maturity neared, Dunning drew to the attention of Alberta's Treasurer the adverse consequences to the market from political statements originating in the Alberta capital. On March 17th, Dunning cabled Cockcroft:

> Your letter requesting Dominion loan to assist you in meeting April first maturity reached me simultaneously with the Premier's announcement that Province was about to introduce legislation reducing interest rates on outstanding debt apparently without reference to proposed Loan Council (STOP)
>
> *Announcement has already had serious adverse effect on market particularly for Western Provincial bonds and proposal if carried out would nullify all efforts already made and proposed to be made by Dominion to protect credit of the Provinces and the Dominion as a whole* (STOP)

> In view of the action contemplated by Province, I do not see how I could justify to Parliament and to the country the loan for which you are now asking.[31]

In throwing down the gauntlet and, in effect, challenging Alberta to comply with the Dominion's desire to protect its own creditworthiness, Dunning ran the calculated risk that default would seriously harm the Dominion's credit standing domestically and abroad. However, in the wake of the default, Western bond prices slumped while Dominion bonds held steady indicating that the calculated risk had been successful in isolating Alberta's credit from that of the Dominion.[32]

On April 1, 1936 the Province of Alberta became the first, and only, provincial government in Canada's history to default on the principal of a maturing obligation.

Rationale for Default

As Professor Mallory noted, this about-face on the position of the Alberta Government towards the Loan Council left Treasurer Cockcroft in an embarrassing position.[33] Why had Cockcroft's commitment to the Loan Council been torpedoed? In all probability, the major factor that determined this about face was the incongruity of the world's first Social Credit government surrendering control over a key element of its financial affairs to a central bank and the senior order of government. Given the deep-seated, agrarian suspicion of the "fifty big shots," of "corrupt" eastern politicians and hostility to the "money power," such submission to financial tutelage would have raised a storm of protest inside the province, the Social Credit party and the Government caucus. Secondly, as the Province claimed, it simply could not meet its principal payment—it did not want to default but it would not submit to Ottawa's ultimatums. Thirdly, default corresponded with the need to refinance the debt at much lower rates. In Aberhart's mind, the orthodox proposals of Ottawa meant going further and further into debt without any visible benefits accruing to the debtor government. The arbitrary reduction of interest was a way of living within one's means and was also consistent with Aberhart's speeches concerning the evils of usury. Finally, default was premised on the grounds that sacrifices should be borne equally. If teachers and civil servants must sacrifice, why should the money power not sacrifice? The austere budget brought in on March 1, 1936, which raised taxes also demonstrated the Government's commitment to balancing its budget and spreading the pain. However, these measures in a time of depression would have to be matched by sacrifices of bondholders.[34]

Bank of Canada and the Dominion Government

A few days before the April 1st deadline, a view similar to Charles Dunning's March 17th cable was received by Governor Towers from S.R. Noble, assistant general manager of the Royal Bank.

> Unquestionably, something must be done to control the expenditures of the Provinces, but the Western ones particularly have had a very severe lesson in the last few years and a default would create a serious situation and set back recovery very materially. *It would, it seems to me, very seriously prejudice our reputation abroad, which we have maintained at tremendous cost.*[35]

A few weeks after the actual default, Towers, reflected upon the Alberta default and Western situation:

> the Alberta default did not cause any important disturbance in the market for bonds of the Dominion of Canada or of eastern provinces. Even though the Minister of Finance stated that Social Credit did not have anything to do with the Dominion's decision not to assist Alberta, both foreign and domestic markets have *tended to regard the Alberta situation as a very special affair.*[36]

In formulating alternatives to the broader question of the western provinces' predisposition to default, Towers recognized that default was inevitable (with the possible exception of Manitoba) unless financial assistance was made available by the Dominion. A loan council was problematic in Towers's opinion because "it would be extraordinarily difficult for Saskatchewan and Manitoba to accept a position which would be called one of tutelage at the same time that Alberta and British Columbia were acting independently." What was needed in Towers's view was a policy that bridled "local opinion" and which called for "more of the benefits as well as the odium of default." Towers argued that the benefits of default calculated to be approximately $6.5 million in interest per annum were far outweighed by the damage to the Dominion's credit structure.

> It would be penny wise and pound foolish to allow an upset to be caused by western defaults which would not provide more than a fraction of the relief required by the country as a whole, and would, on balance, cause a loss to the country as borrowers abroad, and to the Dominion Government as borrowers anywhere. *It must not be overlooked that Dominion Government requirements for new money and refunding during the 1936–37 year are extremely large.*[37]

This underscores the Governor's understanding that the credit of provincial and Dominion governments were interdependent, particularly in the minds of international finance capital, and his acute sensitivity to provincial governments' leanings to default.

Unsettled markets in the wake of the Alberta default forced the Dominion to delay a proposed loan in early June 1936. According to Deputy Finance Minister Clark:

> The Alberta development and the worsening situation in France make it inadvisable to go ahead with the issue next week. We propose, however, to have everything in readiness in order that we may make the public offering on Wednesday next if conditions appear satisfactory on Monday morning. On Monday the French Chamber meets and the new Government takes office, and the early morning cables will give us the necessary information on which to make our decision. Prices cannot, of course, be determined definitely until that time.[38]

Bond prices rallied during the summer of 1936, but at the end of August the Alberta Social Credit government brought down a series of measures that brought more nervousness to markets. These measures included a cut in interest by one half on all outstanding provincial securities[39] and municipal securities,[40] a retroactive cancellation of all interest owed on farm mortgages since 1932,[41] and the establishment of an "Alberta Credit House."[42] That winter, the Canadian cabinet was confronted with a dilemma. Should the Dominion rescue what some, including King, believed to be an impossible situation by pouring in "good money after bad" or permit Alberta's neighbouring province, Saskatchewan and Manitoba, to default? As Towers stressed earlier the "generosity" of the Dominion was necessary to ensure the very success of the refunding operations during the coming fiscal year. According to Professor Neatby:

> Charles Dunning who had shown so little sympathy for provincial administrations a year before, had now shifted his ground because as Minister of Finance one of his major responsibilities in 1937 would be refunding of more than three hundred million of federal bonds. He hoped to sell the new issues at 3 per cent instead of the 5 per cent or higher on the maturing issues, for an annual savings of some six million dollars, but much depended on the federal government at the time. He preferred not to have provincial governments defaulting while he was refunding the federal debt.[43]

Indeed by the beginning of 1939, the Dominion had advanced to the western provinces some $100 million in direct relief and grants in aid to keep the western provinces (Alberta excepted) afloat by ensuring that timely interest and principal payments were made.[44] These actions by the Dominion underline the understanding by government finance officials of the interdependence of federal and provincial credit-worthiness.

Another example of the nervousness of Dominion officials about the western situation is provided by R.B. Bryce in his history of the Finance Department during the Depression. Bryce records a series of discussions between Manitoba and Saskatchewan premiers and Clark, Dunning and Towers. Dominion officials were strongly opposed to unilateral reduction of interest rates by the provinces, particularly at a time of falling interest rates as disturbances to the market would rebound negatively on the Dominion. Manitoba Premier Bracken, who depended on the minority support of Social Credit to govern had *"found that the suggestions Manitoba might be forced to follow Alberta's example and repudiate the interest on its outstanding obligations had a noticeable impact on federal representatives."* The result of these discussions was a Bank of Canada study of the financial problems of the western provinces and the provision of Dominion funds to meet the financial obligations of Manitoba and Saskatchewan.[45]

Response of the Chartered Banks

Soon after the initial legislative program of the Social Credit government became known in April 1936, the CBA solicited the views of Graham Towers and Clifford Clark on the crisis.[46] In May, Towers advised the banks that they should seek representation on the Bondholders' Committee and participate actively in its activities.[47] In June, Clark's ideas were tapped. Initially, the deputy felt "Section 138" ought to be applied on the matter of "prosperity certificates."[48] Clark later expressed some reservations about disallowance, suggesting the Province should "learn from actual experience that it (dated scrip) could not be operated successfully." Both Towers and Clark believed that banks would be well-advised not to accept these certificates with Towers advising that the "practical difficulties" be stressed.[49]

It was not until the reduction of interest payments on the provincial debt was proclaimed on May 30, 1936 that a meeting was held of institutional bondholders in Toronto. At this informal meeting of 25 representatives of insurance, mortgage, trust and loan companies and chartered banks, there existed grave misgivings as to "what length the Alberta Government eventually might go unless some group (naturally the bondholders) discussed the whole matter with the Government."⁵⁰ The banks thought it necessary to solicit Towers's opinion on the matter. Towers replied he believed the committee was "greatly needed" and that bank representation would "strengthen" the situation. George W. Spinney of the Bank of Montreal was named the Association's representative. However, apart from the report sponsored by the Bondholders' Committee known as the "Elliott-Walker Report," meetings with the Government grew fewer and fewer as the Aberhart Government became embroiled in various legislative schemes to vitiate creditors' claims.

In September 1936 H.R. Milner, a prominent Edmonton lawyer and businessman, recommended a clandestine funding arrangement to funnel moneys to anti-Aberhart news and information organizations. Milner's recommendations are interesting because they reflect a greater awareness of the animosity directed at the banks by the Alberta population than that of bankers cloistered in Montreal and Toronto. Moreover, he was aware of the great organization, oratory, public relations and commitment on the part of the Social Credit forces.

> An Alberta committee [wrote Milner] is exceedingly dangerous. The money should be collected in the East and from the Western people who are interested, and should be given to one man whose name should not be known to more than two Eastern men at most and everything should be left to his judgment.⁵¹

Thus, the seriousness of the situation is illustrated by the suggestion of a clandestine money raising operation. In analysing the prospects for using media outlets and influencing news, Milner observed that of the rural dailies and weeklies run mainly by independent operators, only three or four should be used. While *The Calgary Herald* was supportive, the *Calgary Albertan* was under Aberhart's control and *The Edmonton Journal* lacked "intestinal fortitude." Milner recommended the purchase of a controlling interest in the Calgary radio station "Voice of the Prairie" for about $35,000.⁵² The foregoing reveals the sweeping plans recommended to combat the threat of expropriation of institutional creditors' security interests and how this strategy recognized the importance of influencing the dissemination and interpretation of news stories.

On September 1, 1936 the lieutenant-governor gave Royal Assent to several bills including *The Reduction and Settlement of Debts Act* and *The Debt Adjustment Act*. The former Act limited interest and principal owed after 1932, while the latter established a Debt Adjustment Board whose arbitration decisions between debtors and creditors were deemed to be final.

In response to this massive intrusion into debtor-creditor relations, the CBA retained counsel in Edmonton (H.R. Milner), Toronto (W.N. Tilley), and Montreal (R.C. McMichael) to prepare the banks' case against provincial intrusion into the sphere of credit and banking. In a 16-page "draft brief" to the governor-in-Council requesting disallowance of these Acts, the Dominion was urged not to construct too narrow a view of its powers and overriding responsibilities for "peace, order, and good government."

> ...it is apparent that the question of Dominion intervention by way of disallowance or a reference to the Supreme Court of Canada does not rest solely upon the constitutional validity of the Alberta legislation, but upon the serious consequences to the citizens of Canada as well as to Confederation itself, if a unit of Confederation is permitted to evince such disregard of contractual obligations, of fundamental rights, of the stability of financial institutions, and of the very terms of Confederation as crystallized in the *British North America Act*.[53]

In sum, peace, order and good government were reduced to the preservation of the existing financial order. Underpinning the banks' case was the assumption that any violation of the sanctity of contract would harm the general public through a general weakening in the economic order.

Public Relations Initiatives

In October 1936, the CBA in attempting to win its case with the Alberta public, requested bank managers to report cases of actual hardship of those suffering under "Mr. Aberhart's doctrines."[54] The stated objective was "a view to bring home to the electorate the damaging effect of such legislation, not only to those possessed of means, but as well to the man in the street."[55] In the case of The Bank of Nova Scotia's canvas only two instances of hardship were obtained including one news clipping. F.G. Burr reported:

> As you can well surmise, we hear all sorts of stories of hardships that have been caused by the Provincial legislation in this Province, but it is practically impossible to pin these stories down to any actual cases. I have made discreet enquiries from trust and loan companies and lawyers, but have not been able to get anything that would be of value to you.[56]

This finding should have been no surprise in a region where only a relatively few individuals would suffer from reductions in interest payments or those who had placed all their savings in Alberta government obligations.

The importance of a stronger media voice to counter Social Credit agitation culminated in the Canadian Bankers' Association's announcement in December 1936 of the appointment of Vernon Knowles, former managing editor of the *Winnipeg Tribune,* as "Public Relations Adviser."[57] In aiming to counter Social Credit's message, CBA ads were directed at refuting the fallacies spread by Aberhart and others about commercial banking and credit. One such advertisement emphasized that "bankers cannot perform miracles."[58] In rebutting the monetary reformers' accusations of a money power, Knowles pointed to the new institutions of the Bank of Canada and inspector-general of Banks to emphasize that banks were no longer a power unto themselves, if they ever were. Another advertisement opined, that "any group of responsible citizens who will get $500,000 in capital subscribed and half of it paid up, and who fulfil the requirements of the *Bank Act,* can start a bank."[59] This claim was made in spite of the fact that a bank charter had not been issued in Canada for over a decade; hardly a record that suggested competition and free entry into the business of banking.[60]

Another dimension of the banks' publicity was to convince the public of the dangers of the socialization of credit. "Credit—It belongs to you—the community does not own it," read one ad, which appealed to freedom-loving, enterprising individuals who were responsible and a sound risk. As well, the banks stressed their fiduciary role by stating "because of the bank's responsibility to its depositors it can make loans only where repayment is certain."[61] The banks during this period were promoted as secure financial bastions protecting the lowly individual's hard-earned credit and savings against the claims of the undeserving masses seeking special favours. In this crusade to redefine their function as trustees of the savings of the ordinary folk, the banks were solidly supported by the financial press who omitted to mention who owned or controlled the banks that "looked after" the savings of millions of Canadians.[62]

The other major facet of this campaign of advocacy advertising purported to present "A Few Candid Words About Bank Earnings." Readers were informed that "half of one per cent a year on total assets is not much of a profit margin for any business, corporate or individual." The reader was then apprised of the banks' central role in Canada's economic life in terms of payroll expenditures, employment and tax payments.[63]

While it is difficult to estimate the impact of this campaign and similar radio messages upon the Alberta population, in retrospect, it seems safe to say its impact was minimal neither strengthening or weakening the resolve of the devoted Social Crediter or the staunch bank supporter. The CBA's decision to hire a public relations adviser is instructive for it indicates the seriousness with which Social Credit was regarded by central Canadian bankers. No longer were august annual sermons to shareholders' meetings, published in many Canadian dailies, sufficient to ward off thoughts of repudiation and Social Credit. The Aberhart movement certainly forced the banks to take a more active role in shaping the public's perception of their role in the Canadian economy.

Plans for Retribution

The gravity of the situation in the winter of 1936–37 is apparent when examining the various alternatives circulating through CBA offices at that time. These proposals included "intimation" of a lower deposit savings rate for Albertans or an actual reduction, a "turnover charge and closing of 50 or 60 branches," as well as "lending at the current rates of interest, by way of discount wherever possible."[64] However these proposals were not universally endorsed. The Nova Scotia's H.F. Patterson called these reductions "inadvisable and impolitic."[65] Yet by July 1937, despite some internal resistance, ads were being readied for the press to announce the reduction effective August 1, 1937. Only the wise counsel of the Bank of Canada's governor served to postpone a move which, at this time, would surely have been "impolitic" and would have been perceived by Albertans as intimidation. When conferring with general managers in July 1937, Towers expressed "surprise at hearing this for the first time, and pointed out how awkward a situation might have been created if our first news had been from some reporters who enquired what we thought of the new development."[66]

This proposal was abandoned only to resurface a year later after more Social Credit legislation was introduced to raise bank taxes dramatically. The Nova Scotia's Patterson stood by his earlier position, arguing:

> It would be inadvisable for the banks to take steps to recoup themselves in any particular province for excessive taxation levied by it. We feel that whatever explanations the banks may make, they rather than the Government, would be the target of public criticism and it is still our opinion that to take retaliatory measures in Alberta would only provoke reprisals on the part of the Government.[67]

When learning of a second move to lower deposit rates in the summer of 1938, Towers cautioned CBA President S.B. Dobson to "think twice" before embarking on such a course. The reasons for so doing are outlined below.

> ...the banks should fight on the line that *there was one banking system for Canada*, and that the terms of business should be approximately equal throughout the Dominion. That does not mean, for example, that loaning rates must be the same in the case of all borrowers, but there should certainly be no dividing line as between one province and another...I mentioned that Mr. Dunning was generally in agreement with what I said to this point, and then went on to say that if the banks consistently fought on the line of Dominion-wide banking, so to speak, *the Dominion must inevitably protect them in the event of an emergent or an intolerable situation developing*—unless the Dominion abrogated its responsibility for banking, a surrender which I did not believe could take place.[68]

In short, the central bank sought to maintain the constitutional and financial status quo. The central bank's role in preventing what might be termed a colossal blunder enabled the banks to retain their credibility with the Dominion government. This contact and unity of purpose to protect the federally-regulated banking system allowed the chartered banks to put forward a united position to the Alberta Government. Towers's counsel underlined a strong commitment of the Bank of Canada to both the constitutional and financial status quo.

Debt Moratoria Legislation

During the August 1936 session in which the issue of prosperity certificates was authorized, the Legislature passed *The Reduction and Settlements of Debts Act*. The Act was motivated by the perceived arrogance and intransigence of lenders and their refusal to reschedule debts originally contracted when commodity prices were high. The Act, which was declared *ultra vires* the following June, caused *The Monetary Times* to thunder:

> At the recent session of the legislature, however, which met on August 25 and prorogued on September 1, it was evident that he (Premier Aberhart) had lost control and that the back benchers in the party under the leadership of Honourable Lucien Maynard were pushing him into measures which **not** *only strike at the very roots of credit and monetary security, but seem to be heading towards the establishment of a Soviet government in the prairie province....* The extremists were in the saddle and from the direction in which their achievements showed them to be riding, they are heading for something akin to Sovietism, if not the genuine article.[69]

The Act reduced all debts incurred prior to July 1, 1932 by applying all interest payments after that date to the reduction of principal. Another unusual feature of the Act was the inclusion of Section 16 that read "the provisions of this Act shall not be construed as to authorize the doing of any act or thing which is not within the legislative competence of the Legislative Assembly." This disclaimer did not make the Act immune from the courts which held that this section could not stop the judiciary from ruling on the constitutionality of the Act. Significantly, at about the same time, Saskatchewan's Liberal government also introduced sweeping debt reduction legislation which limited maximum interest chargeable on all farm mortgages to 6 percent (clearly *ultra vires*) and wiped out all interest arrears to January 1935.

Legal Analysis

Although the banks' total holdings of Alberta Government securities, including bank pension funds, was very small (about $3.4 million or 0.1 percent of all their assets), legal opinions sought by the CBA recommended a legal challenge. W.N. Tilley believed the courts would not allow the abrogation of valid contracts in the guise of interest reduction on municipal debts.[70] As far as the bankers were concerned, the *Municipal Securities Interest Act* would inflict serious harm on the municipalities' borrowing ability since "there is no means whereby lenders can be forced to extend new credit where the interest rate is inadequate."[71] Thus the withholding of credit was seen as a legitimate response to defend the banks financial interests.

As far as the *Reduction and Settlement of Debts Act* was concerned, this too was regarded as unconstitutional. Opined King's Counsel Tilley:

> A Provincial Act cannot authorize anything to be done which is not within the competence of the Legislative Assembly. The proper construction of an Act is for the courts and the question the courts must decide is not whether it professes to authorize something to be done not within the competence of the Legislature.[72]

In Tilley's view, this Act was clearly beyond the competence of the provincial legislative assembly.

Tilley recommended reference to the Supreme Court of Canada for a quick decision that would avoid accusations of heavy-handedness that might raise Aberhart's standing with the Alberta voters. However, from a strategic point of view, Tilley added:

the main application to the Government should be for disallowance and that it should be pressed strongly. If it is acceded to, the result will not be unsatisfactory. If it is not, the Government would be more apt to refer the matter to the Courts as a concession. But I think nothing should be done to indicate to the Government that any other view is entertained than disallowance and reference should only be suggested as an alternative.[73]

This assessment was not shared by H.R. Milner who thought that disallowance would be playing into Aberhart's hands. As there was no organized demand for federal intervention into the debt settlement area, it was better to let the legislation be challenged in the courts. Milner added the warning:

The Federal Government by now should realize that it is being, or soon will be, *faced with a national emergency* brought on by Aberhart's efforts to encroach on the Federal jurisdiction. *What he does today may very well subsequently be done by other provinces.* The failure of the Federal Government to disallow the Ontario Hydro contract legislation will present the chief obstacle to disallowance in Alberta.[74]

The CBA did prepare a draft brief to the governor-in-Council petitioning for disallowance of this legislation. The brief stressed the serious consequences to the Dominion and its citizens of this flagrant disregard for contractual obligations. Milner's view of a social credit contagion also found its way into a brief to Justice Minister Ernest Lapointe from W.N. Tilley.

The Government might also well bear in mind that there is a real danger of the ideas of repudiation of debt, embodied in the Alberta legislation spreading to other provinces, where governments may be forced to follow Alberta's lead. It is therefore important that any action which the Dominion Government may see fit to take be not deferred too long. The indirect effect of such intervention would not be confined to Canada, *but would undoubtedly improve the credit position of Canada and her provinces in the money markets of the world.*[75]

The implications were clear: the Dominion must prevent the social credit contagion from spreading. To do so would maintain and, possibly strengthen the Dominion's credit standing in world markets. The banks were clearly sending a message to the Dominion government that they expected the Dominion to protect its constitutional terrain and thereby its credit-standing.

The Dominion remained cautious in its approach; making the distinction between protecting financial contracts and overruling legislation widely popular with the western population (which had elected a great many Liberals the year before) was a difficult political dilemma.

Further Social Credit Initiatives

Declaration by the courts in February 1937 that a number of Acts[76] were beyond the competence of the provincial legislature did not bring peace to financial institutions operating in Alberta. The manager of The Bank of Nova Scotia in Alberta, F.G. Burr, informed his general manager that the court's decision "is only going to make Mr. Aberhart go a little farther, and we are hourly expecting a proclamation of a general moratorium given him in the *Debt Adjustment Act* passed at the last session."[77] Indeed, on February 23rd, an Order-in-Council was passed declaring a 60-day moratorium on all debts assumed before July 1, 1936.[78]

That June, the Legislature passed *The Postponement of Debts Act* authorizing the Cabinet "to postpone debt payments, prohibit issue of processes in courts of the Province and to stay proceedings in all civil actions."[79] If the Government was unable to insulate the citizen's property (and civil rights) from the jurisdiction of the courts, it would prevent creditors access to courts to satisfy their claims under the province's constitutional responsibility for the administration of justice. Similarly *The Debt Adjustment Act, 1937* also purported to limit the activities of creditors subject to the Debt Adjustment Board's permission and reaffirmed the Board's powers against the court's remedies of injunction, prohibition, *certiorari*, or *mandamus*.[80] This Act was disallowed in June 1938 shortly after the Liberal election victory in Saskatchewan so as not to send too strong a message that the federal Liberal government was unsympathetic to debtors' rights.[81]

Another ingenious statutory device employed to free debtors from their creditors was *The Judicature Amendment Act, 1937*, an omnibus bill, subsequently disallowed, that barred all courts from hearing legal challenges to provincial Acts unless the provincial cabinet agreed.[82]

The following April, *The Homeowners' Security Act* was passed to protect the mortgagors of farm homes and urban residences. The legislation protected the latter from foreclosure by requiring the creditor to deposit with the Court Clerk $2,000 in order to proceed with his legal claim. Without the deposit, action was automatically stayed. Should the creditor comply by depositing $2,000 and successfully repossess the home, the $2,000 would then be released to the dispossessed enabling the person to purchase a new home.[83]

Thus the creditor was caught in a "Catch-22" position and the debtor in the envious position of receiving $2,000, which in those days was usually sufficient to buy a home outright.

This measure was especially irksome for the banks because they held between $16 million to $20 million of collateral mortgages in Alberta, that is, loans secured by residential property.[84] In addition, an amendment to *The Limitations of Actions Act, 1935* would further handcuff creditors in realizing on their assets.[85] Tilley, in an internal CBA memorandum sketched out the alarming implications of this new legal device introduced by the Social Credit administration.

> In other words, bank debts incurred before that date (1 July 1936) where the debtor has not signed a renewal note and refuses to do so, will be outlawed in slightly over two years. It is evident that if debtors take advantage of this legislation to any great extent the effect upon the banks will be serious.[86]

This measure, in conjunction with amendments being made to the *Debt Adjustment Act*, would, according to Tilley, make its "practically impossible for a bank to institute any legal proceedings in Alberta, without the consent of the Debt Adjustment Board" known to favour debtors' interests. Tilley believed it essential that the legislation be stopped.

> While this statute is now in force, the effect of its provisions is not yet generally realized. It is important, therefore, that if anything at all is done to affect its operation, it should be done speedily for as soon as Alberta debtors become generally aware of its provisions [it] will be almost impossible for the banks to obtain signatures to renewal notes or other agreements of that nature.[87]

The fears of the past two years were now being confirmed—no longer were the banks' security only indirectly subject to depreciation, but they were being confiscated.

A growing frustration about the Alberta situation was apparent in a letter sent Finance Minister Dunning by CBA President Sydney Dobson in May 1938. In referring to the *Limitations of Actions Act*, the *Homeowners' Security Act* and the 1938 *Securities Tax Act*, Dobson asserted:

> Such legislation as this is purely confiscatory and is designed to assist debtors without regard to the rights of or its effects on creditors of any class. It is intended to force creditors generally to compromise

with their debtors, on such terms dictated by the latter and approved by the Debt Adjustment Board. In a word, this is bankruptcy legislation which interferes with banking as well as with long term lending and with trade and commerce between Alberta and the other parts of Canada and other countries.[88]

Dobson also added these laws were "progressively disruptive of the moral fibre and common honesty of Canadian citizens in Alberta and neighbouring provinces."

Throughout the 1936 to 1939 period, Alberta's Social Credit government placed Canada's banking system on its heels. With the reins of power and with access to sophisticated legal advice of the attorney general's department, the banks were forced to mobilize both legal expertise as well as media expertise in order to combat Social Credit's legislative initiatives. The archival records illustrate the close coordination between the CBA and Governor Towers. This coordination is hardly surprising since the banks and central bank shared similar, if not identical views on the nature of lending, perfection of security and legal recourse when a borrower defaulted. Having served as a senior officer with the Royal Bank of Canada and therefore having associated with other senior Canadian bankers, Towers was no doubt regarded as a critical ally for the banks in their quest to limit the impact of Alberta's Social Credit. Towers and the institution of a central bank proved invaluable to the chartered banks in the sense that bankers had a trusted ally with access to the highest levels of the political system. It may be argued that the Alberta situation was the first major test of Towers's mettle as the new governor. His action in warning the banks against a foolhardy course of action confirms this allegiance to the status quo.

INTERNATIONAL FINANCE CAPITAL

The segment of foreign markets trading Canadian bonds was also sensitive to news about Canada's trade balance, national income, government revenues and expenditures, and the domestic political situation. The election of William Aberhart's Social Credit government and the deteriorating fiscal position of the three prairie governments posed serious concerns for the Dominion. From an international creditors' perspective, it was believed that the Dominion, especially the new central bank, should make every effort to prevent Alberta's default from spreading east and west.

London

Shortly after the Bank opened for business, Towers wrote Sir Montagu Norman, governor of the Bank of England, outlining the difficulties facing the western provinces and probing Norman on their possible consequences for Canadian credit. "In a way," wrote Towers, "it is foolish for the Dominion Government to continue to foot the bill on the present basis. It simply means that the Dominion Government is indirectly paying interest at higher rates." More particularly,[89] Towers wished to know the impact on the Dominion's credit rating should the federal government step in to guarantee provincial refinancing.

In London, the Alberta default did not have a major effect on Canadian credit as might be expected. Towers was correct in observing that Alberta would be treated as an exceptional case. Lester Pearson in a June 1936 dispatch to O.D. Skelton, undersecretary of State for External Affairs, noted that British anxiety centred on Alberta while Dominion bonds were trading nearly on a par with British Exchequer issues. Pearson reported that questions were being asked of the secretary of State for the Dominions as to the steps being taken by His Majesty's government to protect the holders of Alberta and City of Vancouver bonds.[90] In November 1936, Towers visited London and met with Sir Montagu Norman. Sir Montagu expressed the view that "any form of western default (was) unwise," and argued for efforts to keep these debtor provinces afloat.[91]

These conversations and others illustrate the close connection foreign bondholders drew between the Dominion's and provincial credits. There also appeared to be a set of expectations built up about Ottawa's decision-makers; expectations that aberrant behaviour, namely default, repudiation or social credit, must be discouraged, and preferably eliminated. A document prepared by the Finance Department for the 1937 Imperial Conference entitled "Interest Reduction Legislation of the Province of Alberta," attempted to address these concerns and supports the view that foreign bondholders and governments expected that Ottawa's decision-makers should police the unorthodox activities of certain provincial governments.

The following passage, presumably written with the input from the Department of Justice, traces the use of the federal power of disallowance, which allowed the Dominion government, through the lieutenant governor, a Dominion appointee, to veto provincial legislation. The power prompted expectations, particularly from countries with a unitary system of government, such as the United Kingdom, that the Dominion would rein in "radical" governments.

Though the power of disallowance has been frequently exercised in the past, it is important to remember that no provincial statute has been disallowed in recent years. A different conception in regard to the disallowance of provincial statutes has grown up and it is now widely believed that disallowance is not the proper remedy except in very exceptional cases. If a provincial statute is unconstitutional, the remedy lies in attacking the validity of the legislation by an action taken in the courts in the ordinary way. If, however, a provincial statute is clearly constitutional but is objectionable for other reasons it is one of the consequences of the granting of responsible government that redress should lie with the electorate of that province. Any other view would place the Dominion in an intolerable position and require it to judge of the propriety of statutes passed by a province in relation to the exclusive legislative authority assigned to the province. The Dominion does not admit, however, that the power of disallowance is obsolete and could not now be exercised if a proper occasion arose *but it should be understood that the power of disallowance is likely to be exercised only in exceptional cases when no other remedies are available, and the interest of the Dominion is directly affected.*[92]

Here the Dominion was clearly hedging its bets—it could plead "provincial rights" when it came to ignoring Duplessis's attacks on Communists or it could disallow legislation that "directly" affected the Dominion's interests regarding its credit standing. As events unfolded, foreign investors' expectations played a part in pressing the Dominion to act "responsibly," to use its constitutional powers and, if need be, its financial resources to safeguard the capital of foreign bondholders and thus preserve its credit standing.

New York

In addressing himself to the problem of best protecting the integrity of the Dominion's and the nation's credit, Towers drew a distinction between the default in Alberta and the situation in the other western provinces. Towers thought it "penny wise and pound foolish" not to preserve the Dominion's and the country's credit intact by meeting, on an ad hoc basis, calls from the other western provinces for loans to meet approaching principal and interest payments.[93] This fundamental requirement to protect foreign bondholders' Canadian investments was based on Towers's reading on the bondholders' preoccupations:

> Investors in that country (the United States) have bought western bonds right up to recent times on the general assumption that they were Canadian obligations, and therefore safe. Doubtless they should have exercised more discrimination, but not having done so, I am afraid that default will change their attitude toward all Canadian obligations from general faith to general distrust. They will fear—perhaps with a good deal of justification—that the default complex will move east. No one should attempt to lay down the law on a matter of this kind where the psychology of markets plays such an important part, but I have no hesitation in saying the situation I have outlined is the *probable* one. *United States investors in Canadian western bonds constitute a very influential group, and if a general western default makes them form an adverse opinion on Canadian securities as a whole, the situation would be extremely serious and damaging for the Dominion.*[94]

The Dominion was caught between the fears of foreign investors and the constitutional division of powers that gave Ottawa virtually no authority to police provincial government debtors.[95] It seems reasonable to presume that the Loan Council concept[96] was a response to both domestic and international finance capital's reluctance to buy provincial paper. Thus the solution proposed to ease bondholders' anxieties was a new institutional framework under federal auspices to control provincial borrowing and thereby provincial credit-worthiness, which in turn would assist in protecting the Dominion's credit standing.[97]

In an encounter between W.C. Clark and a New York investment banker, the connection, in the eyes of international finance capital, between Dominion and provincial credit was often raised. In December 1936, Clark drafted the following memorandum recording his discussion with Harry Morgan of Morgan Stanley.

> I had a private discussion with Mr. Morgan in regard to the Western provincial situation, pointing out the fact that there was no legal connection between our credit and provincial credit (which he admitted, although stressing that there was a definite psychological connection which was of importance to the investor), and pointing out also how difficult it would be to make any statement which would not involve one in speculations that might prove untrue or that might not lead one to go on from a discussion of provincial credit to municipal credit, to almost anything under the sun.[98]

Later, when visiting Washington and New York in April 1939, prior to the sale of $20,000,000 in two-year notes, Towers sounded out Washington official Alvin Hansen and Canadian-born economics professor Jacob Viner and officials at Morgan Stanley on the effects of a possible Saskatchewan and City of Montreal defaults. Hansen and Viner were "unanimous that a combination of the two would be very bad."[99] This seemed to confirm the conventional wisdom within the federal bureaucracy that default must be contained in the interests of the Dominion's foreign and domestic debt management operations.

In attempting to ensure that defaults would not spread east to other provinces, the Dominion Government provided considerable sums to Saskatchewan and Manitoba for relief and the maintenance of interest payments and continued to roll over Alberta's short-term obligations. Indeed, the tax rental scheme worked out during the early part of the war was designed to avoid an expected default by Manitoba in June 1941, the arbitrary reduction of interest by Saskatchewan which, when combined with the Alberta situation and municipal defaults, would have a decidedly negative impact on the Dominion's credit at a time it required vast sums of cash.[100] In Alberta's case, some aid was forthcoming but it was given sparingly. Alberta's requests made directly to the Central Bank were always spurned with the rider that advances would only follow a reconciliation with bondholders.[101]

Alberta's Social Credit's election, the April 1, 1936 default and debt moratoria legislation posed a serious threat to Canada's financial system and, consequently, to the Dominion's credit standing in the world's capital markets. Both domestic and international finance capital quickly recognized this threat and the importance of isolating Alberta as aberrant debtor. The response taken was a measured one and largely directed by Canada's brand new central bank that could make more objective judgments than chartered bankers whose profits were at stake. The careful management of the Alberta situation by Governor Graham Towers was premised on the shared assumptions of maintaining calm in the capital markets. Calm in the capital markets was vitally important as the Dominion remained dependent on favourable markets for selling Dominion securities.

5 | Broadening the Ownership of the Debt and Bank Resistance, 1935–1939

Debt Management and the Central Bank of Canada

The major objectives of debt management after the Bank was created were to take advantage of lower interest rates, to establish a broader and deeper market for government debt and to encourage a more finely tuned, impersonal set of market relations. This meant an end to private consultations with the banks preceding new Dominion issues. The achievement of these goals was a *sine qua non* for monetary policy based on open market operations requiring a highly sensitive, broad market in government debt, which was lacking at this time. The goal of broadening the market for government debt was designed to drive an effective wedge between the Dominion as prime borrower and the institutional purchasers of bonds. According to Governor Towers:

> ...our position versus the commercial banks and the security market is a very special one. For example, we can never obtain opinions from any outside source when we are formulating our advice to the Government regarding new issues. Thus we never enquire the views of anyone outside the bank. A central bank must be independent and impartial, which means that on most occasions it must play a lone hand.[1]

This "lone hand" effectively meant the elimination of the previous consultations or negotiations with the chartered banks. Henceforward, the Bank's policy initiatives and the Dominion's borrowing costs would be based on the central bank's policies in response to Government's needs (as interpreted by Finance and implemented by the Bank) and the movements of domestic and international financial markets. International financial conditions had a significant effect on the ability of the Dominion to borrow at lower costs in international markets. Looser monetary conditions in London and New York also assisted the Dominion in lowering domestic rates. From August 1935, when long-term rates neared 4 percent, rates fell gradually to near 3 percent during the summer of 1939 before inching up prior to the declaration of War.

Lower Interest Rates

During 1936, attention was directed towards funding the debt. In a memo, W.C. Clark outlined for Charles Dunning the variables to be taken into account when determining the term to maturity structure. These variables included the direction of interest rates and tailoring the term and rates to ensure investor receptivity.

> If the objection to a 3 1/4% coupon rate is a real one with you, the alternative would be to try a 12 to 15 year issue, which we could do at slightly better than 3% if the [m]aturity were less than say 14 years and slightly above 3% if the maturity were 14 or 15 years. A 12 to 15 year maturity would probably be too long *to attract bank buying in any volume and it would not give a rate of return that would be attractive to the insurance companies.* To make sure of the success of the issue we could combine it with a shorter issue, say a six or seven year maturity, but the objection to this is that we probably should retain as many short term maturities for use a little later when we have to refund issues maturing in a period of higher interest rates. In other words, when the trend in interest rates turns upwards we will probably prefer to issue 3 to 7 year bonds rather than to tie ourselves up for say a 15 to 25 year period at the prevailing higher interest rates.[2]

The desirability of funding the debt at the prevailing low rates also preoccupied the Bank of Canada. In June of 1936, Towers speaking of the banks' and life insurers' lack of enthusiasm for long-term issues, noted:

> We believe that their resistance is breaking down and that they would be ready to accept a longer term, say 30 years, for the sake of the additional yield. It is a moot question whether they will regard a 3.30 yield as attractive; but the Government cannot, and should not, offer anything better, and the prospects for success are, in our opinion, sufficiently good to make the attempt worthwhile.[3]

This assessment laid the groundwork for another Bank initiative led by Securities Advisor K.A. Henderson that resulted in the sale of $55,000,000 of perpetuals delivered in September 1936. In a "Very Secret and Confidential" (undated) memorandum authored by Clark, there was some doubt in the deputy's mind as to the success of the proposed operation. Clark believed it would be safer to insert a hedge in the form of a 10-year, 2 percent bond, just in case the market did not accept the perpetuals. "While, I, myself, would feel more comfortable with such a hedge," Clark advised his minister, "the Bank officials are confident that the perpetual will sell readily and that a hedge is unnecessary." Clark had confidence in the judgement of the Bank's officials and felt the initiative would meet the needs of "other financial institutions" (nonbank sector) and was consistent with "future plans for consolidation of our national debt."[4] The Bank's advice was taken and the $55 million in perpetuals were successfully marketed along with a $45 million medium-term issue.

The intermediary role played by the Bank as fiscal agent however put the central bank in a somewhat schizophrenic position between the capital markets, institutional investors and the Dominion. In 1937, this schizophrenia became evident during discussions between Finance Minister Dunning, Deputy Minister Clark and Governor Towers. Normally the central bank advanced proposals in the form of recommendations to the minister and his officials on the tranches and rates to be offered on new issues. That October, Towers recommended a 3.5 percent bond at par which Clark believed would be "construed as an admission and crystallization of a higher rate structure, and it was too early to take any such action." In reply, the Governor believed this rate "during the *present unsettlement in the markets* could not be construed as a definite admission of permanently higher rates."[5] Several days later, Clark suggested that if the 3.25 percent rate proved to be a flop the Exchange Fund Account managed by the Bank might take up the residual. For Towers, this action would have had the effect of deceiving the market and "a great many people will say that the Government had got into a fix by endeavouring to pare things down too fine."[6] In Towers's view, it was essential that the loan be a complete success during this period of market uncertainty and a 3.25 percent rate "would not sell in sufficient volume to constitute a success."

> We had feared that no more than, say, $35 millions might be taken, instead of the $50/60 millions which was probably needed....certainly I hoped that would be the case. Our recommendation for the 3 1/2s was based on the feeling that they gave much greater certainty of success at a time when failure would be a bad thing, and they did not represent an unreasonable cost so far as the Government was concerned.[7]

What is revealing about this discussion was the Governor's strong desire to ensure a warm market reception for the bonds. This expectation, "the greater certainty of success," is consistent with the expectation that emphasizes that market issues *must* be successful. "Failure" was not an option in these matters. Clark and Dunning meanwhile, from their institutional standpoint, feared a possible market reaction to a higher rate structure would be detrimental to future borrowing. This is not to say that the Governor and his officials were totally indifferent to the borrower's desires for a reasonable rate for borrowing. In a memorandum prepared in May 1936, the Governor wrote:

> But what we are trying to recommend is a procedure which, in the end, will be the most satisfactory and the most economical to the Government. I feel that this point is extremely important because if any impression—even a subconscious one—grows up that we are casual in our attitude towards costs or possible savings, there must necessarily be a tendency to discount any advice we may be able to give.[8]

The central bank then, in tendering advice to the Dominion on interest rates and terms, had to be both accurate in its appraisal of the market expectations and "appetite" and, at the same time, sensitive to the borrower's requirements for low rates.

Smaller Investors

With the creation of the Bank in 1935, a far more positive attitude was taken to the sale of government debt to smaller subscribers. The main impetus for a broader distribution of the debt came from the central bank's Securities Department, which had close, daily contact with the securities market. Early in 1937, Assistant Deputy Governor Saint-Amour advised his superiors of the trials and tribulations of "the small investor (who) may put in his subscription a few times but if he is turned down on each occasion he will soon take it for granted that his money is not wanted, and will assume that Government bonds are monopolized by banks, insurance companies, etc."[9]

In the Bank's 1937 *Annual Report*, it was announced that to promote wider distribution of bonds the period elapsing between the offering and the opening of subscriptions was being extended. "This procedure gives small investors, particularly those who are distant from the large centres, a better chance of participating in a new issue," the Report commented.[10]

Behind the scenes, officials in the Securities Department promoted the idea of issuing bonds in smaller denominations. In February 1938, W.H. Budden reported a strong demand from small subscribers for a recent CNR issue. Budden counselled the Governor: "the availability of registered bonds in small denominations with the interest paid direct to the owner by cheque would not only provide an improved outlet for savings but would also have a salutary effect of developing a wider interest in and support for government securities."[11] The Securities Department followed this up by calling for the issue of bonds in denominations of $100, $500, and $1,000 in registered form "to facilitate a wider distribution of Dominion of Canada long term bonds" in response to a "progressively increasing demand."[12]

The foregoing can be better understood in the context of discussions taking place between the central bank and the investment dealers at this time in an attempt to improve the marketing and distribution of Dominion securities. This initiative to draw in a wider group of middle-class subscribers is also related to what was perceived to be a distortion in the bond market caused by certain classes of investors, including institutional investors, who had monopolized the ownership of tax exempt bonds.[13]

RELATIONS WITH INVESTMENT DEALERS

In correspondence and meetings with Bank officials, members of the Investment Dealers Association consistently stressed the need for higher commissions "to stimulate sales" and to provide the organization for a wider distribution of bonds—the latter, a policy espoused by the central bank.[14] From the Government's perspective, commissions represented an off-the-top, one-time only, charge for placing the bonds. A high commission would be an inducement to sell as many bonds as possible but Towers saw that too large a commission might have marginally diminishing returns. When discussing the 1937 Refunding Loan of $100 million, Clark proposed an additional 0.25 percent underwriting commission on top of a 0.75 percent sales commission. Towers rejected this disguised commission, adding the extra commission "would not add greatly to the Dominion's reputation for seriousness and plain dealing in matters of finance."[15]

With respect to the issue of allotments, dealers were anxious to purchase a sufficient quantity of both bonds to meet clients' demands and for inventory purposes, with which to turn a quick profit if the issue traded at an early premium, which was often the case. One of the first tasks of the new central bank was to devise a set of procedures for the marketing of public debt. The elimination of "padding" was a major concern of the Bank's. This practice saw "salesmen of larger houses…telephone to stock brokerage friends asking them to put in orders…such orders immediately assume that the loan is to be a big success and put in some orders of their own."[16] Often the names entered on the subscription lists were fictitious, a practice which was difficult, if not impossible, to detect. As Towers remarked in a letter to Charles Dunning, "padding takes on a ridiculous scale, with the result that the more daring padders get a disproportionate amount of the bonds and the orderly marketing of the issue to investors is thereby prejudiced."[17] Padding guaranteed that the padders would secure sufficient bonds to be able to meet customers' demands and more, which enabled the firm to sell bonds into a rising after market to turn a quick profit on their own account. To prevent this practice, the Governor was prepared to sell bonds into a runaway after-market to curb this form of unhealthy speculation.[18]

The real impetus to change these speculative practices began in early 1938. In a memo prepared by the general manager of the Bank of Montreal, the pernicious effects of a "flood of subscriptions from small dealers for amounts which the inexperienced eye could identify at once as being far beyond the capacity of these bond houses to take care of" was sketched.[19] As a result of this complaint, discussions were held with the Investment Dealers Association (IDA). The IDA pressed for the exclusion of non-IDA members, the creation of an "exempted list" for institutional investors with a commission to be pro-rated among IDA members, a 1.25 percent commission to IDA members and 0.5 percent to sub-agents.[20]

The history of this pooled commission concept may be traced to Fry, Mills, Spence and Company proposal to the Dominion government in October 1930. Fry, Mills, Spence and their associates recommended the pooling of commissions for financial institutions (trust and insurance companies) when converting government stock. This suggestion for an exempt list of institutions would have eliminated dealer line-ups outside treasurers' and investment officers' offices seeking to arrange the proposed conversion.[21] This suggestion was again put forward this time by the IDA President, J.E. Savard in May 1936 to bank officials.[22] The IDA desperately sought official recognition as the sole distributing group for Dominion issues along with the banks. The group also sought a type of controlled competition for its members through an exempt list that was eventually implemented during the War.

There were some in the Bank, including the Governor, who believed that stockbrokers, as opposed to investment dealers, should be removed from the list thus strengthening the role of the IDA.[23] However, in the minds of Bank officials and Dunning, the Association had to "clean up its act" before being granted this virtual monopoly. Dunning was apparently prepared to regulate against the abuses of the 1926–1929 period under the trade and commerce clause if the dealers were unwilling to institute a satisfactory form of self-regulation.[24]

Ultimately a decision was reached by which the Bank offered bonds "firm" to an approved list of distributors, including stockbrokers, with a 5 percent deposit required to discourage unnecessary and speculative padding. In addition, the Bank instituted a rule preventing the sale of bonds *below* issue price until the bank lifted the restriction. This restriction was usually lifted after the delivery of bonds. The dealers were eventually able to get around this trade restriction by "over-trading" or entering into swap arrangements with customers. This allowed the dealer to sell the bond at issue price but in return the dealer received a bond that was priced below its market value.[25] It was also decided by the Dominion that firm allotments would be based primarily on the placing record of the various firms—past performance would determine future allotments.

The importance to a firm of allotments is reflected in correspondence between dealers and the Government concerning the Dominion's domestic and foreign placements. In February 1936, Mr. Weldon of Midland Securities petitioned Clark to have his firm's allotment increased. The deputy did acknowledge that he had called "attention to the fact that the amount which it was proposed to allot to your firm did not, in my opinion, represent its placing power, and I suggested that the amount should be increased."[26] Weldon in turn requested further assistance from Clark who replied that he had done all that he possibly could do to bring this to the attention of the authorities at the Bank of Canada.

Canadian dealers also hoped to use their "citizenship" to receive favoured treatment from lead underwriter, Morgan Stanley in U.S. transactions. In 1938, Clark received several petitions from R.W. Gouinlock of Bell, Gouinlock & Co. Ltd. and W. C. Pitfield of Pitfield and Company to have Morgan Stanley give a fair and sympathetic consideration to Canadian houses in general.[27] In reply to Gouinlock, Clark stated:

> Frankly, I do not see that we can be the judge in these matters. Our bankers, Morgan Stanley & Co., are responsible for the success of any issues they underwrite and they must give us a guarantee of performance of their underwriting associates. We feel that we cannot insist on such a guarantee if we are to interfere in the selection of their associates [28]

Gouinlock, not entirely satisfied with this explanation, reiterated the expectation "that we have a right to ask our own Government, when they are arranging a loan of this character, *to have us taken care of in the purchase group in view of our past record* in the field of Government and Provincial financing."[29]

Nationality however was not as important as pricing and placing of bonds in these matters. The deputy minister had to manage these applications diplomatically as advocating "jobs for the boys" would have a damaging effect on the Dominion's all-important "reputation" on Wall Street. The Dominion, in pressing these special claims on the venerable investment bank, which was well paid for its work, advice and distribution capacity, would likely have found this special pleading to be counter-productive.[30]

Dealers Relations with Banks

Competition from the banks in the bond distribution business was a long-standing complaint of the dealers. This conflict originates in the distinct nature of the two types of businesses. Dealers were responsible for distributing new debt and equity issues that had the practical effect of removing funds from the banking system and converting these moneys into instruments which could be freely traded in the secondary market. Banks were principals primarily concerned with yields and liquidity. Another dimension to the conflict was that the banks' maturity preference was short term whereas the dealers were responsible for mobilizing funds over the long term in the form of debt or equity.

After the Conversion Loan of May 1931, the Investment Bankers Association of Canada (IBAC) approached the Canadian Bankers' Association to inquire about press reports that banks promoted the distribution of these securities. The CBA did acknowledge that some bank managers may have been over-zealous taking business away from the dealers, yet the CBA claimed it was not in a position to bring the thousands of branch managers into line. The banks also maintained that they performed an essential role in distributing securities to persons in remote areas where no brokers or dealers were situated.

The extent of this keen competition may be ascertained from the following letter written by an Ottawa-based dealer to the Bank's Securities Advisor. "The worst and most destructive competitor we have," wrote the dealer, "is the manager of the Ottawa office of the 'B. of M.' which I think should be 'ticked off'."[31] The territorial rivalry also related to the financing of underwriting. In their "Brief No. 2—Banks Engaging in the Bond Business" presented to the Macmillan Royal Commission, the IBAC claimed:

> The presence of banks in underwriting syndicates has on numerous occasions created situations where the security dealer is deprived of the confidential relationship which he shall have with the commercial bank which he does his banking. At the present time when bidding

or negotiating for new issues dealers often find it impossible to consult with their bankers in order to arrange loan accommodation and foreign exchange coverage and other details because the bank is likely to be a member of an opposing syndicate and it is of course out of the question for the dealer to disclose his plans to a competitor.[32]

The investment dealers also called for legislation that would limit banks to the "receiving of subscriptions or receiving of instructions for the client."[33] It was the general view of the dealers that it was in the public interest that the industry be protected lest the banks take over this retail brokerage function—a reality which came to pass 50 years later.

Constraints

Limiting the Banks' Influence

From March 1935 when the Bank of Canada was established, the chartered banks were excluded from the planning and preparation of bond issues. Meetings organized between the general managers of the banks and the governor and his officials (direct discussions with Clark and the minister were unusual) dealt with credit policy, international and domestic financial and political events, but never specifically on debt management.

Bank of Canada documents support the thesis that leverage exercised by the banks was founded upon their large holdings of maturing government paper. The creation of a central bank was seen as a partial wedge by which to give the Government more flexibility in refinancing. This could be done by eliminating negotiations and also via larger central bank holdings that would reduce the relative market holdings of the "Big Four" or "Big Five." It remained a slow and arduous process to break institutional behaviours developed over half a century or more of "negotiating" the terms of loans. In the cases to be discussed the banks' holdings were viewed as a major obstacle in refinancing.[34]

In a memorandum dated February 4, 1936, K.A. Henderson, the head of the Securities Department, wrote:

> Of the remaining items the most important are $45,000,000 Dominion of Canada 1 and 1/2% bonds due 15th September 1936, $63,336,000 Dominion of Canada 2% bonds due 15th October 1936, and $79,535,200 Dominion of Canada 5% bonds due 15th November 1936. These maturities total roughly $188 millions and it can be taken for granted that possibly $150 to $160 millions are held by the chartered banks in Canada. The Government is, therefore,

in the position of having to deal at maturity with the banks in a refunding arrangement which might be contemplated at that time. *(The experience of last year in similar circumstances was not one which we would particularly like to have occur again.)*[35]

That May, Governor Towers observed that:

…it would be necessary to have indications from the banks that the terms of the offering were such that they would convert the bonds held by them. While we should not assume that their views would be definitely unreasonable, they might differ from those of the Government by an amount which would not be sufficient to give grounds for a quarrel, but which might easily add to the Government's cost of financing by an amount of, say, 1/20th of 1%…. If the offering is made on a pure conversion basis, I am afraid that the results might be unsatisfactory. *For one thing, as the banks hold a substantial majority of the maturing bonds, might they not expect that the Government would sound them out on terms before proposing a conversion; and would failure to do so set up resistance on their part?*[36]

A further example of the market power wielded by the banks is revealed in correspondence between the general manager of the Bank of Montreal, Jackson Dodds, and the minister of Finance, Charles Dunning. The correspondence shows the Bank of Montreal presented for conversion during the June 1936 loan $44,000,000 or almost one-third of the total conversion offer.

In the Fall of 1936, Dodds sought a return to the previous regime of distribution that favoured conversion holders over new subscribers. In explaining his bank's position, Dodds wrote:

It would seem likely that at some time within a reasonable period before the due date the holder will realize upon his maturing securities so long as a premium exists and in doing so if large holdings are involved the price level on short-term securities is *bound to be affected to the disadvantage of the borrower.*[37]

What Dodds apparently wanted was preferential treatment from the Government for the half dozen large holders of maturing debts who wished to be able to convert their holdings into the tranche that most closely suited their needs and not the needs of the issuer. Dunning, in reply, stated that it would be unacceptable to allow holders two opportunities to convert their holdings. Instead the converters would be given preferential treatment but only once.[38] Dodds's prompt response highlighted the Montreal's vast market power, its preference for a short-term tranche, and the certainty of its conversion privileges.

> It is perhaps worth noting that of the total conversion of $135,000,000 obtained by the Government in June the Bank of Montreal produced $44,000,000, that is, about one third. We fully realize that in converting $43,000,000 of our own bonds out of a total of $78,000,000 maturing we were running the chance that such issue as the Government would see fit to offer in the autumn loan, whatever the term might be, the principle of giving preference to the holders of maturing bonds would still govern.

While agreeing with the Dominion's policy of funding, Dodds proposed that preference still be given to subscribers "who might indicate that they proposed paying for the new issue by surrendering the old."[39] Dunning, in replying to the Montreal's general manager, stated "we feared that preferential allotment on preferred subscriptions would make it necessary to issue a larger proportion of short term bonds than we thought desirable."[40]

From the banks' perspective, knowledge that a follow-up conversion would take place gave the holder greater flexibility. If rates were expected to fall, the bank could convert most of their holdings at existing levels. Or, by holding on to the higher yielding paper, the banks could dispose of the bonds at a premium before maturity. Should rates be expected to rise, banks would simply hold on to the securities until maturity to avoid selling bonds in a declining market at a loss and then convert to a new, higher rate.

In April 1937, discussions on a possible refunding loan were held with Minister Dunning, Deputy Minister Clark, Deputy Governor Osborne, Chief Henderson, and Governor Towers. Towers "pointed out the strong position of the banks as holders of the great majority of the maturing bonds, and said that we thought a 3 1/2 per cent new long term issue would be necessary to attract buyers and *promote redistribution.*" Towers added:

> We did not want to make a *direct arrangement* with the banks, *in view of the probable costs involved*; yet a refunding offer now, containing only banking maturities, would not work. At the worst, it might be dressed up with a longer term offering to get away from the suspicion of an issue designed for banks but on which they were not consulted.[41]

As a result of these discussions it was decided to go ahead in May with an offer in three tranches with two banking issues (a 2-year and 5-year issue) totalling $80,000,000 and a 12-year tranche accounting for $33,500,000. This offering was indicative of the difficulty the Government still faced in trying to refund the debt, which was largely in the hands of the chartered banks.

Further examples of the importance to the Dominion of the banks converting their holdings occurred in 1938. In May, Henderson, in a memo to Deputy Minister Clark, stressed the "formidable" financing requirements that were "rendered more difficult because of the distribution of $90 million 2% bonds due October 15th." Henderson estimated that over $70 million of the bonds were held by the major banks.[42] That December, the issue of further conversion offerings was broached at a meeting of the governor and a committee of the CBA. Towers referred at that meeting to the Government's "painful experience" in the autumn of 1935 when "faced with the immediate necessity of refunding a relatively large issue, practically all of which was in the hands of the banks."[43]

The foregoing illustrates the enormous influence of the banks at the "short end" of the market. One of the ways in which this market power of the banks was gradually muted was the central bank's technique of advance refunding a maturing issue by "being in the market" for bonds which were maturing in the near future.[44] This could be also be achieved by "switching," that is, by selling long-term bonds from its portfolio in exchange for the maturing issue. This process produced a situation in which, perhaps one-half of the maturing issue was in the hands of the central bank, thus largely obviating the need to worry about the banks' intentions.

Weaning banks away from routine, past behaviours, that is, of the privileged access previously enjoyed, was a slow process. Correspondence between Towers and Clark over the Bank of Montreal's usage of the term "fiscal agent of the Government of Canada" in London is instructive. In September 1935, the Governor suggested amending the Montreal's title to "paying agent."[45] No formal response was received from Clark until Towers raised the issue two years later. Towers was particularly opposed to the Bank of Montreal using this title for advertising purposes. Clark's noncommittal reply expressed agreement with the basic complaint, "but I do not think," wrote Clark, "we can make any change for some time."[46]

Foreign Borrowing

> Canada must therefore have particular regard for the effect of its policies upon the confidence of foreign investors. Nervousness there would quickly manifest itself in the domestic investment market in a damaging rise of interest rates.
>
> Graham Ford Towers[47]

Foreign investors, particularly banks, were keenly interested in the liquidity, term to maturity and interest rates offered on securities. In the broader capital markets of London and New York consisting of hundreds, not dozens of large brokers, dealers, and bankers, the type of offering—a private versus public offering was also a critical determinant in the cost and success of a borrowing operation.

The success of borrowing in foreign markets depended on several factors, most notably credit-worthiness, credibility of the government and government representatives and the political-economic context in both the foreign state and the borrowing state. One instance of political factors intruding on the timing decision is found in correspondence from Nevil Ford of The First Boston Corporation to Clark. Ford advised Clark in December 1935 to file a prospectus early with the Securities and Exchange Commission since "[A]s you doubtless know, our Congress goes into session right after New Year's and there is every indication that a great many bills will be introduced which are *liable to be disturbing to the financial markets.*"[48]

After the Bank of Canada commenced operations, it acted as the main conduit for foreign market intelligence between international finance capital and the Dominion. In August 1938, G.L. Harrison, of the Federal Reserve Board of New York advised Governor Towers "that an issue during or very shortly after the elections might encounter a disturbed market, although he did not make this in any way a prognostication."[49] That September, Towers observed "if the London situation continues so uncertain that no plans can be made in respect to that market at this date, we have to evolve some arrangement which leaves a certain latitude and does not put us in a position of having a London commitment...."[50]

In October, with the European situation so unpredictable, the Governor sought some direction from Harrison who cautioned Towers that "it was desirable for us to keep away from the market in December, or even in the last days of November, in our own interests. In the event of a clash, we would probably be the losers."[51] Based on this information, the Dominion went to market on the fifteenth of November. On this particular occasion, events in Europe conspired to dampen the market with the result that Morgan

Stanley was forced at the last moment to drop the sales price 25 cents. This occurrence is a further illustration of the market's acute sensitivity to political crises.[52]

The Bank of Canada was instrumental in strengthening the Dominion's debt management function. The Bank, led by Graham Towers, was staffed with an elite corps. Keeping close contact with the street (dealers, bankers and insurance executives) and representatives of international finance capital, gave the Dominion a strong source of market intelligence. This intelligence and professionalism led to important initiatives to widen the distribution of the debt and to deepen the market in Dominion securities. The Bank's creation, just prior to the war, was of great assistance as important international financial issues arose during and immediately after the war.

Since Towers and many of his staff (Donald Gordon, Thomas Bradshaw on the board) were respected members of the Canadian financial community, they knew the incentives driving the business and the dynamics between the players. Thus they were quite capable of separating special pleading from good policy decisions. The professional cadre and the daily contact with markets enabled the staff to balance the practicalities of the situation (e.g., banks' heavy holdings of maturing issues) with gradualist policies to reduce banks' influence over the pricing of issues. The personalistic set of market relations in government securities was gradually being phased out. However, the magnitude of financial requirements for the war effort, again required careful diplomacy with the banks.

6

Wartime: Conscription of Capital If Necessary, But Not Necessarily Conscription, 1940–1945

INDEED, THE CRUCIAL PROBLEM OF WAR FINANCE, is to dislodge money from its customary channels and guide it into the public treasury, in a manner that provides enough income incentive to shift resources and nevertheless avoids undue hardship for any group.[1]

The Economy and Economic Policy

During the Second World War, all sectors of the economy grew dramatically, most notably the government sector that, by 1943–44, accounted for nearly one-half of the national income as opposed to one-third during the First World War.[2] By 1942, the share of national income controlled by the agricultural sector had been almost restored to its pre-Depression level and profits were growing at the expense of the wage-earning population.

The challenge facing Dominion officials in wartime was to increase national income, to bring the country towards full employment, and to encourage investment without immediately raising taxes so high as to retard the growth of national income. Hence, resort was made to bank financing in the autumn of 1939 for "its expansive effect," the uncertainty of a successful public offering of bonds, and as a stopgap to allow the market to adjust to new conditions.[3]

Officials and ministers were consistent in their view that the war could be financed employing three methods: inflation, borrowing or taxation.[4] By positing the question of war finance in this way, these three alternatives were effectively reduced to two—borrowing and taxation. During the First World War, when financing became unavailable from Great Britain, resort was made to bank credit there being insufficient savings to finance the necessary expenditures. In 1917 and 1918, bank notes and bank deposits rose by 40 percent. Not surprisingly, the cost of living rose by 34 percent between 1916 and 1918. This policy penalized wage earners and those dependent on annuity income. Beneficiaries were debtors, frequently large corporate borrowers and governments, who could pay back debts from rising revenues. This precedent, well remembered by the Dominion's policy-makers, was a policy to be eschewed. Another precedent of equal importance during the Great War was the introduction in 1917 of a "temporary" income tax by then finance minister, Sir Thomas White.

Taxation

In November 1940, Clark pressed his minister for a firm commitment to a program of "drastic taxation" in the upcoming budget based on the need to offset the inflationary consequences of bank borrowing.

> If such a program is followed, we will be able to argue that it will offset the inflationary influence of short-term financing, and the short-term financing can be justified by the technical considerations (I mean the undesirability of offering a public loan immediately before an income tax payment date, the desirability of concentrating on one large public loan a year when the co-operative plan of organization is being followed, etc.) and by the need of expanding bank deposits to provide the additional working capital required by the rapid expansion of business activity.[5]

Both Clark and Governor Towers pressed for a policy of heavy taxation which would reduce unnecessary consumption and take pressure off capital markets. To avoid a recurrence of inflation, it was the original intent of the Government to finance the war through taxation as opposed to borrowing. Central to this strategy was a policy aimed at reducing private consumption. According to Governor Towers:

> This is the all important factor—abstention from consumption. If a person does that but does not subscribe to a War Loan his action is nevertheless useful. But if a person subscribes from past savings in the bank, but does not keep his consumption as low as it should be, he has not really benefited the country.[6]

The proper balance between providing incentives for business and taxing away "excess" war profits was a thorny problem for the Government. Deputy Finance Minister Clark, in an internal memo addressing some of the political implications of war taxation, argued:

> Profit incentive must be maintained and there must be special rewards to induce business efficiency and enterprise, but at the same time

the Canadian public will probably not stand for the profit levels by businessmen which cannot be justified in comparison with the human sacrifices that will have to be asked from individuals.[7]

An "excess profits tax" was introduced in the September 1939 budget and was immediately criticized because it would not be effective until 1940 and the legislation allowed for liberal tax allowances on capital investment.[8] However, as profits continued to increase through into 1942, the Government developed a more elaborate scheme to increase the excess profits tax, only to return 20 percent of the tax collected after the war. Clifford Clark's key policy advisor, R.B. Bryce, doubted the long-term wisdom of this course, observing:

> However, the proposal is open to the very serious objection that we are proposing to continue after the war *the same domination of industry by big monopolistic corporations that plagued us before the war*. It may be argued with some justice that the people who will gain the most from these provisions will be firms like International Nickel, Consolidated Smelters, The Aluminum Company, General Electric, the automobile companies and others who are well established and making very large profits. The 20% returned to them on the condition that they must re-invest it, will help further to establish them in the Canadian industrial picture and enable them to consolidate their gains and achieve even more dominance than before the war.[9]

Inflation

Between March and September 1941, prices rose steadily at nearly twice the rate experienced in the preceding 15 months of war. One explanation for this phenomenon was offered by Professor Parkinson:

> When the economy begins to approach a condition of full employment, therefore, the combined effect of increased exports and increased government expenditures financed by bank credit will have inflationary consequences unless a large proportion of the induced increase in private incomes is simultaneously drained away to the Treasury by taxing and borrowing.[10]

During the summer and fall of 1941, pressure mounted on Prime Minister Mackenzie King to approve a price control scheme, which was finally announced on October 18, 1941. The program called for a universal price ceiling and a variety of subsidies on such necessities as basic foodstuffs and coal. In November, a wage ceiling was introduced along with a cost of living bonus plan. Bonuses were paid in July 1942 and November 1943.[11]

The Wartime Prices and Trade Board was generally successful in keeping prices for consumer goods in check from 1942 to 1945. The universal scheme was adopted for reasons of "promptness, in applying an effective remedy, equity, administrative manageability, and political acceptability." Import prices were regulated via an import subsidy program for essential goods.[12]

Politics

Political discourse on debt management during the war period can be grouped into three categories: (1) the necessity for lower interest rates and the conscription of capital, (2) the concentrated holdings of the debt, and (3) the conduct of borrowing campaigns.

Lower Interest Rates and the Conscription of Capital

Initially politicians from western Canada pressed the government to lower interest rates via monetary expansion to finance the war. Social Credit believed that the initial monetary expansion sanctioned by the Government in the Autumn of 1939, should be continued. As J.H. Blackmore noted: "What consistent excuse can be given by this government for allowing that $200 million to be registered as a debt against the Canadian people?" Blackmore then went on to say, "if $200,000,000 can be created, the ordinary man on the street will say 'Why not have more than $200,000,000?'"[13]

Another Social Credit member, F.C. Casselman (Edmonton East) believed it was outrageous that money would not be forthcoming without the promise of interest. Casselman suggested that noninterest bearing bonds be cashable on demand, like savings certificates.[14] Casselman's colleague, Anthony Hynkla (Vegreville) also ridiculed those "patriots" who loaned money to the Dominion at 3.25 percent. "Patriotism," Hynkla imparted, "surely has a nobler meaning than that."[15] Blackmore continued the Social Credit assault on the moneyed classes who seemed only interested in the security of their investments and not in the security, vitality, and welfare of the Canadian people. Blackmore disputed the minister's "pay-as-you-go" wartime policy.

> The tax structure is being prepared to bleed the Canadian people of every last drop of spending power possible of extraction from their emaciated bodies for the next generation. And for what? To pay 3 per cent interest on a twelve billion dollar debt to a few favoured ones.[16]

Significantly, around the time these statements were being made in Parliament, Towers wrote George Spinney, chairman of the National War Finance Committee:

> Quite apart from the intrinsic undesirability of bank financing on this scale, I believe the repercussions on Parliament and the public would be such that a strong movement would develop for newer methods. What these new methods might be can, for the moment, be left to the imagination.[17]

In May 1940, CCF leader M.J. Coldwell presciently warned of the possibility that during an "inevitable post-war depression," the small investors' bonds would be sold at a discount to plutocrats, thus anticipating the debate amongst policy-makers a few years later.[18] In October 1940, King's diary records a discussion in Cabinet on the financial situation with Clark present. On this occasion, Clark was reassuring in his view that a rapidly expanding national income would be able to service the mounting government expenditures and mounting public debt.[19]

CCF leader Coldwell not only advocated very low rates of interest but, in addition, he pressed for the "conscription of capital." Coldwell believed in equality of sacrifice and was disturbed by the thought that vast accumulations of personal and corporate wealth might be amassed over wartime.[20] In February 1941 and again in January 1942, Coldwell moved resolutions calling for interest-free loans on the accumulated wealth of individuals and corporations.[21] These proposals went further than Keynes's compulsory savings plan on which a low rate of interest would be paid by the state.

By 1942, the whole complexion of the war effort had changed and circumstances demanded even greater sacrifices in both human and financial terms. As the CCF and the Social Credit called for *interest free* loans from the wealthy and financial institutions, that is, conscription of wealth, armed services conscription reared its head. In February 1942, King argued before caucus the case for conscription of wealth if "human life" was to be conscripted. King drew the analogy between voluntary subscriptions for service and the voluntary purchase of a bond. The prime minister believed if armed services conscription would be required, so too was wealth conscription necessary and politically defensible.[22]

Distribution of the Debt

In May 1940, the CCF member from Melfort, Saskatchewan, P.E. Wright argued that the published bond campaign data indicated a small group of persons and corporations were gaining control of the national debt. Wright feared that this ownership would give a minority command over the services of the majority, nonbondholding public who, would "pay tribute not only for one generation but for generation after generation." In an emotional address, Wright asked: Were the people going to tolerate a small minority of coupon clippers demanding the service of men and women "who fought to make those coupons worth the paper they are written on?"[23]

Social Credit member Victor Quelch also maintained that a comparatively few were snatching up the debt.[24] Quelch stressed the dangers of heavy ownership of the debt by financial institutions and, anticipating the Canada Savings Bond, recommended the sale of nonmarketable bonds that could be easily redeemed.[25] Quelch's colleague, J.H. Blackmore, stressed the postwar dangers inherent with refunding debt issued during the war. Foreseeing a debt of $14 billion or more, Blackmore conjured up images of a group of men manipulating the interest rate to their own advantage.

> Suppose the rate of interest was increased to 3, 3 1/2, 4 or 4 1/2 per cent; imagine what would be the condition of the people with a contractual obligation of that kind, which is supposed to be as sacred as though it came from the *sanctum sanctorum*—the holy of all holies of all time.[26]

This perspective was also echoed by F.D. Shaw from Red Deer who reminded the Commons that the growth of interest charges had, by 1943, exceeded prewar Dominion revenues.[27] Shaw emphasized the difficulty facing the Dominion from the heavy fixed interest charges which had to be met before any consideration could be given to social and economic reconstruction.

Sales Campaign

Perhaps the most partisan attack on the Government's debt management program came in November 1940 when Conservative member R.B. Hanson (York Sunbury) blasted the minister and his officials for the failure of the Second War Loan that Hanson described as a "flop."[28] In his sweeping attack, Hanson listed five reasons for the "flop" including (1) lack of war fervour; (2) lack of war casualties; (3) heavy taxation; (4) lack of involvement by provincial war finance committees; and (5) the public's perception that government spending was, as usual, "extravagant."

In March of 1943, Social Crediters complained of the "high pressure" sales tactics of banks and bond dealers to force persons to use credit to purchase bonds by exploiting patriotic sentiment. F.D. Shaw was especially outraged by his constituents' claims that persons who did not buy bonds were being branded as "subversives" by sales personnel.[29]

"Subversion" frequently was cited as one of the main obstacles to a Victory Loan's successful marketing. An extract from a "Statement of J.L. Ilsley, Minister of Finance regarding the marketability of Fourth Victory Loan Bonds," in May 1943 provides some support to Social Credit's charges.

> Before every Victory Loan we are deluged with rumours all of which seem to attempt to impair the sale of bonds. The Fourth Victory Loan is no exception. Such rumours are false, vicious, and subversive. I urge Canadians everywhere to do everything in their power to stamp out such rumours.[30]

Later in the war, Victor Quelch again demanded that the hard sell be stopped and that current, rather than "borrowed" savings, be employed for purchases.[31] These points were acknowledged by both sides of the House who also took exception to the practice of banks and other marketing agents employing credit as a way of meeting their sales objectives. On several occasions, the Minister informed the House that these activities were not encouraged, noting, however that it was difficult to put a halt to this practice when over 100,000 people were distributing war bonds.

BORROWING STRATEGY

Well before war was declared on September 10, 1939 the Bank of Canada had been working on a system of exchange controls. Foreign exchange controls were established on September 15, 1939.[32] In anticipation of a shortage of U.S. currency, the Bank's open market operations had been directed during the months leading up to war to the purchase of optional payment securities with a view to reducing the nation's requirements for U.S. dollars.[33]

The main objectives of the Bank, the Finance Department and the National War Loan Committee were firstly to finance the war at as low a cost as possible and secondly, to ensure a wide distribution of the debt thereby minimizing reliance on the banking system (including the central bank) and thus avoiding inflationary consequences. The goal of achieving as wide a distribution as possible of the national debt was associated with the need to (1) mobilize the large volume of idle bank deposits in the hands of individuals and corporations;[34] and (2) to restrict consumption by voluntary methods to ensure that all the physical resources required were made available to the war machine being put in place by C.D. Howe, minister of Munitions and Supply.

Clark was unequivocal on the question of financing the war at low rates of interest. In a memorandum dated September 5, 1939, Clark, estimating a deficit in the neighbourhood of $100,000,000 for fiscal 1939–40, underlined the absolute necessity for a massive reorientation and reorganization of the tax system. Clark also wrote of the need:

> to retain confidence and enable the huge borrowing operations which we will be compelled to proceed with to be carried out at reasonable interest rates—*and by reasonable rates I do not mean anything like the interest rates which prevailed during the last war. We will have to keep effective control of our capital market,* but to maintain such control many devices will be necessary and in addition we will need to show the investing public that we take a most serious view of the real sacrifices which must be made by the Canadian public in the form of tax levies.[35]

For Clifford Clark, low interest rates were not a matter of "public opinion" or politics, but a matter of necessity if Canada was to end up after the war in a financially secure position. Hence, the deputy minister resisted all movements that portended the crystallization of rates at a higher level.[36] In September 1939 during a meeting with life insurance executives, Clark declared "a four per cent rate would create a revolution in this country."[37] Clark apparently was never loathe to advance political considerations when it came to arguing the case for lower interest rates.

The achievement of lower rates of interest was also the subject of a memorandum prepared by the Toronto investment dealer, Stanley Nixon who served on the National War Finance Committee. In Nixon's view "a favourable market background for public borrowing operations" was required "to keep long-term rates at or below current levels." This favourable market background could be achieved in Nixon's mind:

> If investors, particularly the "professional" groups, *develop confidence in the intention and ability of the government to hold long-term rates around a 3% level,* some portion of the current demand for short and medium-term issues will be withdrawn, and some holdings of these issues will be sold, in favour of higher yielding long term securities.[38]

Nixon's statement underscored the market's need for assurances from "official sources" that medium to long-term interest rate policies would favour the purchase of longer term instruments *that would hold their value.* Nixon's memo also indicated the existence of an important trade-off between the objectives of extending the term to maturity of the debt at higher interest rates versus interest rate minimization through shorter-term issues.

Interest rates dropped during the war holding below 3 percent at the end of the war (see Appendix E).

VICTORY LOAN CAMPAIGNS
Broadening the Distribution of the Debt

Wider distribution was deemed essential in the achievement of the twin goals of reducing unnecessary consumption and limiting bank financing. W.A. Mackintosh in his 1940 memo "Budget Considerations" recommended in the event that "inflationary indications should develop, the Dominion should be ready to restrict the volume of purchasing power by 'over-borrowing' (i.e. borrowing from the public to pay off obligations to the banks) pending legislative action to increase taxation."[39]

In September 1939, a Working Committee composed of bankers and dealers was established to investigate the possible methods of raising loans. During 1940, a War Savings Committee and the Dominion War Loan Committee were created to oversee the sale of savings certificates and war loans respectively. The first organization was responsible for the sale, on a continuing basis, of savings stamps and certificates in small denominations, while the latter group was responsible for the organization and marketing of the large war loans over a three-week period every Spring and Autumn. In March 1942, the two groups merged to become the National War Finance Committee under the chairmanship of G.W. Spinney, general manager of the Bank of Montreal.

In the *Report of the Working Committee, Dominion of Canada War Financing* the "desirability and necessity for the widest possible distribution of the issue to the individual buyer from one end of the Dominion to the other," was posited. The Working Committee underlined the "vital necessity that the first loan should be an outstanding success." This view was shared by most of the officials involved including Towers who recommended that a "broad national organization must be created to ensure that all Canadians who are financially able to subscribe to War Loans shall be directly approached."[40] The Committee, which was composed largely of bankers and dealers, predictably called for "adequate compensation" to ensure the success of the enterprise.[41]

In recommending a competitive, rather than co-operative, mode of marketing the Working Committee advocated the setting of a satisfactory commission "to provide for the organization and selling costs involved in a nation-wide sales effort, and to assure that these bond selling organizations shall be available for the larger and more difficult operations which are to be expected."[42] In this respect, there can be little doubt that by 1939 the dealers were restless in waiting for the heralded economic recovery and desperately needed a financial shot in the arm. This is implicit in the following letter from D.I. McLeod to Clark in which McLeod argued that the Government had a *direct* stake in maintaining the dealers' organization intact.

> I do not think that the Canadian investment dealers desire to think at all in terms of profit at a time like this. On the other hand, for their own preservation, I do not think that they can keep intact for a very long period their machinery for the intensive distribution of securities unless they know fairly definitely that the services of their organizations will be required by the Department of Finance at not too remote a date in the future.[43]

After the rapid inflation experienced between March 1941 and September 1941, the Government launched a campaign to sensitize the public to the dangers of bank borrowing and to the necessity of a broadly based loan campaign. In August of 1942, Clark addressed a meeting of the National War Finance Committee and representatives from various labour organizations. The deputy minister praised the approach taken by Ilsley (on Clark's recommendation) of high taxes saying "it would have been easier for Mr. Ilsley to follow the practices of medieval kings and issue new money or borrow from chartered banks or from the Bank of Canada. But, Mr. Ilsley took the hard way because he had a conscience."[44]

At about this time, the National War Finance Committee produced a booklet for the chartered banks entitled "The Budget and You—How Your Taxes and Savings Help to Win the War." It was ostensibly designed to "clear up much misinformation on the subject of war finance and to promote clearer thinking on the principles of governmental borrowing."[45] This document advanced the Government's preference for borrowing from current and "dormant" savings with a final resort to the banks and in the last instance to the central bank. Another publication issued several months later drew a similar picture of the dangers of bank borrowing, so much so that George Spinney, a banker, wanted the booklet withdrawn thinking certain sections of the text were overdramatized.[46]

By the end of December 1941, however, it had become obvious that the Government's reliance on bank financing, particularly the expansion of Treasury bills and Treasury notes, had to be stopped. In order to lessen reliance on bank financing, the chartered banks' aid was enlisted. The CBA president urged bank managers to recommend the purchase of Victory Loans. If consulted "it would be your duty to commend it without hesitation."[47] However, there was some resistance among branch managers to recommend the purchase of bonds for they saw deposits disappearing from their own branches. This led to the preparation of a booklet by the National War Finance Committee on "The Role of the Chartered Banks in War Finance" that spelled out for these bankers the manner by which deposits withdrawn to purchase Victory Bonds soon found their way back into the banking system through government deposits with the chartered banks and expenditures on goods, services, salaries and, of course, interest.[48]

George Spinney, chairman of the National War Finance Committee, urged his fellow bankers to bring small investors into the market for Victory Bonds. "There is," remarked Spinney, "a limit to what we can get out of the institutions and individuals in the Special Names group and it seems to me that the limitations are even more definite on what the Government can expect to borrow from the medium-salaried class." Spinney then went on to state:

> As large holders of Government bonds it is in the interest of the banks that as many people as possible throughout the length and breadth of the country should have a stake in the Government debt even though the individual holdings are not on a large scale it is sometimes difficult to get the public at large to realize that any development which might harm the investment portfolio of banks and insurance companies is against their own interests. *It is less difficult, however, to convince a man that his own interests are imperilled if some move is on foot which might affect the worth of a War Savings Certificate or Bond which he has in his own bureau drawer or safety deposit box.*[49]

This revealing quotation underlined the bankers' perspective that a widely distributed debt would be *helpful in maintaining the value of the banks' bond portfolios.* Wider distribution could likely constrain the Dominion in pursuing a high interest rate policy for fear of alienating the millions of Canadians whose bond holdings would be depreciated. In other words, a wider distribution was political protection for the banks and other institutional investors against sudden bond price fluctuations.

Another technique used to ensure a wider distribution of the bonds was the heavy use of advertising with very strong appeals to patriotism and conscience. A typical advertisement, which ran in papers during 1943, stated:

You know that it is possible for this war to go on and on. But you also know that buying Victory Bonds now…buying and buying and buying them as you never did before…is the best way you can help to bring the boys back home sooner. Don't let it be on your conscience!

Other ads included a sketch of Adolf Hitler kicking a chair after reading that Canadians had once again oversubscribed to another Victory Loan. The underlying theme of other advertisements suggested that those who did not subscribe were helping the Axis win the war.

Results

Was the Dominion successful in marketing its debt to a broad segment of the population? Individual subscriptions ran to more than three million on four separate loan campaigns, representing sales to more than one-quarter of the Canadian population. In Canada, the probability that an individual would subscribe to a Victory Loan was twice that found in the United States whose Government placed more of its debt with the banking system. Still, an analysis of the Special Names Canvass reveals that a very small proportion of subscribers purchased the bulk of the debt. For example, 7,787 subscribers accounted for about two-thirds of the Second Victory Loan. Only 5,700 of 3,178,275 subscribers to the Eight Victory Loan purchased nearly 50 percent of the securities issued. Typical of these big purchasers were the Canadian Pacific Railway ($15,000,000), the Canada Life Assurance Company ($12,000,000), the T. Eaton Company ($5,500,000), Metropolitan Life ($22,000,000) and the Ford Motor Company ($6,000,000) during the Fourth Victory Loan campaign.[50] However, it should be remembered that life insurance companies and other financial intermediaries were acting as salaried trustees in their role as investors of depositors or annuitants' funds. Indeed large financial intermediaries were expected to be heavy purchasers of these instruments if the loan campaign was to be a success.

The strength of the special names canvass set the tone for these campaigns, although some concern was expressed that the publicity surrounding these large subscriptions was detrimental to the campaign directed at smaller savers who believed their money was really not needed. Another dimension of the distribution was the regional breakdown of sales. Ontario and Quebec, being the home of the major financial institutions and Canada's moneyed classes, accounted for 46.8 percent and 28 percent of total sales, respectively.

In general, the war loan organization was successful in that it widened the distribution of the debt to millions of Canadians in small amounts who had never known what a government bond looked like before. Whereas in

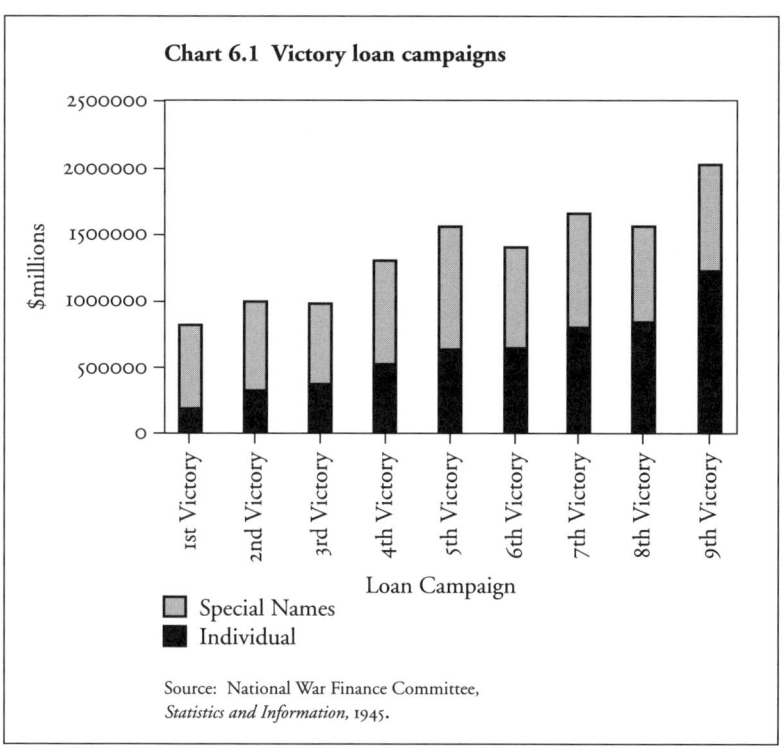

World War I, tens of thousands of Canadians purchased war bonds, in the Second World War millions bought Victory bonds. Paradoxically, the wide placement of the debt in the hands of a financially unsophisticated public, who did not understand the price fluctuations of bonds, proved to be a thorny political problem in the postwar period. This was less so in the United States where institutions, which lacked a "direct" vote, were the major holders.[51]

Price Maintenance

In a letter dated May 10, 1944 to Mr. C.A. White of Vancouver a policy of price maintenance for Victory bonds was tacitly affirmed. Towers did not anticipate a large sell-off of Victory bonds after the war. If there was a great deal of unemployment and selling out-paced institutional buying, Towers gave assurances that: "Under such circumstances, however, the Bank of Canada would normally want to engage in open market operations in order to promote an expansion of credit. There should, therefore, *be no difficulty in absorbing such Victory Bonds as people may need to sell.*"[52]

Towers, as late as the summer of 1944, had "no qualms" about the Bank's and Dominion's capacity to carry out a cheap money policy consistent with maintaining par for the 3 percent Victory Bonds. The Governor felt certain that the commitments made to the millions of small investors could be kept. "In other words," the Governor wrote to Finance Minister Ilsley, "if need arises, we can see that the cash position of the banks is such that they [the banks] will, over a period, be ready buyers of securities."[53]

Clark also shared Towers's view. In a letter to Ontario's Deputy Provincial Treasurer Chester Walters, Clark did not see how it was administratively possible to guarantee that marketable bonds could be sold and bought at par, which had been suggested by the CCF. Nevertheless, he went on to reiterate his belief that bond prices would remain stable, adding "we believe also that post war conditions are not likely to be such as to justify a rise in interest rates; if I believed that potential demand for capital and savings was going to press heavily upon the supply of capital or savings, I would be far less worried about the dangers of unemployment than some people appear to be."[54]

The Dominion and the central bank were tacitly pledged by war's end to an accommodative monetary policy and to the defence of that policy by stabilization actions in the bond market. These commitments however limited the Bank's open market operations in the early postwar period to an unrealistic defence of a 3 percent long-term interest rate.[55]

Deposit Certificates

As early as 1941, the Bank was the largest single player in the secondary market for Dominion securities holding slightly more than 10 percent of the unmatured debt. This market power required that the chartered banks maintain cordial relations with the central bank for if a bank wished to sell off bills or bonds to write new loans, the central bank was an important buyer. Alienating the central bank and largest trader of Dominion securities when one wished to unload some bonds was not "politic." As the Bank's very close working relationship with Finance gave the governor and his senior officials the opportunity to advise on economic policy (taxation, expenditure) and on amendments to the *Bank Act*, this meant banks needed to be very tactful when dealing with Towers and his staff.

The working relationship between the Bank of Canada and the chartered banks came under considerable strain during the war as a result of the sale of deposit certificates (DC). Because of the timing difficulties associated with Victory Loan campaigns, the Government required bank financing to meet its short-term cash requirements but was also concerned with the inflationary consequences. The initial idea for deposit certificates was formulated by the Department of Finance. The DC was modelled after a low-yielding, short-term instrument employed by the British Treasury and sold to the banks at the outset of the conflict.

In Canada there appeared, initially, a difference of opinion between the governor and the Finance Department over what a suitable rate of interest might be on these short-term instruments. At a meeting on December 6, 1940, the central bank's opposition was based on an assumption that the chartered banks *must earn a profit* on their dealings with the Dominion. As events transpired, this was not what Finance Department officials necessarily had in mind. Towers's record of the meeting reflects this disagreement.

> ...we pointed out that a 1–1/2 per cent basis allowed the banks a gross profit of a little more than 3/8 of 1 per cent. This figure was arrived at after an estimate of .9 percent, covering interest which the banks would have to pay on deposits which channelled through to savings accounts (assuming that 60 per cent of the money got into savings accounts and that the savings rate was 1 1/2 per cent). Allowance was also made for the cost of carrying cash reserves of 10 per cent. The profit, therefore, of 3/8 plus per cent would be reduced by additional expenses incurred by the banks in dealing with an additional $250 millions in deposits. While we stated that the 1–1/2 per cent basis seemed as low as one could fairly ask the banks to go, I stated, in response to a questioning attitude by Clark, that if he could persuade the banks to agree to a better deal—fine. But we would not argue for it.[56]

Several months later, Towers again went on record as being opposed to any scheme that would foist on the banks:

> additional non-earning assets....which they would have the expense of deposit interest and so forth. The proposal would, therefore, mean a discriminatory tax on the banks which they would have to pass on to their depositors, shareholders or employees. I do not believe that one could justify a discriminatory tax of this kind by any saving in interest costs which it might achieve.[57]

With the approach of armed services conscription in 1942, it was decided to go ahead with this proposal. That July, Towers sounded out the idea with chartered bankers who were, predictably, not favourably disposed to the plan. According to the record kept by Vernon Knowles, the Association's Public

Relations Adviser, the Government was "out of cash" and needed $500 million between July and the October financing (Third Victory Loan).[58] Towers proposed a new, fully registered, short-term, interest bearing instrument to be allocated on the basis of the increase in bank demand (chequable) deposits. This security would "freeze" bank assets by the proposed $500 million indefinitely and would be inconvertible. The Government's commitment to buy back these securities was given only if the primary distribution among the banks was wrong. Towers admitted that the practical effect of the measure was to have the banks loan the government money at 3/4 percent *for an indefinite period.*

CBA officials expressed worry that this low cost Dominion financing "would affect the borrowing desires of every province, Mr. Dobson observing that every province would want a reduction in its interest rate." Towers deflected these arguments by evoking the inflationary "remedies" advocated by some politicians and citizens. "The pressure on the Government to finance through the Bank of Canada," Towers is reported to have stated, "is quite heavy. Of course there is not any prospect in the near future of the Government cracking in on it but to the layman it looks so easy. He doesn't really understand the evils of such a course."[59]

Not surprisingly, the bankers were not easily convinced. They understandably wanted to hold a marketable instrument that could be readily disposed of. The low, punitive rate was also disturbing. "Mr Logan observed," the CBA record reads, "that once a low rate is set it would be impossible to get it back up again. All governments are going to have to borrow more and lean upon the banks more in the future at as low a rate as they could get." Towers reiterated his expectation that the banks too should be willing to make sacrifices for the cause. He then went on to say "If during the war our entire relations with the banks could be shown to be fair to both sides, not representing an undue cost to the Government and *enabling the banks to get along without resultant war profits, that would be desirable.*"[60]

This difference of opinion was finally settled at a meeting between Finance Minister Ilsley and members of the Association a week later in Ottawa. At the meeting, the main bone of contention was the rate of remuneration, the question of the nonnegotiable character of the deposit certificates having apparently been agreed to. Rates charged the Government were based on the imputed cost of deposits or liabilities of the banks. The Government believed the rates to be 0.55 percent, while the CBA claimed their deposit costs to be considerably higher and therefore desired a higher return on these obligations. Finance Minister Ilsley rejected a rise in bank compensation on the grounds that it would "evoke from monetary experimenters in the House criticism not only of the Government but of the banks." Ilsley believed that the 3/4 percent rate was being seen as a type of service charge that would satisfy the demand by some monetary experimenters for bank loans without interest.[61]

Political Leverage

Minister Ilsley and the Government could effectively use the spectre of radical demands of Social Credit monetary experimenters and the redistributive policies of the CCF as leverage during discussions due to the political situation in early 1942. In January 1942, CCF leader M.J. Coldwell advocated the direct national control of all financial institutions, compulsory interest-free loans imposed on the accumulated savings of rich individuals and corporations as well as a 100 percent excess profits tax.[62]

An indication that Coldwell's recommendations were seriously considered by the Government is revealed in a remarkable document prepared by Lord Keynes's former student, Bob Bryce. Bryce's recommendation for the establishment of controllers for banks, insurance companies and the like was premised on the belief that sacrifices should be spread equally or at least more equally between labour and capital. Noting that no formal controls had yet been imposed on capital, Bryce stated:

> There is already a widespread feeling that there should be some form of *conscription of wealth* in addition to the normal and orthodox forms of taxation, which are after all conscription of income rather than wealth. *If these demands for some application are not met sensibly they are apt to grow and to force later the Government into some radical action, while in the mean-time creating a considerable amount of ill-will.* Therefore I would suggest that in dealing with the problems of financing and of liquidity the Government should be prepared to invoke the principle of conscription of wealth as an instrument to attain certain ends, and also as having a value in itself at this time.[63]

While the policy alternative suggested by Bryce was never implemented, both Towers and Clark read the document and it is not improbable that Ilsley also saw the memorandum.[64] This memo indicates a readiness on the part of Finance policy-makers to consider a wide range of heretofore radical, policy options. In wartime, previous taboos about interfering in markets had vanished opening up to the young policy-making group in Finance a broad range of questions and issue areas. This document also lends certain credence to the view that veiled threats, intimations or suggestions did carry some force—they were not idle blusterings. During the War, the Dominion did seem prepared to overturn "business as usual" to ensure the efficient financing of the war effort.

In December 1943, the CBA president when broaching the question again of the low-yielding DCs held by the banks was given a stern lecture on the benefits of low interest rates by Towers. The Governor stressed the "psychological effect" of a proposed reduction in the bank rate from 2 1/2 percent to 1 1/2 percent and intimated that if the banks preferred not to finance short-term government paper "on an appropriate basis, it would be necessary for us to go into the business ourselves by purchase and resale agreements with dealers."[65]

Governor Towers also used the issue of "bank profitability" on several occasions as leverage. When discussing the deposit certificate situation in July 1942 the Governor reminded bankers of their vulnerability with respect to bank profits. Given the atmosphere of wartime, claims that the banks were reaping huge profits would be valuable political fodder for the banks' enemies in Parliament. The banks had to be seen as co-operating, Towers asserted, adding "bank profits published and taxable were one thing *and that the internal situation was another.*"[66] In another conversation with S.M. Wedd, Towers "expressed the view that the absolute amount of remuneration (for Victory Loans) was getting too high."[67]

At a meeting in February 1944 the Governor offered some advice to the effect that it would be in the banks' own interest to provide improved financial reporting. "The public," Towers stated, believed "that the banks were tremendous money earners and that *this view might impede proposals for the revision of The Bank Act,*"—hardly a subtle reference to the decennial problems faced by the bankers during Commons' committee hearings. Towers also mentioned that it would be politic to reduce remuneration for Victory Loan campaigns by one-third for the banks' rising commissions were increasing "to a point where there was a possibility of embarrassment."[68]

Resistance to Holding DCs

Throughout the Fall and Winter of 1942–43, the banks petitioned the Government to reduce the volume of DCs outstanding. In September 1942, the CBA president wrote Towers to remind him of their understanding that the "Dominion Government will make a very substantial reduction in the banks' holdings of these certificates from the proceeds of the forthcoming Third Victory Loan as soon as the funds are available."[69] The following February in correspondence leading up to a crucial meeting with the governor, the assistant general manager of The Bank of Nova Scotia recorded his bank's displeasure about the existing state of affairs.

> It seems to us that the proper course for the Government to follow is to recognize the situation and replace the unpaid portion of the Certificates of Deposit with longer term obligations and bearing a rate of interest in keeping with the term, e.g., if a two year maturity were decided upon we would suggest a rate of 1 1/2%.[70]

This concern for yield led CBA President St. Pierre to bring these complaints to Towers, who was more likely to be sympathetic than the minister or Clark. The Government's cash requirements, wrote St. Pierre, should be funded "with an appropriate rate." He added "that the Government would not have to finance on such a substantial scale throughout the period contemplated *if it did not act as banker for its war contractors.*"[71] Not only was the Government borrowing from the banks at or below market rates; to add insult to injury it was taking lucrative commercial lending away from the banks!

In February 1943, the ceiling for deposit certificates agreed to the previous summer was more than doubled to one billion dollars. In return for holding these low-yielding instruments, it was suggested at a June 1943 meeting that the "banks should obtain a better rate on some other securities in compensation." There was general agreement among the assembled chartered bankers that the government should borrow "longer" and disappointment that the promised issue to banks of 1 1/2 percent bonds had been put off.[72] Yet, by early summer, a decision was taken by Clark to *increase* the volume of these short-term instruments. This set the stage for a heated exchange at the Mount Royal Club in June between the Governor and assembled bankers. The Royal Bank's Dobson expressed "shock" that the Government was not prepared to honour its commitment of February to issue a two-year, 1.5 percent bond. Eventually a compromise was reached that called for the sale of an additional $100 million in two-year notes earning 1.5 percent and maturing in September 1945.[73]

As late as September 1948, with only $100,000,000 in deposit certificates outstanding, bankers still sought the elimination and/or increase in the yields of these instruments. The Towers's papers contain a memorandum of a conversation between the general manager of the Bank of Toronto, Mr. Gillett and Towers on the subject of DC rates. The general managers "were 'hot and bothered' by reason of the fact that they had simply received routine notices in regard to the renewal of the Deposit Certificate issue maturing September 3rd."[74] Towers tactfully reminded Gillett an arrangement had been made and the Government was "entitled to expect that it held good."[75] Towers then called Gillett's bluff by proposing to pay off the banks by reducing the Dominion's bank balances with the chartered banks that "from an earnings point of view would hardly do the banks much good." Gillett argued that it would not be "politic" to suggest the banks would not renew, but Towers insisted that the facts be put on record. The $100,000,000 in maturing certificates were renewed at 3/4 of one percent, above the old 5/8 percent yield.

In May 1944, the Governor of the Bank of Canada in testimony before the House Standing Committee on Banking and Commerce declared that "there was not any element of forced loans" insofar as the deposit certificates were concerned.[76] This interpretation is somewhat at variance with official records cited here. It is highly doubtful whether this operation could have been achieved without the apparatus of a central bank, the wartime political context and the insistence of a Clifford Clark.

Taxation Problems

In the April 1941 budget a proposal to levy a 15 percent withholding tax, recommended by Walter Gordon, was roundly condemned in domestic and American finance circles and substantially modified.[77] Towers believed:

> the lender may well regard the payment of a lesser sum as a form of repudiation. In some cases, of course, companies issuing bonds have covenanted to refund any tax which might be deducted, at least up to a certain specified percentage. To the extent that this takes place, Canada saves no U.S. funds, and unintended taxation is placed on Canadian companies.[78]

George Spinney, National War Finance Committee chairman, believed the tax was "a bad one, and should be cancelled."

At a meeting on May 5, 1941 with Walter Gordon and Ilsley present, Towers delivered a lecture apprising them of the fact that substantial refunding operations were being conducted that would be "adversely affected by the narrowing of the market which results from charitable organizations, mutual life companies, banks and others not being interested because of the tax." This understanding of the motivations of international finance capital on the part of the Bank was affirmed over the next several days as Towers received a half a dozen phone calls from major U.S. institutions demanding a reversal of the proposal. One life insurance executive told Towers "they would have to whittle down their (Canadian) holdings—as a matter of self-interest, and not in any vindictive spirit."[79] Harry Morgan reported that the Investment Bankers' Association and the National Association of Security Dealers were contemplating the lodging of a strong protest.

It was not only international finance capital that was opposed to the change. A.R. Wood, president of the Sun Life Assurance Company, a firm having very large investments and operations in the United States, feared reprisals by some states leading to the disqualification of Canadian bonds for deposit under their insurance regulations.[80] Chester Walters, Ontario deputy provincial treasurer, representing the constituency of major provincial borrowers, was also upset when he reported "the bottom had dropped out of the market for Ontario bonds."[81] After the markets' reaction and extensive discussions, the Government decided to water down the proposal by excluding interest on bonded indebtedness from the tax. Instead the legislation passed placed a 15 percent withholding tax on nonresident royalties, rents and similar payments deriving from the use of property or patents.[82]

This episode confirms the Bank's conservative stance in these matters and its support for the sanctity of financial contracts. This high drama is illustrative of the complex web of relations between domestic borrowers dependent on present or future access to foreign markets, domestic institutions with major operations abroad (banks and insurers), and international finance capital whose near instantaneous and universally hostile reaction thwarted the Government's desire to increase taxation on finance capital. International finance capital had a very powerful stick with which to strike at the Canadian government discounting the bonds trading in the secondary market "though not in a vindictive spirit."[83] Although the Dominion itself was relatively less reliant on these markets, the provinces' financing requirements made the Dominion reluctant to challenge these financial interests. While it is quite true that in April 1941, Canadian governments could not borrow new cash abroad, the substantial refunding operations that occurred made provincial treasurers and their deputies understandably nervous regarding any taxation proposal of this kind.

Wartime allowed governments virtual *carte blanche* to take control of or direct all kinds of resources: human, physical and financial. In Canada, as well as in other Allied nations, the banks due to their strategic value and international connections were immediately enlisted. Policy-makers, cognizant of the mistakes of the past war and concerned with avoiding a heavy debt burden, which could create an uncertain future where depression might return, opted for a balanced policy of borrowing and taxation. As human conscription loomed in Canada, the unthinkable began to be mooted—the conscription of capital. Given the high value of predictability, stability and marketplace relations, this type of thinking could only have taken place at the war's nadir. Its quiet implementation, through the deposit certificate vehicle, was a testament to firstly, the Bank of Canada's professionalism as agent to the government despite its initial disapproval of the plan and, secondly, the Dominion's all embracing powers to consummate the war effort. This episode is a reminder of the ultimate power of the state to expropriate, in the sense of lower returns to finance capital, even in the most developed market economies.

7 Attempts to Keep Faith with Bondholders, 1946–1952

The Economy and Economic Policy

The main problems that plagued the Canadian economy during the early postwar period were inflation and the threat, or perceived threat, of unemployment. In Canada, the United States, and the United Kingdom plans were well advanced before the surrender to create a viable international monetary order and to promote the necessary business confidence through the introduction of "full employment" policies. The bias towards full employment was obviously premised on the fear that a return to the economic chaos and social turmoil of the 1930s would lead to the undermining of western political institutions. This bias was reflected in a talk given by W.C. Clark to businessmen at the Chateau Montebello in Quebec in October 1942. Clark gave his audience the following preview of what postwar economic policy might be:

> *What will be needed is to safeguard against deflation, not prevent inflation.* If we are to avoid a long depression and mass unemployment, the policy required will be one of stimulation of the economy, one that will create expansionist tendencies, one that will provide incentives to expansion, one that will encourage the consumer to spend and expand his purchasing power, in short, one which will keep the national income from falling to abnormally low levels.[1]

This palpable fear amongst politicians, their policy-makers, and the public of a return to the high prewar levels of unemployment was to inform government policy over the next four decades. The lowering of the Bank Rate in February 1944 was a signal the Bank was prepared to continue its cheap money policy that was also designed to make the servicing of the national debt more manageable.[2]

The "White Paper" on Employment in April 1945 provided a general framework with respect to surplus and deficit budgeting. While no explicit policy was ever enunciated, a coherent pattern emerged. The pattern of budget making consistently underestimated the budget surplus. Finance Minister Douglas Abbott and his officials consciously followed this strategy knowing full-well that the publication of larger surplus projections would encourage Liberal backbenchers to call for tax cuts, which the minister, his officials, and the central bank did not support.[3] This approach resulted in a fall in the national debt from $18.96 billion at March 31, 1946 to $15.585 billion at the end of March, 1949. With such surpluses, the Dominion, through its Securities Investment Account, soon found itself a substantial purchaser of the debt.[4]

Complicating the management of the public debt was the extremely high volume of debt issued through the war and held by the general public. By 1945, the Dominion's debt represented about one and a half times the productive capacity of the economy. Fortunately, the efforts to maintain interest rates at very low levels meant a minimal interest rate burden. Also by issuing long-term Victory bonds the Dominion did not face significant refinancing until 1950.

With the lifting of price, wage and production controls beginning in 1946, a consumption-led boom financed, in part, by the selling of Victory Bonds, was widely predicted. This development, combined with banks liquidating their government securities to finance business credit, would likely force up interest rates. Given these considerations, the Government was urged to maintain existing levels of taxation to run up large surpluses to purchase the bonds held by the public and in the banking system. This program, in conjunction with a moderate rise in interest rates, was recommended to check inflation.[5]

From 1946 to 1948, consumer credit and consumption rose by 25 percent. Consumer prices increased at a similar pace prompting the appointment, in February 1948, of a Royal Commission on Prices, chaired by Professor C.A. Curtis of Queen's University. The commissioners were loathe to point the finger at any one group responsible, but they did feel that taxes were too low, budget surpluses were not sufficiently large to drain off purchasing power, and monetary policy was regarded as being too easy.[6] The latter policy was clearly prompted by the authorities' desire to keep interest costs within reason and the fear of a recurrence of depression.

During the 1946 to 1950 period, employment trends continued to be generally favourable. The addition of nearly 900,000 jobs in the nonagricultural sector was partially offset by a major decline in agricultural employment—a drop of 300,000 workers in six years. Unemployment predictably rose during demobilization but this trend was arrested during the consumer-led boom of 1947–48. Afterwards, unemployment began to build up until the Korean War broke out peaking at 144,000 unemployed during the winter of 1949–50.

Most importantly for interest rate and exchange rate policies, Canada's trade position with the United States ran into deficit after the war. Imports, relative to exports, continued to grow with this trend particularly pronounced in 1947 when imports grew 20 percent as against an 11 percent rise in exports. By November 1947, Canada's official reserves were dangerously low, which allowed the Government virtually no room by which to manoeuvre. The resulting exchange crisis was exacerbated by the continuing repatriation of foreign debts and by a reduction of exports to the United Kingdom. After 1948, a decided improvement in Canada's reserves was observed as a resumption of selling bonds abroad coincided with a comprehensive program introduced in 1948 to preserve Canada's U.S. dollar reserves by limiting travel and imports from the dollar zone.

Canada Savings Bonds

It was during the Second World War that suggestions for a savings instrument that could be cashed on demand were mooted. The CCF and the Social Credit went on record as favouring such an instrument that permitted the holders to sell the bond without a capital loss when cash was required. Early in 1940, W.A. Mackintosh, Queen's University economist and special assistant to Clifford Clark, recommended the development of a special registered bond for smaller savers. Mackintosh's analysis favoured the creation of a debt instrument with a definite maturity date that could be cashed at an earlier date in case of definite need.[7]

Later, E. Fricker, chief of the War Savings Division of the Bank of Canada, proposed the issue of a "tap" bond (issued continuously throughout the year) for a term of 10 to 15 years to yield about 3 percent. The bond would be nontransferable, taxable, and redeemable on a sliding penalty scale.[8] This tap issue would also offer an important outlet for current savings between Victory Loan issues. However, the proposal was rejected on the grounds that the overhead registration costs were too high for the anticipated sales making the whole venture uneconomical. While these suggestions were shelved initially, the enormous success that greeted the payroll savings plan towards the end of the war assured its continuation in another form after the war. The object was to "get as many people as possible to maintain the scale of their present pay deductions."[9] The maintenance of this form of predictable savings was also viewed as an anti-inflationary measure, a method of keeping latent purchasing power in savings, not consumption.

During the early postwar period the development of the Canada Savings Bond instrument was a key priority of the Bank and Finance Department. In furthering the goal of soaking up excess purchasing power, the National War Finance Committee commissioned a survey of employers in 1945 to determine the extent of support for a continuation of the program. The survey found that nearly six of every seven employers favoured such a continuance.[10]

In March 1946, Towers and Henderson met with Bob Bryce and Clark to discuss the form of the proposed savings instrument. At this meeting it was decided to create an instrument to be sold as a tap issue. The instrument would be sold in denominations of $50, $100, and $500 redeemable at par at banks, without a waiting period, to a maximum limit of $2,000 for each purchaser. A single annual coupon of 3 percent was contemplated that would be taxable.[11]

At the end of June, Towers revealed details of the forthcoming Autumn issue to bankers in Montreal and "expressed the view that a passive approach by the banks would not produce satisfactory results and urged the appointment of something equivalent to the Victory Loan officers."[12] That September, Towers sent a letter to bankers to counteract "any impression that the operation of this autumn will be in the nature of a very low pressure campaign." While the approach would "differ materially" from the war loans that relied on appeals to patriotism (and conscience), Towers stressed "vigorous salesmanship" and promotion on the basis of "self-interest."[13]

The lukewarm reception of the banks was based on two reasons. Firstly, savings bonds were nontransferable and therefore could not be held by the banks as collateral for loans. Secondly, opposition was based on the traditional perception of bank managers that deposit withdrawals were lost to the banking system.[14] Even within the Bank of Canada there was some debate as to the proper development and place of this nonmarketable debt instrument. On the positive side, the savings bond promised a wider distribution of the debt and it also would minimize the monetization of the debt in the banking system. Some supporters claimed it would lead to a public better informed about government finance. Other advantages included limiting the maximum purchases to several thousand dollars, which meant the Government could be assured all daily demands for cash could be met quite easily following the traditional banking maxim of maintaining daily reserves sufficient to meet the expected demands for encashment.

A major reason against creating the Canada Savings Bond was that this borrowing vehicle gave the Dominion ready access to a vast pool of untapped savings. From a central banker's perspective, this could be unhealthy insofar as it might encourage profligacy in government spending when governments realized they could raise large amounts of cash by offering a "sweetener" to the population. Another problem area was the cash redemption on demand feature that was potentially inflationary should panic set in among the largely, unsophisticated holders. Related to this question of redemption on demand was the feeling that holders would tend to redeem bonds before the maturity dates and that this run-off and the higher administrative expense of these campaigns far outweighed the benefits of this savings instrument. Finally, some observers thought that placing too heavy a reliance on nonmarketable debt insulated from interest rate movements would make the debt manager less sensitive to price fluctuations in the capital markets.[15]

The Canada Savings Bond was first issued with a 2.75 percent coupon sold at par from 1946 to 1950. The rate was increased to 3.25 percent in 1951 and to 3.75 percent in the autumn of 1952. Sales ranged from a high of $483 million in 1946 to a low of $235 million in 1948. With the secular rise in rates beginning in early 1948, cashing in of the bonds commenced. By March 31, 1953 of the $1,533 million in savings bonds issued at 2.75 percent only $581 million or 38 percent remained outstanding. This development demonstrated that the majority of savers were indeed sensitive to market rate trends and cashed bonds in when changes in the rate of interest made other investment options more attractive.

The Effect of U.S. Interest Rates

The most formidable obstacles in the way of maintaining stability in the bond markets were market developments in New York and moral commitments made during the war to maintain long-term rates at or below 3 percent. Both of these factors conspired towards the end of 1947 to force the Bank to gradually lift the lid on interest rates.

In July 1946, the Canadian dollar, which had been pegged at 90 cents U.S. during the war, was repegged at par. However, as interest rates climbed in New York during 1947, questions were raised in the House about Canada's interest rate policy. In responding to a question from Conservative A. Cockeram (York South) in April, a confident Finance Minister Douglas Abbott replied that the situation would "be handled as a matter of government policy which will be announced in due course."[16] In May, Conservative Finance critic J.M. Macdonnell doubted the Government and central bank would be able to keep interest rates down given that rates were rising in New York. Macdonnell advocated an increase in interest rates by arguing that higher rates were necessary for the middle classes' economic well-being and the middle classes always acted as a preservative for democratic government.[17]

That June, Stanstead Conservative J.T. Hackett asked the minister for information on the level of Canada's official foreign exchange reserves. No information at this time was forthcoming.[18] Subsequently, it was revealed that during the first half of 1947, Canada was losing foreign exchange on the order of $70 million per month.[19]

During the summer of 1947 a massive run-off of Canada's foreign exchange reserves continued that became the subject of speculation and questions in the House of Commons. Parliamentarians and academics were perplexed by the Bank and Government's position, which held that "a drastic increase in interest rates which would be likely to create a situation that might hamper, and even prevent, essential forms of capital investment which Canada needs."[20]

In August, Towers and Lester Pearson met with Prime Minister King to discuss the looming exchange crisis. King granted Towers permission to initiate discussions with the U.S. Treasury Department, provided Abbott was in agreement. King recorded in his diary: "I pointed out, once we borrowed, we would find it increasingly difficult to loan abroad or make further advances for relief, etc. This may not be a misfortune. The sooner the country or more the Gov't realizes that we can't go on spending at will the better."[21]

The Dominion however was not yet prepared to see rates rise to combat the capital outflow that would decrease the price of outstanding issues of Victory bonds. Nor did it contemplate allowing the dollar to float freely (as it eventually did in 1950), so it eventually resorted to borrowing in New York. As a stopgap, during the fall of 1947, the Dominion used its budget surplus to buy up large quantities of Victory Bonds and so had the central bank.

In December 1947, Governor Towers met with Sproul of the Federal Reserve to discuss interest rate conditions in the context of discussions for a U.S. dollar loan due to the urgency of the exchange situation. Sproul indicated that the banks were short of cash, meaning sales of government paper to the "Fed" would bring about a "firming" or rise of interest rates. This upward trend became apparent in subsequent discussions with private bankers who were not in a mood to lend long at rates that Towers considered reasonable in the circumstances.[22]

Towers initially pursued discussions on the basis of a private placement with New York banks. Winthrop Aldrich of the Chase Bank advised Towers the banks would be unwilling to lend for more than four years at approximately 2.5 percent. Towers thought that a two-year maturity was no good and that the $75 million proposed

> ...hardly seemed a respectable amount for Canada to do in the circumstances. He (Aldrich) did not agree on the question of amount, but said that he would reopen the thing with the banks on the basis of three, four and five year maturities. In that case the rate would be higher. National City had suggested 2 3/4 per cent on the two, three and four year deal. I said that I was sure that 2 3/4 per cent could not be accepted by the Canadian Government. Aldrich said it might be 2 5/8. I said I felt that was still high, and that 2 1/2 was the right level [23]

Towers later met with Messrs. Burgess and Pfeffer of National City Bank who also doubted that a longer term tranche at 2 1/2 percent could be arranged. Towers's record indicates that arranging a private, as opposed to a public, placement gave the lenders more opportunity to exert leverage with respect to the price.[24]

> Pfeffer spoke to me alone on my way out, and said that in confidence he wished to express the view that the sounding out of banks was not a very good procedure from the Canadian standpoint. The banks were in a frame of mind to ask questions, express doubts and generally hum and haw. If on the other hand we did a public issue, it was much more likely that people would buy on their general belief in Canada's credit standing without bothering too much about details.

At the opening of the Fourth Session in December 1947, made necessary by the exchange crisis, it was announced that Canada was seeking a $300,000,000 loan from Eximbank. Conservative leader John Bracken asked the minister whether any terms or conditions would be attached to the loan, as well as information on the present status of Canada's foreign reserves. Abbott dodged the question about reserves but stated categorically that no conditions had been placed on the loan.[25]

However, on December 16th, Abbott announced, to what must have been an incredulous House, a series of drastic measures to conserve foreign exchange, (*viz*. U.S. dollars). In underlining the urgency of the crisis, he drew to the Commons' attention Canada's shipment of $75 million in gold to the newly created International Monetary Fund and a $145 U.S. million loan repayment as factors that had aggravated the situation. The import restrictions announced were sweeping, ranging from poultry and eggs to most household appliances, to cigarettes, soaps, and cosmetics. Quotas were also imposed on citrus fruits, vegetables, textiles, leather goods, among other products. A special excise tax on consumer durables was imposed and a $50 limit on travel expenditures while in the U.S. dollar area implemented.[26]

Abbott in explaining the Government's continuing commitment to maintain the dollar at par (in U.S. funds) and not to allow the dollar to fall, which naturally displeased the export-producing industries and regions, argued that the inflationary consequences of devaluation would be devastating. "Anyone who suggests that depreciation is not an inflationary measure in times like these is living in a world of fantasy," stated the finance minister.[27]

In speaking to the $300 million loan, Abbott was well aware that this served only as a "temporary solution."

> It merely provides a supplement to our exchange reserves to take care of a temporary deficit until the constructive longer-run measures which are going into effect get into full operation and produce a more reasonable balance in our commercial and financial relationships with the dollar area. Not only does it give more time for the constructive solutions, but it also permits the adoption of a program less upsetting to business than would be necessary. Without the additional latitude which a loan provides, the program of restrictions would have to be much more severe which would cause undue dislocations to the Canadian economy and to many of our suppliers in the United States.[28]

In providing interim details on the actual loan, Abbott observed that Eximbank, a government agency, and not private banks had been tapped because of "the magnitude of the sum required" and the necessity for a quick decision.[29] This was only partially true for it was rather the rate of interest that was the stumbling block with American banks as well as the term.[30] Curiously, at the time of this announcement, the rate of interest "was not known," though Abbott believed it to be "slightly above 1 7/8%." The loan was repayable in "equal instalments in three, four, and five years time."[31] The borrower was permitted to draw down the loan when required so, in a sense, this arrangement was similar to a line of credit with a bank. In June of 1948, Abbott informed the House that drawings to that date were only $140 million.

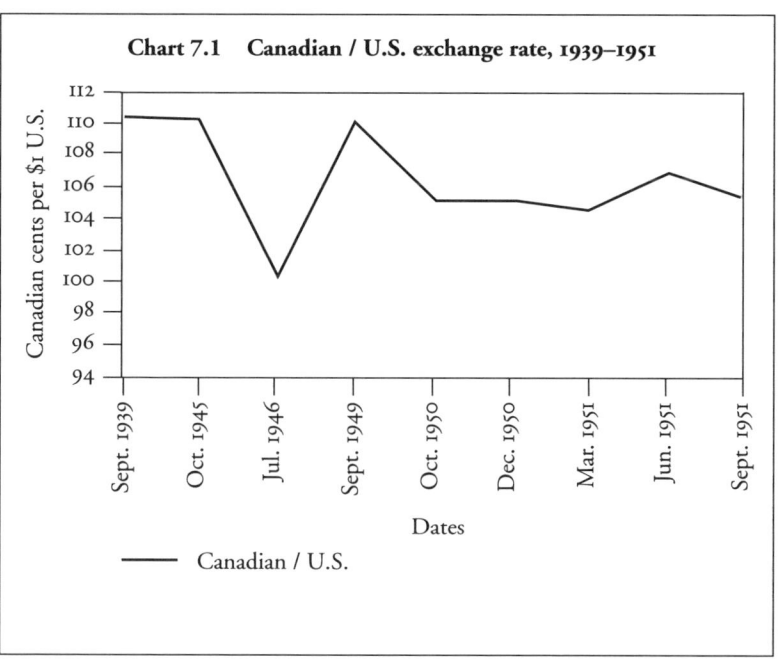

Bond Price Maintenance

By January 1948, the question for policy-makers was whether to carry on a Victory bond price stabilization operation financed by budgetary surpluses or allow market forces to push interest rates upward. Towers and his colleagues had to navigate between the pressures of the market and implicit war-time promises. At a meeting in early January 1948 with Clark, Abbott, Towers, James Coyne, and Donald Gordon present, the pros and cons of letting interest rates rise were debated. From the Bank's perspective, sensitized by its daily contacts with the market, it was futile, if not impossible, to hold bond prices steady. According to the Governor's notes from the meeting:

> The present flurry of selling is inspired by the recent upward move of interest rates on U.S. Government securities. However, even after nervous selling subsides, one must expect that the Stabilization Account will be called upon to purchase a very substantial amount of securities during 1948.[32]

In arguing the case for higher rates, the Governor believed that higher rates might bring under control the current capital boom and at the same time re-establish the traditional 1/2 of 1 percent differential between U.S. treasuries and Dominion paper. Towers then added:

> Finally, as long as Government does not require to borrow in the market, a higher interest rate does not increase the debt cost *and permits Government to buy up its outstanding issues on more favourable terms*. However, a policy of deliberately varying interest rates to favour the Government's own position might ultimately result in higher rates being demanded by investors, or a narrowing of the public bond market.[33]

Towers concluded his presentation with a plea either for a clear mandate for the current policy of price maintenance or a clear change in policy direction.

Abbott and Clark, while recognizing the current rate structure was unrealistic, preferred to see rates go up marginally, by perhaps 1/4 of 1 percent. Bank officials pointed out that such a movement might be interpreted by the market as only a first step in a movement towards a 3 percent rate. This reading by the market might necessitate heavier purchases by the Securities Investment ("stabilization") account. Abbott and Clark recognized the possibility and stated that purchases would be financed from surplus funds and borrowed moneys if required. Complicating this difficult choice was the possibility that war could erupt in Korea and, if the Government did not keep its tacit promises to maintain the value of its bonds, this would make future war financing more difficult with memories of capital losses still fresh in the minds of Victory Loan bondholders.

Soon after the meeting, the Governor advised Clark that steps were being taken "to raise the yield on market issues approximately .22 per cent." To disguise the operation, the Bank abandoned its previous system of a daily list of bids and offers that was replaced by the Bank responding to bids and offers from the market. No statements were to be issued. According to Towers— "If questioned, the answer would be that there appeared to be some unsettlement in the bond market and some firming of interest rates was apparently taking place. No concern would be expressed."[34]

In late January the administered "break" in bond prices occurred with yields, rising some 30 to 35 basis points, slightly higher than was targeted. The success of this policy was premised on a conservative fiscal policy of maintaining high levels of taxation and high budget surpluses. The governor reminded the minister that maintenance of the existing fiscal regime was needed to facilitate the control of credit and to keep the confidence of the market.[35]

Later that year, the Dominion arranged a private placement with three major U.S. life insurance companies to repay the Eximbank loan. These two essentially private funding operations precluded participation from other U.S. investment houses which prompted Nevil Ford of The First Boston Corporation to counsel the Dominion to refund callable issues through a public placement.

> Many investors are greatly perturbed by increasing restriction of opportunity to invest in Dominion securities...we and group including Canadian houses who have served Dominion in past and consistently provide principal market and distribution of Canadian securities in U.S.A. are convinced that public offering and distribution of a Dominion long term loan in amount sufficient to refund these issues can be made on terms at least equal if not more favourable to government than can a private placement restricted to a few large investors.[36]

Throughout 1951 efforts again were made to maintain bond prices with purchases by the Securities Investment Account. Proposals were mooted at the time involving swaps with the Government's Exchange Fund Account to provide moneys to purchase the Victory Bonds. During the first nine months of 1951, over $273 million in securities were bought but this activity did not stem the rise in rates which inched upward from 3 to 3.25 percent. By the end of 1951, rates touched 3.5 percent, nearly one full point above the level at the end of 1947. In November, the Government officially abandoned its policy of price support.[37]

The reaction of the public to the capital losses from rising bond yields may be gauged from the following letter of March 12, 1951, from R.H. Cook to Governor Towers. Cook wrote:

> We are now being told that great pressure is being put on our responsible ministers, which I assume would mean the Minister of Finance, and perhaps also on you as Governor of the Bank of Canada, to raise the rates of interest generally, or in other words take away all support from Canada's War Bonds. If this were done, it would probably be the policy of our life insurance companies, for instance, to keep out of the war bond market until these bonds could again, as following the first war, be purchased down in the low nineties, to net the life insurance companies perhaps 4 to 5 %. The Canadian public want nothing of such manipulation, and there

will very soon, in my opinion, be questions asked on the floor of the Commons if the present bonds do not very soon reach par again, and indicate the government's intention to stand by the word of its last responsible Minister of Finance.[38]

That June, the Government's interest rate policy was questioned in the Senate. Conservative Senator Haig attacked the Government's handling of the Victory Bond price support program by pointing to the public's misperception that Victory Loans could be sold at par (100 cents on the dollar) at any time even though "the government had never said the bonds would be maintained at par, (that) there was no legislation to maintain them at par."[39] Several weeks later, Haig returned to the theme of falling bond prices,

> It all comes about by reason of the fact that the Government of Canada is spending too much money; investors in government bonds are afraid of their securities and are demanding higher interest rates. The Dominion Government has now reached the stage—though Mr. Towers will not admit it—where it has not got enough money to liquidate the bonds, and as a result their market value has declined and the general rate of interest is going up.[40]

Haig's comments sparked a former Liberal Cabinet Minister, Senator E.D. Euler (Liberal Waterloo) to observe that falling bond prices were having a damaging effect on provincial hydro bonds. "This destruction of public confidence," Euler remarked, "is to my mind most unfortunate."[41]

During the following session, Newfoundland Senator A.B. Baird returned to the problem of the small investor losing money when selling Victory bonds. Baird quaintly rebuffed Liberal Senator Robertson's claim that these bonds were a good investment if held until maturity, stating this was "saving in another direction." "To buy at 99 and sell at 91," Baird declared, "does not represent my idea of a good investment."[42]

By 1952, Towers was less sanguine about the Bank's ability to resist market pressures for higher yields.

> One final thought: Lacking an overall cash surplus, any purchase of securities for X Account implies (other things being equal) that Government has to borrow money for the purpose. Without suggesting that literally nothing should be done and the market left completely to its own devices, we should point out to the Minister that buying will have be kept to the minimum and the selling pressure, if any, combated in the main by price reductions.[43]

Thus, the regulation of Canada's capital markets had come full circle from a total inability on the part of the Dominion to intervene in setting interest rates to the administered control of rates during the war (with the help of exchange controls) to a postwar return to market forces largely set outside Canada's borders.

Alberta's Debt Reorganization Act: The Dominion's Incentive

Following Alberta's default, the Dominion was unsympathetic to assisting Alberta financially until it made restitution with holders of bonds in default. It was only after Aberhart's death and Provincial Treasurer Solon Low's departure for Ottawa that representatives from Wood Gundy and The First Boston Corporation met with Premier Ernest Manning, Deputy Provincial Treasurer Frank Percival and the Provincial Auditor Keith Huckvale, to work out a debt reorganization plan. On June 6, 1945, the Alberta Cabinet passed Order-in-Council 925/45 that outlined the government's debt reorganization program.

Significantly, this program was two-pronged, the first included revising the existing financial arrangements and taxation agreements between Alberta and the Dominion, the second aspect dealt with curing the 1936 default. The agreement with the Dominion allowed the province to receive an additional $1.7 million per annum under the 1942 Dominion and Provincial Taxation Agreements for the 1941–45 fiscal years and to receive in the future $5.8 million instead of $4.1 million in federal payments. Dominion largesse also extended to repaying the fiscal need subsidy for the years 1937 through to 1941 for a total of $2.4 million. The total payment was $9.4 million, a considerable sum in 1945.

The transaction evolved in an unusual way. Without the concurrence of the Legislative Assembly, the government agreed on a reorganization program to be put to bondholders. According to the Order-in-Council of June 1945, once the Dominion had passed its Order, authorizing the payment of $9.4 million to the province, and sufficient bonds were deposited with the province to justify proceeding with the Debt Reorganization program, the Provincial Treasurer was authorized to make an offer to the holders of outstanding bonds and debentures (including those in default) and Alberta savings certificates (excluding bonds of Alberta and Great Waterways Railway Company). The offer was to be submitted to the minister of Finance of Canada and published in the *Alberta Gazette* and deemed to be in effect upon its publication in the *Gazette*.

It is remarkable that such a plan was undertaken without the consent of the Legislature although the Order tersely noted that a special session of the

Legislature was to be called "...to legalize and validate the Order." Clearly this was a plan that had the involvement and backing of the Dominion Government, the Bank of Canada, and representatives of domestic and foreign bondholders and knowledge of its existence limited to only of few key players in the Alberta government. Indeed, there were sanctions against trading in Alberta bonds after February 1945. In order to prevent insider trading on Alberta bonds then in default, the province was to furnish the Dominion with all such information as the Dominion required to "assist it in collecting any special tax imposed by it in respect of *speculative profits* made by residents of Canada who have purchased presently outstanding obligations of the Province on or after February 1st, 1945." Understandably governments were concerned with a possible scandal where insiders bought up cheap Alberta bonds, which would rise dramatically in value once the debt reorganization plan was made public.

The program worked as follows. As at June 15, 1945 $79.9 million of bonds and debentures were outstanding and $33.4 million in bonds and debentures were in default. The holders of the obligations in default were to be paid out fully plus $6.9 million as adjustments to unpaid interest in cash. The cash required for the principal repayment was provided, in part, from the issue of $29.6 million in serial bonds (2 percent to 3.25 percent) maturing between 1946 and 1960.

Holders of bonds that had not matured were to exchange their instruments one for one for new debentures paying 3.5 percent and maturing from 1961 to 1980 plus a payment of $21.7 million representing adjustments for unpaid interest. Fifty percent of this adjustment for interest ($10.8 million) was paid in cash and the other 50 percent paid in noninterest bearing talons falling due in equal instalments from June 1, 1946 to June 1, 1950. The new bonds would be callable on any interest payment date. In addition the new bonds issued were payable in the same currency or currencies as the outstanding bonds. The $10.8 million in cash for interest payments as well as the $6.9 million in unpaid interest adjustments was financed from Treasury reserves of $8 million, a $300,000 debt service appropriation and $9.4 million in federal payments.[44]

On July 17, 1945 Order-in-Council 1168/45 was passed. This Order authorized the publication of the Debt Reorganization Offer, which served as an offering circular to the holders of outstanding provincial and provincially guaranteed securities. The circular described the issue of four tranches of securities: 840,885 stock in pound sterling; $18.3 million optional payment debentures (Canadian or U.S. dollars or pound sterling); $42.9 million in optional payment debentures (Canadian or U.S. dollars); and $14.5 million in domestic debentures. In exchange for cash and new securities, the new holders were required to sign a letter of acceptance "releasing, waiving, abandoning and discharging all claims" for principal and interest of the outstanding debt.[45]

This complex refinancing was eventually authorized under *The Provincial Debt Reorganization Act*[46] assented to on July 26, 1945. By March of 1946 only $3.2 million of unmatured debentures remained outstanding. In 1947 Moody's revised Alberta's credit rating to Baa from Ba. In 1952, Alberta's rating was raised to A. Thus Alberta had returned to the international capital markets. The war with the "money power" was over. However, the lesson in this significant development was the evident importance that the Dominion ascribed to curing the default. The structure of this transaction showed that the Dominion's payments to the account of Alberta were to be specifically tied to curing the default and thus dedicated to eliminating Alberta's leading role as a pariah to the international financial community.

Debt management in the early postwar period was affected by three issues. The first was the effect of fiscal policy that was producing large budget surpluses. These surpluses meant that new debt issuance was minimal which in turn assisted the Dominion in resisting for a time international pressures emanating from the U.S. to raise interest rates. The second issue was the implicit guarantee to maintain bond prices. While this issue is more narrowly a matter of interest rate policy, the effect of large portions of the debt being held in the hands of a financially unsophisticated public made for difficult political choices. During 1947 and 1948, it was quite clear that political influence constrained bank officials who were more comfortable in seeing interest rates rise. Finally, the large volume of the debt outstanding at the end of the war, 150 percent of GDP by war's end, was a critical factor. It was critical for the debt manager to ensure that capital markets were favourable for the Dominion when it began to refinance maturing Victory bond issues.

8 | Politics, Public Debt and Debt Management

Public Versus Private Debts

A theory of public debt must be capable of distinguishing between "private" and "public" debts, and, at the same time, be sensitive to the meaning of "debt." Governments rarely borrow with requirements to pledge security or to maintain certain debt coverage ratios. Rather, governments at all levels promise to pay out of general revenue, interest and principal to debt holders. In the case of national governments, its power to expropriate, to tax, to borrow and to print money through its control of the central bank makes governments very different from corporations or individuals.

When corporations or individuals borrow, a comprehensive security document is drawn up that requires the borrower to, for example, maintain fire insurance on the home or maintain certain debt service coverage ratios. Quite frequently security, in the form of a house, corporate assets or market securities, is required as collateral to be realized upon in the event of nonpayment. In the case of nonpayment there is a defined legal process by which realization takes place (e.g., foreclosure, Rice Order, bankruptcy proceedings).

As Emerson P. Schmidt, in his examination of private and public debts, noted: "It is not the dissimilarity between private and public debt, which is significant; rather public authority backed by the taxing and other sovereign powers can manipulate purchasing power and resources in ways which are not open to private enterprise."[1] Another key difference between individual or corporate bankruptcy and state "bankruptcy" is that there is really no formal court process whereby the state would be compelled to pay interest and principal.[2] The process of curing a default is a very political one.

Equally significant is the role that public debt comes to play in the capital markets. Public debt, issued by the national government, is the foundation for all developed capital markets. As the primary source of collateral for securities lending transactions, futures and options markets, investment portfolios or for the management of liquidity, government bond trading overwhelms the trading of all other instruments.[3]

Yet private and public debts share one important thing in common, they represent a "promise to pay" and represent an important "bond" between the debtor and the creditor that is mutually acceptable to both parties. Critically important to the politics of public debt and debt management is the fact that these instruments, like corporate debt instruments, are widely traded in diverse markets. Thus, the value of public debt and thereby the cost of borrowing is, during "normal" times, determined by market supply and demand conditions. Resort to the "printing press" in a small open market economy quickly causes exchange rates to weaken and interest rates to rise as investors shift into other competing domestic and international debt obligations that hold their value.

External Versus Internal Debt

External debt obligations, denominated in a foreign currency, are of quite a different character for the government must acquire or earn foreign exchange to meet interest payments. Since the national government controls the means to ration foreign exchange, rating agencies distinguish between foreign and domestic pay obligations based on levels of international indebtedness and domestic fiscal and monetary policies.[4] As such, the availability of foreign exchange to other national borrowers, such as privately owned corporations, is dependent on the sovereign government allocating scarce foreign exchange for "priority purposes." Hence the capacity of such "subordinate" borrowers to repay foreign debts may be limited during times of crisis.

To the extent that the economy has sufficient access to foreign exchange through trade or through additional borrowing capacity in foreign markets to service foreign debts, there is no *a priori* justification to label external debt as "bad." Indeed, under certain circumstances, foreign borrowing may be much cheaper over the long-term, whether hedged or unhedged. The question then becomes "when does foreign borrowing become a method of 'protecting' our reputation or 'lifestyle' as opposed to borrowing to finance productive capital investment?"

In the case of the 1947 exchange crisis in Canada, procrastination by the authorities appears to have been caused by the desire to resist upward movements in interest rates and to combat inflationary pressures from a devaluation of the dollar. This resistance was in large part due to the Dominion government's tacit price maintenance for Victory Loan bondholders. These considerations eventually led to a decision to borrow abroad to protect the value of Canadian currency.

Economics and Politics

In reviewing the Parliamentary debates and other relevant resources about the period, several evolving themes become critical to watch for in the conduct of debt management in Canada. These themes varied somewhat over time. During the Great Depression, the gradual refunding of foreign pay bonds, the removal of the tax exempt feature and the absolute requirement to lower interest rates were central features of the debt management program. This objective was reinforced by the objections of many parliamentarians to the high real rate of interest.

During wartime, interest rate minimization, wider distribution of bondholdings, and the conscription of capital were pivotal issues. Finally in the postwar period the upward drift of yields on securities that were held in small denominations by ordinary Canadians illustrated the influence of international forces on Dominion securities, notwithstanding the virtual repatriation of the Dominion's debt.

The economic turmoil resulting from depression and wartime provided a fertile ground for underconsumptionist theories and conspiracy theories. These economic circumstances were especially conducive to gradual governmental intervention in the nation's economic life. Had it not been for the brutal contraction of credit from 1930 to 1933, a Conservative government would hardly have been expected to have commissioned a study on Canada's banking system. It is equally unlikely that the Dominion would have been able to compel banks to lend the Government money at or below cost had it not been for the existence of exchange controls necessitated by all-out war. Likewise, the international economic boom after the war, which created high demand for credit, necessitated upward movements in interest rates with negative consequences for Canadian holders of Victory bonds.

The nature of Canadian politics changed dramatically during the Depression. The Conservative party was shown to be quite incapable of coping with massive unemployment. The economic dislocation, which was felt severely in western Canada, lead to the demand for a reassessment of Canada's financial system. The scarcity of credit became a political issue. Demands for scaling down of debts were heard from all sides except the Conservative party. Given the international character of the depression it is not surprising that theories of imperialistic or Jewish conspiracies were constructed to accord blame to foreign parties.

Both Sellar and Clark introduced various political arguments in their plea for lower interest rates. As the minister of Finance's most senior and trusted policy advisor, the deputy minister acted as a middleman in interpreting the political significance of statements by politicians, the Cabinet or reactions of politicians to statements of political opponents or provincial leaders. This intelligence passed on to banks and others in the investment community could be used as a signal or as a trial balloon to demonstrate that the government might be prepared to do something "radical." Based on the archival records, it is clear that Deputy Finance Minister Clark and others carefully contrasted the radical views of monetary reformers against the financing needs and economic orthodoxy of the Liberals or Conservatives as a lever in enforcing the drive for lower interest rates. Likewise, the Alberta default galvanized the federal government into acting to ensure that other prairie governments were not tempted to default.

After the Bank of Canada was created, this "political leverage" was further buttressed by a growing market power that gave the Dominion, through the Bank, the ability to make its own interest rate forecasts come true. Moreover, since banking is federally regulated and when the Government holds a majority in the House of Commons, its interpretation of the "public will" is the ultimate form of leverage over the heavily regulated business of banking.

The conscription crisis and the demand by third parties for conscription of capital is also quite revealing about the influence of politics on debt management. Not only were senior Finance officials studying the conscription of capital, King briefed caucus on its merits. While conscription of private capital did not occur, the coincidence of military conscription and the initiation of the deposit certificate program, leave little doubt that assets of the banks were, in effect, conscripted for the war effort. Other cautions were used occasionally by Towers (excess profits and disclosure of hidden reserves) to enlist the cooperation of chartered bankers.

During the Second World War, Victory Loan campaigns designed to appeal to all classes of Canadians were premised on patriotism, "sound finance" and reducing consumption to a minimum. This program recognized that the huge sums involved required that no stone be left unturned to ensure the success of the ever increasing financial demands of wartime. The result for debt managers was to introduce more, rather than fewer, political considerations into the debt management function. The postwar discussions between Minister Abbott, Deputy Minister Clark and Governor Towers are illustrative of the political unease experienced when international interest rates were rising that eventually led to a fall in the value of Victory bonds. The reticence of the central bank, Finance and politicians to see rates rise underpin the implicit pact between governments and bondholders to restrain inflation and thus maintain bond prices.

CENTRALITY OF MARKETS

The behaviour of government debtors and institutional creditors can best be understood as institutions seeking to minimize interest costs (in the case of the government) or seeking to maximize real rates of return (in the case of creditors). This quest for maximizing and/or minimizing the rate of interest are the primary motivations underlying the tension between debtors and creditors. This characterization is broadly consistent with economic models describing the behaviour of profit-maximizing institutions.

Ultimately, it is the market that decides whether an issue will be a success or not. In respecting and "listening to the market," the Dominion's debt managers accepted the fundamental assumption that it is the market that is the most efficient form of distributing wealth.[5] This fundamental assumption holds that governments should not tinker with the market even if it would be in their best interest to do so. The Dominion's "successful" wartime experience with government intervention nevertheless had a continuing influence over government policies of social and economic intervention during the next four decades.[6]

International and domestic finance capital's reaction to domestic political developments was premised on the understanding that the Dominion *must maintain an economic environment hospitable to the claims of foreign and domestic securities holders.* Given the hundreds of investment options available to Canadian and foreign investors, the market was quick to discount bonds of an offending debtor but "not in any vindictive spirit." This practice was effective in constraining, but not dictating, the monetary and fiscal policies of the Dominion even when foreign borrowing was negligible and exchange controls were in place. In spite of the fact that Canadian borrowers could not borrow new cash in New York during the war, the likelihood of future borrowing at higher rates was enough to deter increases in withholding taxes in 1941.

The evidence surveyed does not show that state indebtedness to banks allowed banks to dictate specific economic policies. This debtor-creditor relationship, based on continued borrowing during the 1930s did, however, facilitate Canadian banks' access to key officials. This access was also facilitated as bankers, central bankers and Finance Department officials spoke the same language and made the same assumptions about the economy. Out of this shared world view were developed a set of unstated norms and expectations that guided policy-making. These assumptions included the freedom and sanctity of contract, the supremacy of market forces, and the need to maintain "business confidence." As one former Bank and Finance Department official commented to the author: "you must listen to the market; if you don't, you'll be crucified."[7] The market to participants represented the "good," the true test of creditworthiness.

It was this world view that was held by Towers, Clark and others. Mackenzie King once recorded in his diary how he was struck by the thinking of Towers and the "Finance crowd" during deliberations on the low interest loan to England after the Second World War. King noted on February 18, 1946: "I confess that Towers' statement did not impress me. What did impress me was that as the Governor of the Bank of Canada he was really under the influence of the large financial banking world. It was clear he was influenced by their environment." Several days later, King returned to the same theme, recording:

> Of course I feel that Clark and all his group and all the Finance Department and the Bank of Canada people, the big trade interests and so forth have only one point of view and really are a world of finance—feeling a greater common interest in finance than they do any interest in common with the political world.[8]

This respect and belief in the market and market forces is a conservative force limiting governmental action even when the central bank is nominally controlled by the government. This study shows that there existed an "ideological confraternity" shared by key actors and this confraternity is rooted in the centrality of capital markets. This ideological confraternity complements studies in the field of political culture that focus upon the values and belief systems underpinning society or certain key segments of the society.[9] Thus state indebtedness, especially when concentrated in the hands of large institutions, sends a simple signal to government decision-makers: expropriation of capital or increased deficits will result in the discounting of bonds in the secondary market, leading to higher interest rates and the departure of "worried" finance capital.[10] This study also illustrates quite clearly the support function provided by financial dailies and weeklies in attacking any attempts to renegotiate interest rates or contracts that would favour the borrower.

From the depression years to the postwar boom, the influence exerted by finance capital was more personalistic; today it is more impersonalistic, more diversified in its character but nonetheless pervasive given the internationalization of capital markets. The dominance of deep, liquid markets made up of thousands of well-informed institutional investors linked electronically and motivated by achieving quarterly returns in the first quartile is in sharp contrast to face-to-face meetings with bankers during the 1930s.

International Activities

The principal reasons for gathering information about foreign market conditions was to issue bonds at the most opportune time. The estimation of the most appropriate time was based on several factors including the avoidance of conflict with major borrowers, notably the national government, avoiding dates that correspond to elections or the opening of legislatures, and being prepared to enter the market the minute rates seemed most favourable.

The foregoing description of an often extensive information gathering process is consistent with the debt management maxim of keeping interest costs to a minimum. Had the Dominion entered these markets, particularly during the Depression, without advance preparation there would certainly have been cause for alarm that Canadian taxpayers were paying more than they should for foreign-denominated funds. However, by employing Morgan Stanley and Nivisons, the Dominion was receiving, arguably, the most respected advice in these foreign markets. This advice, along with access to a foreign central bank's thinking, meant the Dominion was able to avoid embarrassing clashes in timing with major governmental and corporate borrowers.

Did foreign borrowing during the 1930–1952 period erode Canada's sovereignty? Or, to rephrase the question: Was Canada's independence violated in any way as a result of its indebtedness to financial institutions and citizens of foreign nations? Certainly Canada's experience was markedly different than that of Latin American and Central American nations whose custom houses were routinely seized in the first three decades of this century.[11] For the most part, international finance capital regarded Clark, Towers, and Liberal and Conservative governments as reliable and therefore credit worthy. Historically, there is very little evidence to suggest that Canada's monetary and fiscal policies were directly determined abroad.

Yet the strenuous objections of international finance capital to the imposition of special withholding taxes also revealed how very sensitive international finance capital was to reductions in their after-tax rate of return that effectively reduced the value of these securities in secondary markets. This facet of investment behaviour leading to a heavy sell-off of the affected class of bonds was the most effective way that international finance capital could discipline the borrower. This leverage was most authoritative when large refunding and/or new market issues were being contemplated. The fate of the 1941 withholding tax proposal is a concrete example of international and domestic finance capital's influence on taxation policy-making. Equally important was the role of both domestic and international financial newspapers in supporting finance capital's attack on what it perceived to be confiscation of property rights.

In the case of Alberta, the central bank acted resolutely in responding to the expectations of foreign bondholders by ensuring that default would be contained and Alberta's "misbehaviour" would not be rewarded through subventions from the federal treasury. Towers was acutely aware of the market's negative reaction to "manifestations of good or bad faith" in the arena of government debentures against which no specific assets are pledged.[12] Knowing that institutional investors, faced with a variety of bonds to choose from, would rarely purchase obligations unless the credit worthiness of the issuer was sound, Towers sought to preserve the trust necessary in the debtor-creditor relationship.

The Alberta Default

The Alberta aberration teaches several lessons about the nature of public debts and the importance of good debt management. First of all, the crisis of Alberta public finance demonstrates the dangers to the issuer of the optional-payment bond and more generally the special difficulties of foreign borrowing.[13] Secondly, Alberta did not follow the maxim of flexibility in managing its debts by ensuring that call features could be available when bond yields fell. To be fair, the Province was not unusual in this respect as investors continued to vigorously resist the call provision. Thirdly, the maturity structure was dominated by too many long-term issues, which again did not permit the debtor to take advantage of declining rates.

The conditions for Alberta's default included objective financial circumstances but also subjective factors such as feelings of alienation and victimization wrought by finance capital and conflicts with the Dominion over financial sovereignty. Equally important was Social Credit's assessment that the opprobrium accorded default and the financial consequences were no worse than maintaining the status quo and might even be better. The crisis demonstrated that the Dominion, motivated by self interest in regard to the refinancing of hundreds of millions of maturing bonds, successfully isolated the Social Credit administration. Dunning and his officials were able to convince international finance capital, which previously regarded federal and provincial credit as synonymous, that Alberta was a "special case," a poor cousin, whose actions were in no way supported by the Dominion.

After analysing the initiatives taken by the Province and the reaction of the chartered banks to these measures, the protection of the Dominion's credit standing could only be served by Alberta's default. The great fear that Social Credit would spread like a prairie fire was implicit in many editorials and communiques by bankers, lawyers and Dominion officials. The Dominion concluded that Alberta, which had moved too far in interfering with federal prerogatives, should be cut adrift in order for the Dominion to maintain credibility with the international and domestic financial communities.

The default also served to build a close working relationship between the new Bank of Canada governor and the chartered banks. This close co-operation preserved the constitutional authority of the Dominion in the sphere of banking, credit, currency and interest.

What then are the conditions under which bankruptcy today would become attractive to a governmental debtor? One of the conditions is the co-existence of a large segment of the population that is heavily indebted with a likewise heavily indebted government. (Heavily indebted would mean debt service costs approaching or exceeding 50 percent of revenue.) How, for example, could a government justify cutting or eliminating welfare, health care or unemployment insurance, as one of its biggest expenditures items, while still remaining current on its interest payment? A second condition is a precipitous fall in income that results in the rise of interest payments as a percentage of spending and revenue. Market collapses are typically associated with such falls in income as the devastation in financial markets flow through to the real economy as liquidity and credit dries up. A recent example would be the collapse of oil prices in Alberta in 1985–86 or the cod fish moratorium in Newfoundland. Historically, this phase could be associated with efforts by the Dominion to withhold economic and financial information from the markets in the early stages of the Depression. This decline in income is particularly important—as the standard of living declines significantly and the interest costs of indebtedness rise disproportionately, finance capital and the evil of usury become "the enemy." In this phase, finance capital may demand either changes in spending policy or require security for borrowing. In the early 1990s, frequent warnings to the federal and provincial governments from rating agencies and subsequent downgrades were instrumental in a shift away from Keynesian deficit financing to neo-conservative policies of privatization and "cutting government waste." At this historical moment another condition is critical—the identification of "external forces" (e.g., Montagu Norman, Bay Street, International Monetary Fund) outside the geographical area as causes of social and economic collapse. An "us versus them" psychological dynamic thus reinforces the "righteousness" of default. Finally, equally important is the emergence of a theory that can be rapidly popularized and translated to the mass public that attaches blame to these external forces. Such a theory, essentially moralistic, boils down to the evils of money-lending. These conditions are more often present in developing countries, such as Peru or recently Indonesia, where default and rescheduling of debts may be perceived as the only alternative to social and political chaos. What is most interesting, from a social-psychological perspective, is the almost total collective amnesia amongst the Alberta population of the province's 1936 default.

DISTRIBUTION OF THE DEBT

The leverage exercised by the banks on the Dominion during the Depression was based on their collective ownership of the biggest share of maturing debt and its effective internal coordination through the offices of the Canadian Bankers' Association. This concentrated portion of maturing debt issues, often well over 50 percent of maturing obligations, gave the banks the opportunity to negotiate privately behind closed doors with the debtor over the term and yield. The banks drive for yield and liquidity was most visible in the bankers' protests against the institution of the deposit certificate. As this study showed, this nonmarket relationship tended to hamper the Government's attempts to lengthen the term maturity of the debt in the face of the banks' own preference for short-term bonds. The creation of a central bank enabled Finance to eliminate the direct head-to-head negotiations previously observed. After 1935, terms were tailored by the Bank on the basis of ongoing market contacts and rates determined largely by secondary market trading.

Finally, the wide distribution of the public debt at war's end had a significant influence on debt management and interest rate policy in the early postwar period. The Canada Savings Bond was a direct result of responding to the different needs of the retail market for a near liquid, nontradeable security. And, the broad distribution had serious implications for interest rate policy. Without the broad distribution it is likely that elected officials would not have resisted to the same extent a rise in interest rates.

Canada's dependence on international capital markets changed significantly after the Great War. From a situation of utmost dependence on London for capital, the Dominion Government was, in effect, reliant on Toronto and Montreal financial institutions and wealthy individuals. The Dominion's foreign borrowing shifted away from London to New York as the Dominion tapped the U.S. dollar market for relatively modest sums. (See Appendix B.) Foreign borrowing mostly was used to refinance maturing issues or to maintain the value of the Canadian dollar, as evident in the 1947 exchange crisis. Over time, and still today, the Dominion's concern is related to the effect of international interest rates, especially U.S. government securities, that serve as a benchmark borrowing rate for Canada.

Canada's evolution as a nation independent from the United Kingdom was not only a political one, it was also financial. As the Dominion organized to become financially self-sufficient, its financial interests were in a sense domesticated. Domestic investment dealers, such as A.E. Ames and Wood Gundy, assumed a bigger role. The whole controversy at the time of the Bank of Canada's establishment—that this institution was part of a conspiracy to put Canada under imperial domination—reinforced Canadians' desire to work outside the control of London.

During the Depression, the financial apparatus of the Dominion was modernized. Ottawa was able to attract a brain trust of remarkable public servants, principally educated at graduate schools in the United Kingdom or the United States, and equipped with the latest economic and financial theories. This nucleus gave the Dominion a new energy and intelligence to address complex financial and economic problems. This team of public servants oversaw the establishment of a central bank, the isolation of the Alberta Social Credit administration, a very successful wartime debt management program, and a new set of financial institutions such as the Canada Mortgage and Housing Corporation.

While Sellar, Clark and Towers were the main operatives in raising loans, they had to be acutely sensitive to their political masters. Government borrowing was never done in isolation from political considerations in Canada. This was because legally, approval was required by Parliament and the Cabinet and politically this debt was directly a charge on the taxpayers of Canada. It was Prime Minister Bennett who changed the institutional structures to strengthen the Dominion's leverage vis-a-vis the banks. It was Prime Minister King and Finance Minister Ilsley who approved the deposit certificate program during the Second World War. These political actions had a direct impact on interest rates the Dominion paid on its debt securities—rates lower than they otherwise would have been had the status quo prevailed. That is the Dominion Government was no longer a relatively passive price taker.

Politics and public debt management are inextricably linked and the debt management programs and policies offer interesting insights about the nature of external parties' influence on government policy over time. Political theory, broadly stated, attempts to understand the dynamic interplay of various "interests," "classes" or "social tendencies." Using state borrowing as a test case for understanding the dynamic interplay of economic interests illustrates the powerful influences of international finance capital—the "money power" as Mackenzie King termed finance capital—over governmental decision-making. This economic "interest" had a pervasive influence on decision-makers in Finance and the Bank of Canada in the mid-twentieth century. Today, the phenomena of globalization, which stripped to its basics is the free mobility of international finance capital, serves as a check to government's financial decision-making. The necessity for governments to access capital markets continually modifies policies in subtle ways. During the Depression, with very high levels of indebtedness, paradoxically, the policy response of the Dominion was to increase state involvement in the financial system to preserve the long-term viability of domestic and international finance capital. In the 1980s and 1990s the policy response has been to significantly restructure the "welfare state" to enable governments to continue to borrow money, or, importantly, to refinance maturing debt issues. *Politics and Public Debt* provides a historical context and methodological framework to examine current trends in the management of Canada's public debt at the federal, provincial and municipal levels.

Appendices

Appendix A
Synopsis of Major Domestic Borrowing, 1930–1952

Date of Issue	Amount $Cdn.	Coupon Rate (%)	Purpose
December 1, 1930	40,000,000	4.00	Refunding
May 1931 *	638,609,300	4.50	Conversion
November 1931	221,198,200	5.00	Refunding/Cash
August 1, 1932	50,000,000	4.5	Cash
October 15, 1932	81,191,000	4.00	Refunding/Cash
November 1, 1932	35,000,000	4.00	Cash
May 31, 1933	40,000,000	3.50	Cash
October 15. 1933	225,000,000	3.5 & 4.0	Cash/Conversion
October 15, 1934	63,336,000	2.00	Cash/Conversion
October 15, 1934	7,933,000	2.50	Cash/Conversion
October 15, 1934	40,409,000	3.00	Cash/Conversion
October 15, 1934	138,322,000	3.50	Cash/Conversion
September 15,1935	135,000,000	1.5 & 2.0	Refunding
June 1,1936	134,703,000	1.5 & 3.25	Conversion
September 15,1936	45,000,000	1.00	Cash
September 15,1936**	55,000,000	3.00	Cash
June 1, 1937	60,000,000	2.00	Conversion
June 1, 1937	20,000,000	1.00	Conversion
June 1, 1937	33,500,000	3.25	Conversion
June 1, 1938	90,625.000	2.00	Cash/Conversion
June 1, 1938	49,225,000	3.00	Cash/Conversion
May 15, 1939	95,500,000	1.50	Cash/Conversion
May 15, 1939	39,000.000	3.00	Cash/Conversion
October 16, 1939	200,000,000	2.00	Cash/Repatriation
February 1, 1940	250,000,000	3.25	First War Loan
May 1, 1940	250,000,000	1.00	Gold sale to FECB
January 2 1941	250,000,000	1.50	Chartered banks
June 15, 1941	193, 286,000	2.00	War/Converslon
June 15, 1941	643,534,250	3.00	War/Conversion
March 1, 1942	57,169,000	1.50	War
March 1, 1942	269,879,000	2.25	War
March 1, 1942	669,658,000	3.00	War

Date of Issue	Amount $Cdn.	Coupon Rate (%)	Purpose
November 1, 1942	144,253,000	1.75	War
November 1, 1942	847,136,050	3.00	War
May 1, 1943	197,455,000	1.75	War
May 1, 1943	1,111,261,650	3.00	War
July 2, 1943	200,000,000	1.50	Chartered banks
November 1, 1943	373,259,000	1.75	War
November 1, 1943	1,197,324,750	3.00	War
May 1, 1944	239,713,000	1.75	War
May 1, 1944	1,165,300,350	3.00	War
November 1, 1944	344,267,000	3.00	War
November 1, 1944	1,365,639,200	3.00	War
May 1, 1945	267,800,000	1.75	War
May 1, 1945	1,295,819,350	3.00	War
November 1, 1945	335,690,000	1.75	War
November 1, 1945	1,691,796,700	3.00	War
November 1, 1946	400,000,000	1.75	Refunding
CSB 1946-47	483,410,000	2.75	Cash
May 1, 1947	200,000,000	0.62	Cash
CSB 1947-48	263,530,150	2.75	Cash
March 1, 1948	145,000,000	1.50	Cash
CSB 1948-49	235,258,360	2.75	Cash
CSB 1949-50	288,904,400	2.75	Cash
August 30, 1950	300,000,000	.875	Cash/Conversion
June 15, 1950	395,000,000	2.00	Refunding
June 15, 1950	350,000,000	2.75	Refunding
November 1, 1950	300,000,000	1.75	Refunding
November 1, 1950	400,000,000	2.25	Refunding
CSB 1950-51	261,993,600	2.75	Cash
CSB 1951-52	357,649,750	2.0 & 3.5	Cash
July 23, 1952	100,000,000	1.50	Cash/D.C.s
CSB 1952-53	340,304,350	3.75	Cash

CSB sales figures as at March 31 of year succeeding initiation of campaign.
* See Table 3.3.
** Perpetual issue.
Source: *Public Accounts of Canada* (Ottawa: various years).

Appendix B
Synopsis of Dominion Loans Issued Abroad, 1930–1950

Date Issued	Term	Where Payable	Amount	Coupon Rate (%)
July 1	1930–50	London	137,058,841	3.5
October 1	1930–60	New York	100,000,000	4.0
October 1	1932–33	New York	60,000,000	4.0
July 1	1933–34	New York	60,000,000	4.0
September 1	1933–58	London	73,000,000	4.0
May 1	1934–55	London	48,666,667	3.25
September 1	1934–35	New York	50,000,000	2.0
August 15	1935–45	New York	76,000,000	2.5
January 1	1936–39	New York	40,000,000	2.0
January 15	1936–41	New York	48,000,000	3.25
January 15	1937–44	New York	30,000,000	2.25
January 15	1937–67	New York	55,000,000	3.0
November 15	1938–68	New York	40,000,000	3.0
May 1	1939–41	New York	20,000,000	1.25
May 1	1941–43	New York	10,000,000	2.25
January 15	1943–48	New York	30,000,000	2.5
January 15	1943–53	New York	30,000,000	3.0
January 15	1943–58	New York	30,000,000	3.0
December 1947	Eximbank Credit	New York	50,000,000	2.25
August 1	1948–63	New York	150,000,000	3.0
July 1	1949–63	London	54,812,961	3.25
September 1	1949–74	New York	110,000,000	2.75
September 15	1950–75	New York	52,500,000	2.75

Sources: *Public Accounts of Canada*, various years; *Canada Year Book*, various years.

Appendix C
Credit Ratings of Dominion of Canada and Selected Provincial Governments
Moody's Investors Service – 1930 through to 1953

Province	Credit Rating[1]	
Nova Scotia	Aa	1930
	A	1932
	Baa	1935
	A	1939
New Brunswick	Aa	1930
	A	1932
	Baa	1948
Quebec	Aaa	1930
	Aa	1932
	A	1934
	Aa	1938
	A	1948
Ontario	Aaa	1930
	Aa	1934
	A	1934
	Aa	1935
	A	1948
Manitoba	Aa	1930
	Baa	1932
	A	1950
Saskatchewan	Aa	1930
	A	1932
Alberta	Baa	1930
	Ba	1936
	Baa	1947
	A	1952
Dominion of Canada	Aaa	1931
	Aa	1932

[1] At January of each year.

Source: *Moody's Rating Changes for Major Canadian Issuers from 1918 to date*, May 26, 1992, *Canadian Credit Report*, August 18, 1983.

Appendix D
Government of Canada Bond Yields, 1930–1939

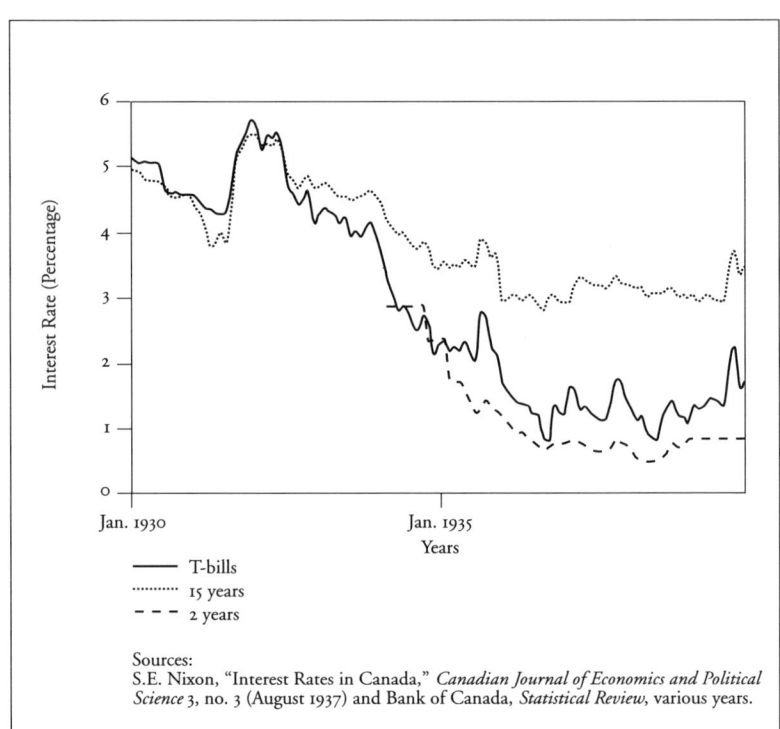

Sources:
S.E. Nixon, "Interest Rates in Canada," *Canadian Journal of Economics and Political Science* 3, no. 3 (August 1937) and Bank of Canada, *Statistical Review*, various years.

Appendix E
Government of Canada Bond Yields, 1940–1945

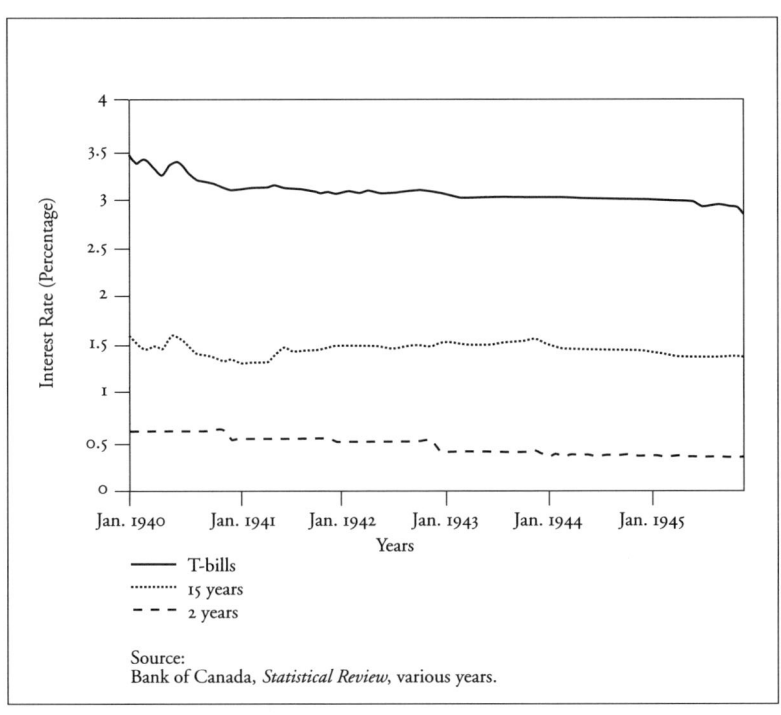

Source:
Bank of Canada, *Statistical Review*, various years.

Appendix F
Government of Canada Bond Yields, 1946–1952

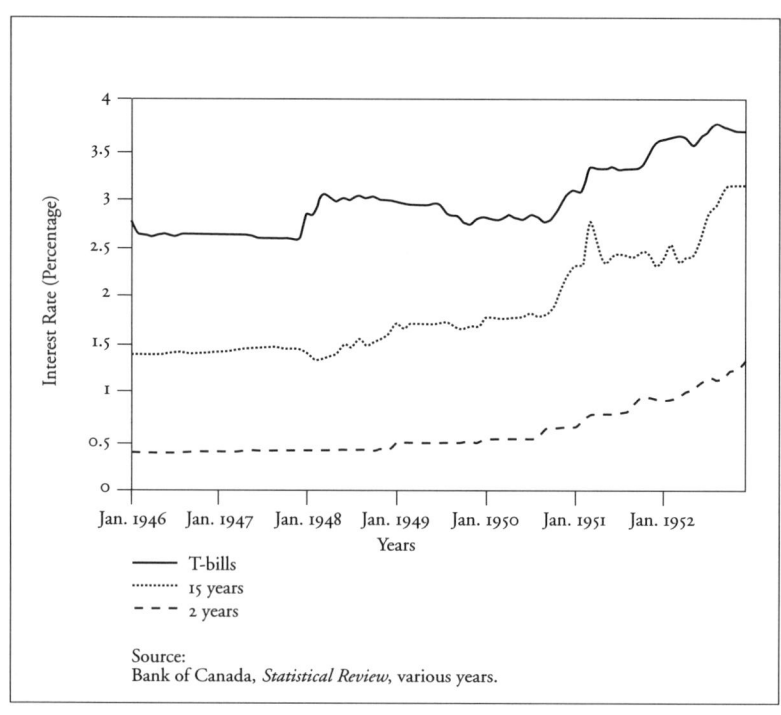

Source:
Bank of Canada, *Statistical Review*, various years.

NOTES

PREFACE

1. For example Harold Chorney of Concordia University.
2. Robert L. Ascah, "The Deficit Debate: A Survey and an Assessment," presented to the Canadian Political Science Association Annual Meeting, Winnipeg, 8 June 1986.
3. C.D. Howe Institute, "Avoiding A Crisis: Proceedings of a Workshop on Canada's Fiscal Outlook," 27 January 1993. Cecil Foster, "NDP premiers urge leadership on debt," *The Financial Post*, 2 March 1993, p. 3. Mel Duvall, "Federal Deficit reaching 'crisis level'," *Calgary Herald*, 30 November 1993, p. D-1 on Premier Roy Romanov's speech to the Calgary Chamber of Commerce. Geoffrey York, "Bold plan would give provinces debt relief," *The Globe and Mail*, 29 November 1993, pp. A-1; A-3. A senior advisor to Premier Bob Rae, Michael Mendelsohn, in a paper to the Caledon Institute of Social Policy, raised the prospect of the federal government *assuming* responsibility for the provinces' $200 billion in debt. See also Lisa Grogan-Green, "Fear of fiscal crisis hangs ominously over bond market," *The Financial Post*, 28 December 1993, p. 16.
4. "The crush of Newfoundland's (and Canada's) debt," *The Globe and Mail*, 5 March 1993, p. A19 (emphasis added).
5. J.J. Moskau, "Canada gets IMF deficit warning," *The Globe and Mail*, 20 April 1993, p. B-1; B-3. See also *Grant's Interest Rate Observer*, an influential investor newsletter "Northward, the IMF," 7 May 1993, pp. 2–8. In a report in *The Wall Street Journal*, Robert Blohm, an investment banker noted that a "debt crisis would begin when provinces could no longer roll over their maturing foreign debt at an acceptable cost." "Canadian Bond Market Teeters While Provinces Fiddle," 23 April 1993, p. A15.
6. Martin Mittelstaedt, "Ottawa seeks way to bail out provinces," *The Globe and Mail*, November 1993, p. A-1. A memorandum from then Deputy Minister Fred Gorbet to Finance Minister Mazankowski entitled "Are Saskatchewan and Newfoundland Becoming Insolvent?" dated 13 March 1992 was released under the federal access to information legislation and a 12 November 1992 federal Finance study of fiscal sustainability of provincial deficits also added to concerns about the financial health of specific provincial governments.

7. Bruce Little, "Cut or be cut, provinces told," *The Globe and Mail*, 18 December 1993.
8. Moody's Investment Services, 16 February 1995. Moody's press release stated that it "was concerned about the medium-term deficit outlook, especially as regards the problems facing Canada's public sector once the next, inevitable downturn occurs." The previous June when Moody's put Canada's foreign currency debt under review the agency stated: "The public sector debt question is complicated by the fact that, in recent years, foreigners have been purchasing an ever larger portion of Canadian public sector debt obligations. The rising concern about the level of public sector finance within Canada appears to pose a risk that, during a period of stress, holders of Canadian dollar-denominated debt might turn those assets into foreign currency assets." At the time of Moody's announcement then Canadian Bankers Association President Helen Sinclair commented in an interview about the difficulties for a country's sovereignty when so much of its public debt is held by nonresidents. "Reduction of foreign-held debt key for economy, banks say," *Edmonton Journal*, 6 April 1995. Not to belabour the "crisis" mentality but rating agencies' statistics typically do not include the huge unfunded liabilities of public pension plans.
9. See for example, Linda McQuaig's, *Shooting the Hippo: Death by Deficit and Other Canadian Myths* (Toronto: Viking, 1995).

I PUBLIC DEBT AND DEBT MANAGEMENT

1. J.M. Keynes, *The Economic Consequences of the Peace* (New York: Harcourt, Brace and Howe, 1920), p. 37.
2. Harold Innis, "The Penetrative Powers of the Price System," in Mary Q. Innis, ed., *Essays in Canadian Economic History* (Toronto: University of Toronto Press, 1973), p. 265.
3. For examples sections 110–116 of the Act.
4. Tom Naylor, *The History of Canadian Business*, Volume I (Toronto: James Lorimer & Company, 1975), p. 26 that borrowed heavily from the earlier work of Gustavus Meyers.
5. Bank of Canada, "Submission by the Bank of Canada to the Royal Commission on Banking and Finance," Ottawa, 31 May 1962, Submission IV, p. 46. See also statement of J.E. Coyne cited in Douglas Fullerton, *The Bond Market in Canada* (Toronto: The Carswell Company Limited, 1962), pp. 60–61.
6. For a recent commentary on debt management objectives and issues facing provincial issuers see Philip Wooldridge, "Financing activities of provincial governments and their enterprises," *Bank of Canada Review* (Spring 1996): pp. 13–29.
7. *Proceedings*, Royal Commission on Banking and Finance, Volume 24, Ottawa, 9 July 1962, p. 2486.
8. Royal Commission on Dominion-Provincial Relations, *Book I* (Ottawa: King's Printer, 1940), pp. 75–76.

9. Ibid., pp. 98–99.
10. *Canada Year Book, Public Accounts of Canada,* various years at March 31.
11. Watson Sellar, "Memorandum for Mr. Bennett," 12 March 1931, National Archives of Canada (originally Public Archives of Canada when the original research was done, hereafter cited as NAC), RG 19, Volume 592, File 155–30, Volume 2.
12. Bank of Canada, *Annual Report, 1937* (Ottawa: Bank of Canada, 22 February 1938), p. 14.
13. *The War Appropriation (United Nations Mutual Aid) Act, 1943,* 7 George VI, Statutes of Canada, 1943, Chapter 17. Mackenzie King saw the hand of the Bank of England in this transaction and thought the Bank of Canada too pliant in these negotiations. King did not want to "give to the British Treasury in advance the intimation, as he [Ilsley] wished, of what we are proposing to do in making a virtual gift of a billion dollars to Britain but to allow me to hold this card in making pleas which I might have to make with Churchill and Roosevelt alike for some recognition of what Canada is doing in discussions pertaining to our right to participate in at least the direction of our own part of the war effort, and not to have it taken altogether out of our hands." Cited in J.L. Granatstein, *Canada's War. The Politics of the Mackenzie King Government, 1939–1945* (Toronto: Oxford University Press, 1975), p. 190. In a note to his successor James Coyne, Towers acknowledged his role, as early as August 1941, in recommending to Ilsley that noninterest bearing loans and a gift should be made to the United Kingdom. Towers Memoranda, No. 401, 2 August 1941, "Major Considerations relating to sale of securities," and "Note for Mr. Coyne," 28 January 1955, with Towers Memoranda, No. 402, Bank of Canada Archives.
14. These were respectively, $446.7 million of the 5.5 percent 1918–33 Victory Loan, $236.3 million of the 5.5 percent 1917–1937 Victory Loan and the $511.9 million 5.5 percent 1919–1934 Victory Loan.

2   Capital Markets and the Players

1. Adam Smith, *An Inquiry into the Nature and Causes of the Wealth of Nations,* Andrew Kinder, ed. (Harmondsworth: Penguin Books, 1970), p. 119.
2. William C. Hood, *Financing of Economic Activity in Canada,* Royal Commission on Canada's Economic Prospects (Ottawa: Queen's Printer, 1958), p. 11 (emphasis added).
3. E.P. Neufeld, *The Financial System of Canada* (Toronto: Macmillan of Canada, 1972), pp. 468–72.
4. S. Sarpkaya, *The Money Market in Canada,* Second Edition (Toronto: Butterworth, 1980), p. 3 (emphasis added). Today the money market is generally considered as consisting of those financial instruments with an original term to maturity of less than one year.

5. J.A. McLeod, "Presidential Address: Problems Facing Canada's Banks," *The Journal of the Canadian Bankers Association* 40, no. 2 (January 1933): 159–65; and Royal Commission on Banking and Currency, *Proceedings* (Ottawa: King's Printer, September 1933), p. 3155.
6. R.S. Sayers, *Central Banking after Bagehot* (Oxford: Clarendon Press, 1957), pp. 112–13. Indeed it was predicted that during the early years of the Bank of Canada's operations the moral force of the Bank would be at its weakest which would be its principal source of power and influence. See testimony of M.W. Wilson on behalf of the Canadian Bankers' Association, *Proceedings*, Royal Commission on Banking and Currency, Ottawa, 14 September 1933, p. 3161.
7. Graham F. Towers, "Review of Post-War Monetary Policy," in James P. Cairns and H.H. Binhammer, eds., *Canadian Banking and Monetary Policy* (Toronto: McGraw-Hill, 1965), pp. 190–99.
8. Bank of Canada, "Government of Canada Treasury Bills," *Bank of Canada Review* (May 1972): 3–13; and Bruce Maclaury, *The Canadian Money Market: Its Development and Its Impact*, Harvard University, Department of Economics, unpublished Ph.D. Dissertation, 1961.
9. When a primary distribution takes place, the issue price is determined perhaps a month before the date that the securities are delivered or sold to the final buyer. During the interim period final legal documentation is prepared and the certificates are printed up for delivery.
10. It should be noted that Henry C. Adams was familiar with Marx's economic writings having read *Capital, Volume I* in a French translation. See Henry C. Adams, *Public Debts: An Essay in the Science of Finance* (New York: D. Appleton and Company, 1898), p. 8n.
11. Ibid., p. 11.
12. Ibid., p. 41.
13. Ibid., p. 50 (emphasis added).
14. D.C. MacGregor, "The Problem of the Public Debt in Canada," *Canadian Journal of Economics and Political Science* 2, no. 2 (May 1936): 167–94; and D.C. MacGregor, "Outline of the Position of Public Finance: Public Debt," in H.A. Innis and A.F.W. Plumptre, eds., *The Canadian Economy and its Problems* (Toronto: Canadian Institute of International Affairs, 1934), pp. 55–61.
15. See Robert L. Ascah, "Testing Theories of Federalism: The Case of the Financial Sector," a paper delivered to the Annual Meeting of the Canadian Political Science Association, Victoria, 27 May 1990, pp. 12–13.
16. *The Exchequer and Audit Act, Revised Statutes of Canada*, 1906, Chapter 24.
17. *Consolidated Revenue and Audit Act*, 22 George V, *Statutes of Canada*, 1931, Chapter 23.
18. CBA Circular 95-U, "Minutes of Meeting with the Prime Minister and Minister of Finance with the Members of the Association held in the Office of the Minister of Finance in Ottawa, Monday, October 17th, 1932," The Bank of Nova Scotia Archives, Secretary's Department Papers, RG018/01/0007/0167.

19. Apparently, Graham Towers believed that one of the conditions Clark set for his appointment was the establishment of a central bank. Interview, Ottawa, 3 June 1982. The extent of Bennett's annoyance towards the banks is revealed in a letter to J.A. McLeod, CBA president in June 1933. Bennett denounced the banks "for driving customers to the wall who are unable to liquidate their liabilities under existing economic conditions" while at the same time reminding him he would be overseeing the dicennial changes to the *Bank Act.* Cited in H. Blair Neatby's *William Lyon Mackenzie King: 1932–1939, The Prism of Unity* (Toronto: University of Toronto Press, 1976), p. 58.
20. House of Commons, *Debates,* 17th Parliament, 5th Session, 21 June 1934, p. 4193.
21. House of Commons, *Debates,* 17th Parliament, 5th Session, 27 June 1934, p. 4365. From *The Financial Post* these comments: "The Bank of England crowd have worked persistently to establish in the Empire a ring of central banking organizations which would be dominated by a keystone institution in London, thus strengthening the grip of a small London group on Empire finance, and making banks in the various Dominions pawns of a gigantic scheme of imperial control through finance. Already their agents have been active in Ottawa, attempting to shape the foundation on which our new banking legislation will be erected." *The Nation's Business,* 21 October 1934. Perhaps the most bizarre exposition of the theory came from Liberal Senator J.P.B. Casgrain who argued that the Bank of England was controlled by Jewish bankers. "The purpose of Mr. Montagu Norman is to try to get the banks in all the Dominions and colonies under the control of the Bank of England. He had good reason for doing that. I do not know whether everybody is aware that the Bank of England is controlled by the London traders. And who are these traders? They are mainly very largely people of German and Jewish origin in many cases German Jews. They are the masters of Mr. Montagu Norman, and if he did not so what he was told he would not keep his place very long." Senate, *Debates,* 17th Parliament, 5th Session, 28 June 1934, p. 604.
22. *The Canadian Who's Who,* Volume VI, 1952–54 (Toronto: Trans-Canada Press, 1955), p. 1054.
23. Douglas Fullerton, *Graham Towers and His Times* (Toronto: McClelland and Stewart, 1986), pp. 55–57.
24. *Vancouver Sun,* "The Passing of a Great Canadian," 13 December 1975.
25. 24–25 George V, *Statutes of Canada,* 1934, Chapter 43.
26. Interview, 11 June 1982.
27. See Fullerton, *The Bond Market in Canada,* p. 110, who succintly states: "Since the Bank often has the power to make its own forecasts come true, the dealer usually listens attentively."
28. Royal Commission on Banking and Finance, *Report* (Ottawa: Queen's Printer, 1964), p. 325.
29. Towers Memoranda, No. 50, December 1936, "Statement Re. Mechanics of Central Banking: for Dominion-Provincial Conference, December 1936," Bank of Canada Archives.

30. Towers Memoranda, No. 129, 3 May 1938, "Conversation with Mr. Howe on subject of his remarks during hearings of Committee on Railways and Shipping," Bank of Canada Archives (emphasis added).
31. With the passage of securities legislation in the United States in 1933 and 1934, Canada like any other corporate borrower was required to file a prospectus. This was, and is, not required for the Dominion or provincial governments in Canada.
32. Smith, 1970, p. 389.
33. Ernest Mandel, *Marxist Economic Theory* (London: Merlin Press, 1968), p. 221.
34. Notice deposits technically required a 30-day notice that funds would be withdrawn although this condition was usually waived for small depositors.
35. For example, "The Banks," *The Western Producer*, 20 April 1933, p. 6. "By running to cover immediately economic disturbances arise, by leaving industry and agriculture to fend for themselves, by withdrawing itself as rapidly and as completely as possible inside of its own comparatively safe retreat—by these means a banking system can come through very difficult times relatively unscathed and owing to the relative immunity from injury, strengthened."
36. J. Douglas Gibson, "The Changing Character of Bank Assets," *The Journal of the Canadian Bankers' Association* 45, no. 2 (January 1938): 149.
37. F.C. Biggar, "Monetary Misconceptions," Speech before the Rotary Club of Montreal, Tuesday, 23 June 1936, p. 6.
38. Bank of Canada, *Annual Report of the Governor of the Bank of Canada and Statement of Accounts*, 1948 (Ottawa: Bank of Canada, 11 February 1949), p. 79.
39. Ralph B. McKibbin to author, 27 April 1982.
40. Adam Shortt, *History of Canadian Banking* (Toronto: Canadian Bankers Association, n.d), pp. 317–60.
41. 62–63 Victoria, *Statutes of Canada*, 1900, Chapter 93.
42. *The Bank Act, Revised Statutes of Canada*, 1906, Chapter 29, Sections 117–123 (curator functions), 99–111 (purchase of bank assets).
43. See C.G. Coote's memorandum in *Proceedings*, Royal Commission on Banking and Currency, Volume 7, pp. 48–49.
44. See S. Sarpkaya, "Counting Canada's Banks," reprint from The *Journal of the Canadian Bankers' Association and ICB Review* (October and December 1978).
45. See B.H. Beckhart, "Fewer and Larger Banks," in E.P. Neufeld, ed., *Money and Banking in Canada* (Toronto: Macmillan, 1964), pp. 196–205.
46. Another significant source of revenue is derived from advisory functions, most notably in the field of mergers and acquisitions.
47. See Testimony of W.C. Pitfield, President, Investment Bankers' Association, *Proceedings*, Royal Commission on Banking and Currency, 11 September 1933, pp. 3094–95.
48. Testimony of Mr. Milner, *Proceedings*, Royal Commission on Banking and Finance, 11 July 1962, Volume 26, p. 2670.
49. Interviews with N.H. Gunn, 26 May 1982, 1 June 1982.

50. Neufeld, *The Financial System of Canada*, p. 25. After the central bank was set up, it acted as the sole jobber in Canada bonds.
51. Investment Bankers Association, Brief No. 2, *Proceedings*, Royal Commission on Banking and Currency (1933), p. 3113.

3   POLITICAL UNCERTAINTY AND NEW INSTITUTIONAL ARRANGEMENTS, 1930–1939

1. W.A. Mackintosh, *The Economic Background to Dominion-Provincial Relations*, A Study for the Royal Commission on Dominion-Provincial Relations (Ottawa: King's Printer, 1939), Table 15, p. 41.
2. See A.E. Safarian, *The Canadian Economy in the Great Depression* (Toronto: University of Toronto Press, 1957), pp. 21–35.
3. Paul Kennedy, *The Rise and Fall of the Great Powers since 1500* (New York: Random House, 1987), pp. 281–83.
4. As Chart 1.1 illustrates there was virtually no term borrowing by the Dominion in New York until after the Great War and even then in very small amounts.
5. William Adams Brown Jr. analysis is recounted by F.A. Knox in "Review Article: The International Gold Standard Reinterpreted," *Canadian Journal of Economics and Political Science* 10, no. 4 (November 1944): 502–7. See also E.L. Hargreaves who also argued that one of the problems underlying the financial crises of the 1920s and early 1930s was the absence of any legal authority to enforce payment. "Debt" in G.D.H. Cole, ed., *What Everyone Wants to Know about Money* (London: Victor Gollancz, Ltd., 1936), p. 437.
6. The Bank of Nova Scotia, "Ten Percent and Two Percent," *Monthly Review*, Toronto (August 1930).
7. Canadian Bank of Commerce, *Annual Report*, 1928, p. 38. See also comments of Mr. Peleg Howland, general manager, Imperial Bank of Canada, *Annual Report*, 1929, p. 16 and testimony of Mr. Jackson Dodds, general manager, Bank of Montreal to the House of Commons Standing Committee on Banking and Commerce, *Proceedings*, 17th Parliament, 5th Session, Tuesday, 27 March 1934, pp. 216–20.
8. R. Craig McIvor, *Canadian Monetary, Banking and Fiscal Development* (Toronto: Macmillan Company of Canada Limited, 1958), p. 130. Also Irving Brecher, *Monetary and Fiscal Thought in Canada, 1919–1939* (Toronto: University of Toronto Press, 1957), p. 33.
9. Watson Sellar to R.B. Bennett, "Memorandum re. Bond Prices," 1 September 1931, NAC, RG 19, Volume 592, File 155–30, Volume 2.
10. Watson Sellar, "Memorandum for Mr. Bennett," 12 March 1931, NAC, RG 19, Volume 592, File 155–30, Volume 2.
11. D.C. MacGregor, "The Threat of Financial Crisis," *The Canadian Forum* 13, no. 150 (March 1933): 206.
12. See W.C. Clark, "The Flight from the Gold Standard," *Queen's Quarterly* 38, no. 4 (Fall 1931): 751–55.

13. Watson Sellar to R.B. Bennett. "Memorandum re. Interest Rates," 21 October 1931, NAC, RG 19, Volume 592, File 155–30, Volume 2.
14. Interview with N.H. Gunn, 26 May 1982.
15. "Memorandum to Minister," 9 September 1932 and "Memorandum to Minister Re. Financing 1932," 12 September 1932, NAC, RG 19, Volume 592, File 155–30, Volume 2.
16. *Proceedings*, Royal Commission on Banking and Currency, Ottawa, 12 September 1933, p. 3095.
17. Alberta's default record was second best to British Columbia's (0.6 percent of total debt) while Ontario's was the highest (19.1 percent of total outstanding debt). See Thomas Bradshaw, "Maintenance of public credit and its relation to the present financial position of many Ontario municipalities," *Canadian Chartered Accountant* (February 1935): 120–22. Bradshaw headed up an Ontario Government inquiry into municipal defaults and later became an original member of the Executive Committee on the Bank of Canada.
18. P.C. 693, 27 October 1931 that authorized valuation at current market prices on 31 August 1931. In Carr, Jack L., G.F. Mathewson and N.C. Quigley, *Ensuring Failure: Financial System Stability and Deposit Insurance in Canada* (Toronto: C.D. Howe Institute, 1994) at pp. 35–36, Carr *et al.* argue that this Order-in-Council was not favourable to the banks as the banks "chose not to use them" and the Order expired in February 1932. They further adduce from the working papers of the auditor of The Bank of Nova Scotia, "the securities were reported at market value and all losses were written off." In addition the authors point to the share value of the Canadian banks to demonstrate that the market regarded the banks as solvent. While this financial explanation may be satisfactory, it does not take into account the psychology of markets and the potential for rumours about insolvency gaining currency. This order clearly gave the banks flexibility if problems arose.
19. House of Commons, *Debates*, 17th Parliament, 3rd Session, 20 April 1932, p. 2214. Coote eventually served on the Board of Directors and Executive Committee of the Bank of Canada as the Alberta member for many years.
20. House of Commons, *Debates*, 17th Parliament, 3rd Session, 11 April 1932, p. 1916.
21. House of Commons, *Debates*, 17th Parliament, 2nd Session, 17 June 1931, p. 2752.
22. Royal Commission on Dominion-Provincial Relations, *Book III, Documentation*, Table 47, p. 122.
23. House of Commons, *Debates*, 18th Parliament, 1st Session, 8 June 1936, p. 3499.
24. See Neatby's *William Lyon Mackenzie King*, pp. 30–34. Professor Curtis of Queen's University prepared a memorandum for King in 1932 on a central bank. According to Professor Neatby, King was "delighted" with the analysis for "a central bank was an institution, not a policy. Opponents of inflation might be persuaded to support the idea of establishing a central bank because it could provide some control over credit without interfering unduly with private enterprise and would not necessarily inflate the money supply," p. 34. King was

also impressed with Jimmy Gardiner's political maxim that electoral popularity in the west could be gained by hammering the Tories and the banks, p. 30.
25. Senate, *Debates*, 18th Parliament, 1st Session, 29 April 1936, pp. 203, 217.
26. Some analysts, including D.C. MacGregor, calculated that the share of national income going to the payment of debts actually doubled in the early years of the Depression.
27. House of Commons, *Debates*, 17th Parliament, 5th Session, 19 March 1934, p. 1605.
28. House of Commons, *Debates*, 17th Parliament, 6th Session, 21 May 1935, p. 2924.
29. *The Monetary Times*, "No bids received for Ontario," 8 June 1935, p. 20.
30. The Province of Ontario Savings Office was established in 1921 by the United Farmers of Ontario Government as a means of providing low-cost financing to Ontario farmers. The Savings Office is still in existence. See E.J. Doak, *Financial Intermediation by Governments*, unpublished Ph.D. Dissertation, University of Toronto, Department of Economics, 1970, pp. 81–85.
31. *The Monetary Times*, "The Business Outlook," 22 June 1935, p. 1. According to one dealer interviewed, there was a fear on the street that Hepburn might move further to repudiate even the bonded indebtedness of the province. The decision taken by dealers not to bid for the bonds was a means of registering a protest against Hepburn's earlier action. Interview with N.H. Gunn, 26 May 1982.
32. House of Commons, *Debates*, 17th Parliament, 5th Session, 19 March 1934, p. 1627 (emphasis added).
33. "These widely heralded statements" include the utterances of one Ian Mackenzie, a Liberal M.P. from Vancouver who called for a reduction of rates on outstanding debts to 2.5 percent, the increase of currency by some $340 million, and negotiations with foreign creditors to lower rates on foreign-pay debts. House of Commons, *Debates*, 17th Parliament, 6th Session, 22 March 1935, p. 1965 (emphasis added).
34. Senate, *Debates*, 18th Parliament, 2nd Session, 20 January 1937, pp. 20–23, 29.
35. Ibid. McMeans also attributed the debt reduction legislation to the fact that most of the western MLA's were debtors themselves (emphasis added).
36. See Victor Quelch, House of Commons, *Debates*, 18th Parliament, 4th Session, 3 March 1939, p. 1519.
37. House of Commons, *Debates*, 18th Parliament, 1st Session, 26 February 1936, p. 559.
38. Ibid., 12 May 1936, p. 2722 and House of Commons, *Debates*, 18th Parliament, 2nd Session, 12 March 1937, p. 1752.
39. J.H. Gundy to Charles Dunning, 31 March 1930, NAC, RG 19, Volume 592, File 155–30, "Financing 1930 (Canada)," Volume 1 (emphasis added).
40. Letter to Minister of Finance from Fry, Mills, Spence & Co., Bell Gouinlock & Co., Ltd., and McLeod Young Weir & Co., Ltd., 15 October 1930, NAC, RG 19, Volume 592, File 155–30.
41. This of course did not prevent the dealers from separately advertising the loan for potential buyers.

42. Sellar to Acting Finance Minister Ryckman, 29 September 1930, Sellar to Ryckman, 12 December 1930, NAC, RG 19, Volume 592, File 155–30, Volume 1.
43. Watson Sellar to Acting Finance Minister A.B. Ryckman, 29 September 1930, NAC RG 19, Volume 592, File 155–30, Volume 1.
44. "Memorandum to Acting Finance Minister Ryckman from Bank of Montreal, Dominion Securities, Royal Bank of Canada, Wood Gundy, A.E. Ames, and Canadian Bank of Commerce," 11 October 1930, NAC, RG 19, Volume 592, File 155–30.
45. B.J. Roberts to Watson Sellar, "New Issue and Conversion," 12 October 1930, NAC, RG 19, Volume 592, File 155–30.
46. Watson Sellar to Acting Finance Minister Ryckman, 13 October 1930, NAC, RG 19, Volume 592, File 155–30.
47. House of Commons, *Debates*, 17th Parliament, 2nd Session, 8 May 1931, p. 1383.
48. Ibid.
49. George S. Watts to author, 28 July 1982.
50. Watson Sellar, "Memorandum to File: Meeting in Committee Room, Bank of Montreal," 27 September 1932, NAC, RG 19, Volume 592, File 155–30. This operation is known as rediscounting in which the banks pledge a security to the Government in exchange for bank notes thereby increasing their cash reserves and, as a result, their commercial loan portfolios. In this instance the Government issued the securities that were then rediscounted under the Act.
51. Ibid. (emphasis added).
52. Eugene Forsey, "Inflation in Canada," *The Canadian Forum* 13, no. 147 (December 1932): 88.
53. Enclosure to CBA Circular 94-Y, dated 29 September 1932; "Minutes of Conference with Minister of Finance at the Bank of Montreal, Tuesday, 27 September 1932," The Bank of Nova Scotia Archives, RG018/01/0007/0167 (emphasis added).
54. S.R. Noble, "The Monetary Experience of Canada During the Depression," *The Journal of the Canadian Bankers' Association* 45, no. 3 (April 1938): 274.
55. Towers Memoranda, No. 254, 4 May 1939, "Reply to Dr. Donnelly's Questions in the House," p. 4, Bank of Canada Archives.
56. House of Commons, *Debates*, 17th Parliament, 4th Session, 11 May 1933, p. 4854 (emphasis added).
57. Ibid.
58. This does not imply that the Dominion could set interest rates over the "objections" of the market but rather that constitutionally the Parliament of Canada was empowered to legislate in this area.
59. "Agenda for Meeting with Bankers, 26 May 1933," NAC, RG 19, Volume 592, File 155–30 (emphasis added) and CBA Circular 104–F, 27 May 1933, The Bank of Nova Scotia Archives, RG018/01/0007/0000/0167.
60. House of Commons, *Debates*, 17th Parliament, 4th Session, 11 May 1933, p. 4856.

61. CBA Circular 108–Q, 16 September 1933, The Bank of Nova Scotia Archives, RG019/01/0007/0000/0167.
62. CBA Circular 108–X, 2 October 1933, Enclosure entitled: "Minutes of Conference held in Ottawa, Wednesday September 27, 1933 with the Right Honourable R.B. Bennett, Prime Minister Relative to the forthcoming Conversion Loan," The Bank of Nova Scotia Archives, RG018/01/0007/0000/0167 (emphasis added).
63. A.W. Rogers to H.F. Patterson, general manager, 20 July 1934, Enclosure: "Minutes of a Meeting of the Minister of Finance [Hon. E.N. Rhodes] and Deputy Minister [W.C. Clark] with the President and Senior Vice-President of the Association, held in the Office of the Minister at Ottawa, on Thursday July 19th, 1934," The Bank of Nova Scotia Archives, RG018/01/0007/0000/0158–9.
64. Ibid., p. 8.
65. CBA Circular 120–P, "Minutes of a Conference Held at the Request of the Minister of Finance at Ottawa on Monday 24th September, 1934 relative to the forthcoming Conversion loan," The Bank of Nova Scotia Archives, RG018/01/0007/0000/0158–9.
66. Enclosure to confidential letter, A.W. Rogers, Secretary, CBA to H.F. Patterson, general manager, dated 25 July 1934: "Memorandum of telephone conversation between the Prime Minister and Mr. Jackson Dodds, 25 July 1934," The Bank of Nova Scotia Archives, RG018/01/0007/0000/0158–9 (emphasis added).
67. Watson Sellar to R.B. Bennett, "Re. Interest Rates," NAC, RG 19, Volume 592, File 155–30, Volume 2.
68. Watson Sellar, "Memorandum to Minister," 9 September 1932 and "Memorandum for the Minister re. Financing 1932," 12 September 1932, NAC, RG 19, Volume 592, File 155–30, Volume 2.
69. Rowe, Swann & Company to Canadian High Commissioner, Hon. George Ferguson, 31 January 1933, NAC, RG 19, Volume 591, File 155–24A, "Dominion Financing in London-General File."
70. Ibid.
71. Ferguson to Rowe, Swann and Co., 2 February 1933, NAC RG 19, Volume 591, File 155–24A.
72. Nivisons & Company, Enclosure in W.A. Bog, Bank of Montreal to W.C. Clark, 6 February 1935, NAC, RG 19, Volume 3978, File F–1–5–1, "Deputy Minister's Files."
73. For instance the $50,000,000 of one-year promissory notes issued by the Dominion in New York in September 1934 were tax exempt in the hands of foreign holders. NAC, RG 19, Volume 595, File 155–34–60. Provincial governments still provide a covenant. See Province of Alberta, *Offering Circular* dated 29 October 1991 at page 5. "The Province, subject to its redemption rights, will pay additional interest as will result in the holders of bonds or coupons receiving the amounts which they would otherwise have received if no such tax had been imposed."

74. Robert B. Bryce, *Maturing in Hard Times: Canada's Department of Finance through the Great Depresssion* (Kingston and Montreal: McGill-Queen's University Press, 1986), p. 104.
75. House of Commons, *Debates*, 17th Parliament, 4th Session, 21 March 1933, p. 3225. In June 1931, R.B. Bennett attempted to introduce a 2 percent withholding tax on interest and dividends paid to nonresidents. This was withdrawn in July 1931. See Bryce, *Maturing in Hard Times*, p. 104.
76. *The Monetary Times*, "Lack of Clarity in Budget Legislation," 7 April 1933, p. 6.
77. *The Monetary Times*, "This Dominion Must Honour its Contracts," 14 April 1933, p. 6.
78. R. Nivison & Co. to General Manager, Bank of Montreal, 25 April 1933, NAC, RG 19, Volume 591, File 155–24A (emphasis added).
79. *An Act to Amend the Income War Tax Act*, 23–24 George V, Statutes of Canada, 1933, Chapter 41, Section 9(b). Also Bryce, *Maturing in Hard Times*, p. 110
80. *The Monetary Times*, "Bond Trading at Standstill," 4 May 1935, p. 22 that observed "interest high in London" about Ontario-Hydro situation.

4 The Alberta Default and Its Impact on the Dominion's Credit

1. C.H. Douglas, *The Alberta Experiment: An Interim Survey* (London: Eyre and Spottiswoode, 1934), p. 95.
2. D.C. MacGregor, J.B. Rutherford, G.E. Britnell and J.J. Deutsch, *National Income: A Study prepared for the Royal Commission on Dominion Provincial Relations* (Ottawa: King's Printer, 1939), Table IX, p. 55; Table IX-A, p. 89 and Table IX-C, p. 90.
3. Government of the Province of Alberta, Executive Council, *The Case for Alberta*, Part 1 (Edmonton: 1938), Table III, p. 16.
4. Royal Commission on Dominion Provincial Relations, *Report*, Book I (Ottawa: King's Printer, 1940), pp. 144–45.
5. W.J. Loucks, House of Commons, *Debates*, 17th Parliament, 2nd Session, 23 March 1931, pp. 234–35, M.N. Campbell, House of Commons, *Debates*, 17th Parliament, 2nd Session, 25 March 1931, pp. 302–3. Testimony of Canadian Bankers' Association President J.A. McLeod, *Proceedings*, Royal Commission on Banking and Currency, Ottawa, 14 September 1933, pp. 3260–63.
6. Government of the Province of Alberta, *The Case for Alberta*, Part I, pp. 196–97.
7. Royal Commission on Dominion-Provincial Relations, *Report*, 1940, Book I, p. 159.
8. Bank of Canada, *Report on the Financial Position of the Province of Alberta* (Ottawa: Bank of Canada, April 7, 1937), p. 8.
9. Ibid., p. 21. During 1936, numerous rumours abounded to the effect that a New York consortium of investors was interested in purchasing the run-down network. *The Calgary Herald*, "Admit Gov't Negotiating for Telephone Deal," 19 March 1936, p. 1.

10. In *The Case for Alberta*, the Province argued that as these projects contributed significantly to the nation's economic life, the Dominion should be willing to absorb its costs, Part I, pp. 69–85.
11. Bank of Canada, *Report of the Financial Position of Alberta* (April 1937), p. 12; and Jacob Viner, *The Debt Problem of the Government of the Province of Alberta—A Report submitted to the Provincial Treasurer*, August 1939, p. 45.
12. Ibid. According to the Public Accounts Inquiry undertaken by the Royal Commission on Dominion Provincial Relations, the small surpluses were more properly accounted for as deficits. Calculations made by the Government excluded interest paid on guaranteed debentures and debenture discount amortization. *Province of Alberta, Comparative Statistics of Public Finance, 1913, 1921, 1925 to 1937*, Appendix J, "Revised," Schedule 4, p. 9.
13. Alberta Taxation Inquiry Board, *Report of the Alberta Taxation Board on Provincial and Municipal Taxation* (Edmonton: A. Shnitka, King's Printer, 30 November 1935), p. 146.
14. A common complaint of the Alberta Government and other western governments was the lack of low-cost financing when banks were liquidating commercial loans and purchasing securities that were soon trading at a premium. In a presentation before the Macmillan Commission, R.G. Read, provincial treasurer, requested "your Commission to note that during the period the Province was unable to sell debentures at a lower cost than 6.76%, the banks were able to borrow under the Finance Act from the Dominion at 3%." "Submission to Macmillan Commission," 21 August 1933, p. 4.
15. Ibid., pp. 6–7. One of the Rowell-Sirois recommendations never acted upon was a Dominion subsidy to make up for provincial exchange losses. Royal Commission on Dominion-Provincial Relations, *Report*, Book II, pp. 123–24.
16. At this time the Bank of Canada was privately owned.
17. G.F. Towers to Thomas Bradshaw, 15 March 1935, "PF2—Provincial Government Financing—Alberta, 1935, 1936," Bank of Canada Archives (emphasis added).
18. Towers Memoranda, 30 March 1935, "Conversations with Mr. Percival, Deputy Provincial Treasurer of Alberta, March 20–22, 1935," Bank of Canada Archives, "PF2—Provincial Government Financing—Alberta 1935, 1936."
20. J.F. Percival to G.F. Towers, 5 April 1935, Bank of Canada Archives, "PF2—Provincial Financing—Alberta, 1935, 1936."
20. Towers Memoranda, No. 10, 5 June 1935, "Memorandum of Conversation with Honourable George Hoadley, Minister of Trade and Industry, and of Railways and Telephones, Alberta, 4 June 1935," p. 2, Bank of Canada Archives.
21. Ibid. Interestingly, it was not until February 1936 that disclosure of this hypothecation to the Imperial Bank was made public. *The Calgary Herald*, "Government Reveals Loans from Chartered Banks Amount to $5,700,000," 12 February 1936, p. 3.
22. A.J. Hooke, *Looking Backward to Go Forward* (Edmonton: A.J. Hooke, 1980), p. 40.
23. Interview with Senator Ernest C. Manning, 13 July 1983. Magor's appointment had the effect of alienating Major C.H. Douglas who had been appointed the

Government's advisor by the previous government and who resented Magor whom he saw as a nominee of the Montreal banks. Douglas, *The Alberta Experiment*, pp. 151–61. It is quite probable that Douglas used the Magor issue as a way of getting out of a situation in which he risked his reputation in a scheme that would, in all probability, be defeated by the Dominion and the federally regulated banking industry.

24. Interview with A.J. Hooke, 12 July 1983; and interview with Senator Ernest C. Manning, 13 July 1983.
25. Indeed, this move was consistent with one of the Social Credit electoral pledges to make government more efficient and to eliminate the enormous waste of taxpayers' money. See Alf Hooke, *30 + 5: I Know, I Was There* (Edmonton: Co-op Press, 1971), pp. 66–69.
26. *The Calgary Herald*, "Provinces Agree on Approval of Loans in Future," 14 January 1936, p. 1.
27. *The Calgary Herald*, "Dominion to Aid Alberta to Meet Bonds," 15 January 1936, p. 1.
28. *The Calgary Herald*, "Douglas Asserts Finance Threatens Canada's Democracy," 10 February 1936, p. 2.
29. *The Calgary Herald*, "Must Accept Loan Council to Get Help—Dominion Guarantees to be Withheld from Opposing Provinces," 4 March 1936, p. 1.
30. *The Calgary Herald*, "Compulsory Refunding Likely," 13 March 1936, p. 1.
31. CN Telegram, Dunning to Cockcroft, 17 March 1936, Bank of Canada Archives, "PF2—Provincial Financing—Alberta, 1935, 1936" (emphasis added). See also correspondence between the Alberta premier, Cockcroft and Dunning tabled in the House of Commons by Dunning. House of Commons, *Debates*, 18th Parliament, 1st Session, 1 April 1936, pp. 1683–87.
32. *The Monetary Times*, "The Business Outlook," p. 1. "The street apparently took the view that as the Dominion was not going to guarantee the province's bonds, its own credit must be strengthened thereby, while the market for Alberta bonds was weakened."
33. James Mallory, *Social Credit and the Federal Power* (Toronto: University of Toronto Press, 1976), pp. 130–31.
34. CBA Confidential Letter, A.W. Rogers to H.F. Patterson, Enclosure: "Report of 17 June 1936 Bondholders Committee and Government," The Bank of Nova Scotia Archives, RG018/01/0007/0000/0266–282.
35. S.R. Noble to G.F. Towers, 26 March 1936, Bank of Canada Archives, "PF2—Provincial Financing—Alberta, 1935, 1936" (emphasis added). These views seem to parallel those of Senator McMeans who demanded that something be done to control the legislation of the western provinces (Chapter 3).
36. Towers Memoranda, No. 14, 18 April 1936, "Memorandum in regard to Loan Councils and certain alternatives to present proposals," Bank of Canada Archives (emphasis added).
37. Ibid. (emphasis added).

38. W.C. Clark to Charles Dunning, 28 May 1936, NAC, RG 19, Volume 3978, File F-1–11.
39. *The Provincial Securities Interest Act*, 1 Edward VIII (Second Session), Statutes of Alberta, 1936, Chapter 11.
40. *The Municipal Securities Interest Act*, 1 Edward VIII (Second Session), Statutes of Alberta, 1936, Chapter 12.
41. *The Reduction and Settlements of Debts Act*, 1 Edward VIII (Second Session), Statutes of Alberta, 1936, Chapter 2.
42. *The Alberta Credit House Act*, 1 Edward VIII (Second Session), Statutes of Alberta, 1936, Chapter 1.
43. Neatby, *William Lyon Mackenzie King*, p. 197.
44. Figures cited in Budget Speech, 25 April 1939, House of Commons, *Debates*, 18th Parliament, 5th Session, p. 3173.
45. Bryce, *Maturing in Hard Times*, pp. 193–95.
46. Initiatives included *The Social Credit Measures Act* that empowered the provincial cabinet "to put into operation any measures designed to facilitate the exchange of goods and services or any proposal which is calculated to bring about the equation of consumption to production and thus to ensure to the people of the Province of Alberta the full benefit of the increment arising from their association." *The Provincial Loans Refunding Act* authorized the cabinet to negotiate with bondholders a reduction of interest and acceleration of maturities. During the fall sitting of the Legislature, legislation was passed to establish social credit, reduce payments on outstanding debts, and to cut by one-half all interest payments on municipal and provincial and provincial guaranteed debts.
47. CBA Circular 157-A, A.W. Rogers to the General Manager, 30 May 1936, The Bank of Nova Scotia Archives, RG018/01/0007/0000/0266–282.
48. Prosperity certificates were issued under authority of the *Prosperity Certificates Act*. Prosperity certificates were a form of "depreciating script" or currency, which were valued at one dollar and acted as a medium of exchange. The holder was required to buy stamps (one cent per week) that were remitted to the provincial treasury to build up a fund from which to redeem this currency after two years. Certificates were used to pay some government laborers but were refused as legal tender by the banks and by many merchants.
49. CBA Circular 158-H, 19 June 1936, The Bank of Nova Scotia Archives, RG018/01/0007/0000/0266–282.
50. CBA Circular 157-A, A.W. Rogers to the General Manager, dated 30 May 1936, The Bank of Nova Scotia Archives, RG018/01/0007/0000/0266–282.
51. CBA Confidential Letter A.W. Rogers, Secretary to the General Manager, The Bank of Nova Scotia, dated 28 September 1936. "Enclosure: Memorandum dated Sept. 18, 1936, prepared by H.R. Milner, K.C.," p. 3, The Bank of Nova Scotia Archives, RG018/01/0007/0000/0266–282.
52. Ibid., pp. 2–3.

53. A.W. Rogers to H.F. Patterson, General Manager, The Bank of Nova Scotia, dated 6 October 1936. "Enclosure: Draft brief to Governor General in Council re. disallowance," 6 October 1936, p. 16, paragraph 24, The Bank of Nova Scotia Archives, RG018/01/0007/0000/0266–282.
54. CBA Circular 163-T, 21 October 1936, The Bank of Nova Scotia Archives, RG018/01/0007/0000/0266–282.
55. J.G. Rogerson, Secretary, The Bank of Nova Scotia, to F.G. Burr, Manager, The Bank of Nova Scotia, Calgary, dated 22 October 1936, The Bank of Nova Scotia Archives, RG018/01/0007/0000/0266–282.
56. F.G. Burr to Mr. Rogerson, Secretary, The Bank of Nova Scotia, 13 January 1937, The Bank of Nova Scotia Archives, RG018/01/0007/0000/0266–282.
57. This move was greeted with glowing praise from *The Monetary Times*, "The Banks Make a Good Move," 2 January 1937.
58. Placed in *The Monetary Times*, 25 June 1938 and major Alberta dailies.
59. Placed in *The Monetary Times*, 9 April 1938 and various Alberta dailies.
60. The last bank chartered in Canada before 1937 was the Barclays Bank, later merged with the Imperial Bank of Canada. Between 1910 and 1928, four banks were issued charters—one in Quebec, one in the Maritimes, and two in Western Canada. Not one of these charters were ever used. Sarpkaya, "Counting Canada's Banks."
61. Placed in *The Monetary Times*, 14 May 1938, and various Alberta dailies.
62. For instance *The Monetary Times*, "Who Owns the Wealth?" 24 October 1936.
63. Placed in *The Monetary Times*, 24 September 1938 and various Alberta dailies. Earlier broadcasts and publications put out by the banks were praised as valuable by Graham Towers during a meeting with bankers in November 1937. Towers Memoranda, No. 77, 23 November 1937, "Governor's Conversation with the Bankers in Toronto, November 18, 1937," Bank of Canada Archives.
64. A.W. Rogers to General Manager H.F. Patterson, 9 Markch 1937 and 15 March 1937, The Bank of Nova Scotia Archives, RG018/01/0007/0000/0266–282.
65. A.W. Rogers to General Manager, 30 June 1937, The Bank of Nova Scotia Archives, RG018/01/0007/0000/0266–282.
66. Towers Memoranda, No. 56, 12 July 1937, "Visit to Toronto, Meeting with General Managers, 7–9 July 1937," Bank of Canada Archives. This near gaffe may have convinced bankers to hire a public relations specialist.
67. H.F. Patterson to President Dobson, 14 April 1938, The Bank of Nova Scotia Archives, RG018/01/0007/0000/0266–282.
68. Towers Memoranda, No. 151, 22 June 1938, "Telephone Conversation with Dobson, C.B.A.," pp. 1–2, Bank of Canada Archives (emphasis added).
69. *The Monetary Times*, "Ottawa Should Disallow Legislation," 12 September 1936, p. 6. This analysis, by no means unusual for the "eastern" financial press is similar to an earlier declaration by this financial weekly that labeled Ontario Premier Hepburn, Aberhart and Vancouver Liberal M.P. Gerry McGeer as the "three musketeers." "It is customary to look askance at the action of Mr. Hitler

in breaking certain treaties and to offer thanks that we are not as others are or even as this Nazi, but when one looks at our own 'kid forward line' of McGeer, Aberhart and Hepburn, we must realize that we as Canadians have not got much to brag about in comparison with Mr. Hitler after all, and that instead of putting one in the penalty box we ought to put four." *The Monetary Times,* "The Business Outlook," 21 March 1936, p. 1.

70. CBA Circular 162-F, 17 September 1936, Enclosure: "Copy of Opinion dated 16 September 1936 by W. N. Tilley, Esq. K.C. re. The Municipal Securities Interest Act (Alberta)," The Bank of Nova Scotia Archives, RG018/01/0007/0000/0266–282.

71. CBA Circular 161-H, A.W. Rogers to the General Manager, The Bank of Nova Scotia, dated 3 September 1936, Enclosure "Draft Brief, Alberta Legislation Restricting Interest on Municipal Securities to 3%," p. 2, The Bank of Nova Scotia Archives, RG018/01/0007/0000/0266–282.

72. CBA Circular 162-A, 16 September 1936, Enclosure: "Opinion of W.N. Tilley, K.C. re. Debt Adjustment Act," The Bank of Nova Scotia Archives, RG018/01/0007/0000/0266–282.

73. CBA Circular No. 162-J, A.W. Rogers, Secretary to the General Manager, The Bank of Nova Scotia, dated 17 September 1936. "Enclosure: Opinion of Mr. W.N. Tilley K.C., dated 17 September 1936, Alberta Legislation, The Reduction and Settlement of Debts Act, Memorandum as to Disallowance, etc.," The Bank of Nova Scotia Archives, RG018/01/0007/0000/0262–282.

74. CBA Confidential Letter, A.W. Rogers, Secretary to the General Manager, The Bank of Nova Scotia, dated 28 September 1936, Enclosure: "Memorandum dated Sept. 18, 1936, prepared by H.R. Milner, K.C.," p. 1, The Bank of Nova Scotia Archives, RG018/01/0007/0000/0266–282 (emphasis added).

75. W.N. Tilley, K.C. to Hon. Ernest Lapointe, Minister of Justice, 9 December 1936, "Re. The Reduction and Settlement of Debts Act, The Debt Adjustment Act, 1936, The Provincial Securities Interest Act, The Municipal Securities Interest Act, The Alberta Credit House Act," p. 9, The Bank Nova Scotia Archives, RG018/01/0007/0000/0266–282.

76. Notably *The Provincial Securities Interest Act, The Municipal Securities Interest Act,* and *The Reduction and Settlement of Debts Act.*

77. F.G Burr to H.F. Patterson, General Manager, The Bank of Nova Scotia, 23 February 1937, The Bank of Nova Scotia Archives, RG018/01/0007/0000/0266–282. See also E.S. Thompson for the Secretary, CBA to the General Manager, The Bank of Nova Scotia, 25 February 1937, who cautioned that in the wake of Mr. Justice Ewing's decision "care must be taken to avoid any appearance of a threat that the banks proposed to withdraw or restrict credit because of the moratorium." The Bank of Nova Scotia Archives, RG018/01/0007/0000/0266–282.

78. O.C. 188/37, 23 February 1937. The move was apparently prompted by fears of a creditor backlash enforcing overdue claims. See CBA Confidential Letter,

A.W. Rogers, Secretary to H.F. Patterson, dated 1 March 1937. Enclosure: "Report of Messrs. J. Walker and Frank Pike, Meeting with Aberhart, 25 February 1937," The Bank of Nova Scotia Archives, RG018/01/0007/0000/0266–282.
79. 1 George VI, Statutes of Alberta, 1937, Chapter 30, section 2.
80. 1 George VI, Statutes of Alberta, 1937, Chapter 9, Section 27.
81. P.C. 1367, 15 June 1938.
82. 1 George VI (Second Session), Statutes of Alberta, 1937, Chapter 5, Section 27(c).
83. 1 George VI, Statutes of Alberta, 1938, Chapter 29, Sections 3–4.
84. A.W. Rogers to General Manager H.F. Patterson, 26 April 1938, The Bank of Nova Scotia Archives, RG018/01/0007/0000/0282–266.
85. *The Limitation of Actions Act, 1935, Amendment Act, 1938*, 2 George VI, Statutes of Alberta, 1938, Chapter 28.
86. A.W. Roger to General Manager H.F. Patterson, 26 April 1938, Enclosure: "Memorandum by W.N. Tilley, K.C. re. Effects of 1938 Alberta Legislation and Recommendations," pp. 8–9, The Bank of Nova Scotia Archives, RG018/01/0007/0000/0266–282.
87. Ibid.
88. CBA Confidential Letter A.W. Rogers, Secretary to H.F. Patterson, General Manager dated 26 May 1938, Enclosure: "Dobson to Dunning, 14 May 1938," The Bank of Nova Scotia Archives, RG018/01/0007/0000/0266–282.
89. G.F. Towers to Governor Norman, 22 March 1935, Bank of Canada Archives, "PF2—Provincial Government Financing—Alberta, 1935, 1936."
90. L.B. Pearson to O.D. Skelton, "Recent British Press Opinion on Canadian Credit and Finance," 17 June 1936, NAC, RG 19, Volume 591, File 155–24A. Another complicating factor in the Dominion's credit standing in London several years later were the activities of Sir Edward Beatty and Sir Edward Peacock of the CPR to thwart C.D. Howe's plan to reorganize Canadian National Railway's capital structure. According to J.W. Dafoe, Beatty launched "an organized campaign to damage the credit of Canada on the ground of the railway situation, in the hope that the government can be intimidated to yielding to Sir Edward Beatty's demand. I was told that no Canadian can stir about in London without encountering this propaganda." Recounted in Robert Bothwell and William Kilbourn, *C.D. Howe: A Biography* (Toronto: University of Toronto Press, 1979), p. 99.
91. Towers Memoranda, No. 43, "Conversation with Governor Norman, London, November 1936," Bank of Canada Archives.
92. June 1937, "PF2—Provincial Financing—Alberta 1937–1944," Bank of Canada Archives (emphasis added).
93. Towers Memoranda, No. 14, 18 April 1936, pp. 3–4, "Memorandum in regard to Loan Councils and Certain Alternatives to Present Proposals," Bank of Canada Archives (emphasis added).
94. Ibid., p. 5.
95. Under section 92(3) of the *Constitution Act*, provinces have the exclusive power to borrow money on the sole credit of the province.

96. The Loan Council concept sought to institutionalize the ad hoc arrangements that had grown up during the Depression whereby the Dominion periodically advanced sums to the provinces for relief to meet payments on principal and interest. Modelled loosely after the Australian Loan Council, the "council," in effect nine separate bodies, one for each province, was to be composed of the Governor of the Bank of Canada, the Dominion's Finance Minister and the Provincial Treasurer of the province concerned. To give effect to the proposal a joint resolution of the Commons and the Senate was needed to amend section 92 of the BNA Act. The proposed amendment would have authorized the "Parliament of Canada to guarantee the payment of principal, interest and sinking fund of any securities which any province of Canada" issued. Should default occur, the Government of Canada could meet payments to creditors out of subsidies normally granted to the province in default. Senate, *Debates*, 18th Parliament, 1st Session, 14 May 1936, pp. 2795–96.
97. In order to work this domestic problem out amicably between the provinces and the financial interests, Towers also proposed a refunding corporation whose stock would be owned by the Dominion, the central bank, and private finance capital. This new corporation would enable provinces to introduce legislation to call in bonds with the highest coupon rates for redemption. However, this proposal never received the support of the financial community nor apparently the Department of Finance. Towers Memoranda, No. 31, "Notes on a Refunding Corporation," 20 October 1936, Bank of Canada Archives.
98. W.C. Clark to Charles Dunning, 31 December 1936, "Discussion with Harry Morgan," NAC, RG 19, Volume 3978, File F-1-7, "Deputy Minister's Files."
99. Towers Memoranda, No. 251, 18 April 1939, "Visit to Washington and New York, April 15–17, 1939," Bank of Canada Archives.
100 Towers Memoranda, No. 377, 2 March 1941, "Advisability of Some Declaration of Policy Respecting Dominion and Provincial Fields of Taxation," Bank of Canada Archives.
101. For instance, J.A.C. Osborne, Deputy Governor, Bank of Canada to Charles Cockcroft, Alberta Provincial Treasurer, 28, 30 October 1936, Bank of Canada Archives, "PF2—Provincial Government Financing—1935, 1936."

5 Broadening the Ownership of the Debt and Bank Resistance, 1935–1939

1. Towers Memoranda, No. 50, December 1936, "Statement Re. Mechanics of Central Banking: for Dominion-Provincial Conference, December 1936," Bank of Canada Archives. Also quoted in Chapter 2 in regard to relations with commercial banks and investment dealers.
2. W.C. Clark to Charles Dunning, 4 February 1936, NAC, RG 19, Volume 3978, Deputy Minister's Files, File F-1-6 (emphasis added).
3. Towers Memoranda, No. 19, 26 May 1936, "Considerations in regard to possible conversion loan, June 1936," Bank of Canada Archives.

4. W.C. Clark to Charles Dunning, "Re. Proposed Dominion Financing for $100,000,000," n.d., NAC, RG 19, Volume 3978, Deputy Minister's Files, File F-1-11.
5. Towers Memoranda, No. 72, 26 October 1937, "Memorandum of Conversations with Mr. Dunning and Dr. Clark in regard to proposed loan," Bank of Canada Archives.
6. Towers Memoranda, No. 74, 28 October 1937, "Re. discussions on 1937 autumn loan," Bank of Canada Archives.
7. Towers Memorandum, No. 75, 29 October 1937, "Conversation with the Hon. C.A. Dunning," Bank of Canada Archives.
8. Towers Memoranda, No. 19, 26 May 1936, "Considerations in regard to possible conversion loan, June 1936," Bank of Canada Archives.
9. Memorandum to the Governor and Deputy Governor from Assistant Deputy Governor, 21 January 1937, Bank of Canada Archives, DG 400, "Dominion Government Financing, 1935–1937."
10. Bank of Canada, *Annual Report*, 1937 (Ottawa: Bank of Canada, 22 February 1938), p. 11.
11. W.H. Budden to Governor Towers, "Re: Desirability of Issuing Smaller Denominations, Particularly in Registered Form," 7 February 1938, Bank of Canada Archives, DG 400, "Dominion Government Financing, 1938."
12. Ibid.
13. Ibid., and Ralph B. McKibbin to author, 27 April 1982.
14. J.E. Savard, President, Investment Dealers' Association to K.A. Henderson, 21 May 1936, Bank of Canada Archives, DG 400, "Dominion Government Financing 1935–38," and "Meeting with Representatives of the Investment Dealers Association at Bank of Canada," 29 November 1938, DG 400, "Dominion Government Financing 1935–37," Bank of Canada Archives.
15. Towers Memoranda, No. 75, 29 October 1937, "Conversation with the Hon. C.A. Dunning," Bank of Canada Archives. It is informative to note that criticisms about the level of remuneration were directed at the oligopolistic banks and not towards the rabidly competitive dealers. After the Bank's creation, commissions were set by the Bank on behalf of the Government. The commission was based on whether new cash was received (higher rate) and the term (longer term, higher rate).
16. See "Memorandum on Dominion Government Loans," 25 May 1938 and "Memorandum of Discussions," 13 June 1938, Bank of Canada Archives, DG 400, "Dominion Government Financing—1938." (Presumably authored by the Securities Advisor, K.A. Henderson.)
17. Towers to Dunning, 20 December 1938, NAC, RG 19, Volume 589, File 155-0-97.
18. See "Memorandum of Discussions," 13 June 1938, Bank of Canada Archives, DG 400, "Dominion Government Financing—1938."
19. Jackson Dodds Memoranda, "Dominion Government Loan," 26 May 1938, Bank of Canada Archives, DG 400, "Dominion Government Financing—1938."

20. K.A. Henderson to Dr. Clark, "Memo re. suggestions received regarding Offering of Dominion issues by Bank of Canada," 22 December 1938, NAC, RG 19, Volume 589, File 155-0-97.
21. Letter to Minister of Finance from Fry, Mills, Spence & Co., Bell Gouinlock & Co., Ltd., and McLeod Young Weir & Co., Ltd., 15 October 1930, NAC, RG 19, Volume 592, File 155-30.
22. J.E. Savard to K.A. Henderson, 21 May 1936, Bank of Canada Archives, DG 400, "Dominion Government Financing, 1935-37," Bank of Canada Archives.
23. "Memorandum of Discussions," 13 June 1938, DG 400, "Dominion Government Financing—1938."
24. Towers Memoranda, No. 136, 13 May 1938, "Conversation with Dunning, Clark and Henderson re. Pringle's letter...," Bank of Canada Archives and K.A. Henderson to Dr. Clark, "Memorandum re. suggestions received regarding offering of Dominion issues by Bank of Canada," 22 December 1938, NAC, RG 19, Volume 589, File 155-0-97. Dunning may have been reacting to reports of some firms having minimal or nil capital.
25. Bank of Canada, *Submission by the Bank of Canada to the Royal Commission on Banking and Finance* (Ottawa: Bank of Canada, May 31, 1962), pp. 50-51.
26. Clark to Weldon, 15 February 1936, NAC, RG 19, Volume 592, File 155-30, Volume 3.
27. R.W. Gouinlock to W.C. Clark, 28 October 1938, W.C. Pitfield to W.C. Clark, 2 November 1938, NAC, RG 19, Volume 604, File 155-71-2.
28. W.C. Clark to R.W. Gouinlock, 3 November 1938, NAC, RG 19, Volume 604, File 155-71-2.
29. R.W. Gouinlock to W.C. Clark, 8 November 1938, NAC, RG 19, Volume 604, File 155-71-2 (emphasis added).
30. After the war, the large Canadian dealer, Wood Gundy sought a position in lead underwriting alongside Morgan Stanley for a U.S. dollar issue. Morgan Stanley's Perry Hall believed that Wood Gundy should not have any priority position or special claim for a joint account by virtue of the fact that it had a firm order for $50 million in bonds. Towers, present at this exchange, declined to express any opinion for this was a governmental (*viz.* a political) decision.
31. 15 December 1938, DG 400, "Dominion Government Financing 1938," Bank of Canada Archives.
32. Royal Commission on Banking and Currency, *Proceedings* (Ottawa: King's Printer, 1933), p. 3114.
33. Testimony of W.C. Pitfield, IBAC President, Royal Commission on Banking and Currency, *Proceedings* (Ottawa: King's Printer, September 1933), p. 3106.
34. Chartered banks' holdings of Dominion and provincial stock grew rapidly between 1935 and 1939 nearly doubling to $1,234 million. *Canada Year Book*, 1946, pp. 963-64. (Figures average of banks' monthly reports.)
35. "Dominion Government Financing Fiscal Year 1936-37," NAC, RG 19, Volume 3978, File F-1-6 (emphasis added).

36. Towers Memoranda, No. 19, 26 May 1936, "Considerations in regard to possible conversion loan, June 1936," Bank of Canada Archives (emphasis added).
37. Dodds to Dunning, 20 October 1936, NAC, RG 19, Volume 589, File 155-0-97 (emphasis added). Dunning later became a director of "Canada's First Bank."
38. Dunning to Dodds, 26 October 1936, NAC, RG 19, Volume 589, File 155-0-97.
39. Dodds to Dunning, 28 October 1936, NAC, RG 19, Volume 589, File 155-0-97.
40. Dunning to Dodds, 31 October 1936, NAC, RG 19, Volume 589.
41. Towers Memoranda, No. 54, 30 April 1937, "Memorandum regarding conversations on Dominion refunding, April 1937," Bank of Canada Archives (emphasis added).
42. K.A. Henderson to W.C. Clark, 10 May 1938, NAC, RG 19, Volume 3978, File F-1-6.
43. "Comments on report of meeting with CBA Investment Committee," 21 December 1938, Bank of Canada Archives, DG 400, "Dominion Government Financing, 1938."
44. *Submissions by the Bank of Canada to the Royal Commission on Banking and Finance*, 1962, p. 48.
45. G.F. Towers to W.C. Clark, 4 September 1935, NAC, RG 19, Volume 234.
46. W.C. Clark to G.F. Towers, 24 December 1937, NAC, RG 19, Volume 234.
47. Towers Memoranda, No. 236, 13 March 1939, "Submission to Rowell Sirois Commission," Bank of Canada Archives.
48. Nevil Ford to W.C. Clark, 20 December 1935, NAC, RG 19, Volume 3978, File 1-1-6, "Dominion Financing, 1935–36" (emphasis added).
49. Towers Memoranda, No. 162, 26 August 1938, "Preliminary Memorandum in regard to financing of loans maturing Jan. 1-July 1, 1939," Bank of Canada Archives.
50. Towers Memoranda, No. 171, 15 September 1938, Bank of Canada Archives.
51. Towers Memoranda, No. 187, 21 October 1938, "Discussions re. Canadian Financing New York, Oct. 18th and 19th, 1938," Bank of Canada Archives.
52. Towers Memoranda, No. 196, 15 November 1938, Bank of Canada Archives.

6   Wartime: Conscription of Capital If Necessary, But Not Necessarily Conscription, 1940–1945

1. Benjamin Higgins, *Canada's Financial System in War* (New York: National Bureau of Economic Research, April 1944), p. 1.
2. If munitions exports during the First World War are excluded, government spending was only 10 percent of national income.
3. W.C. Clark to J.L. Ilsley, 5 September 1939, NAC, RG 19, Volume 3427 and W.C. Clark to J.L. Ilsley, 12 October 1939, NAC, RG 19, Volume 3978, File F-1-11.
4. Donald Gordon, "Some Current Problems," *The Journal of the Canadian Bankers' Association* 47, no. 4 (July 1940): 427; and J.L. Ilsley, House of Commons, *Debates*, 18th Parliament, 6th (War) Session, 12 September 1939, pp. 137–38 in which the "pay-as-you-go as far as practicable" policy was outlined.

5. W.C. Clark to J.L. Ilsley, 16 November 1940, NAC, RG 19, Volume 3978, File F-1-11 (Deputy Minister's Files).
6. Towers Memoranda, No. 371, 24 December 1940, "General Considerations Relating to War Savings Publicity—Methods and Objectives," Bank of Canada Archives.
7. W.C. Clark to J.L. Ilsley, 5 September 1939, p. 5, NAC, RG 19, Volume 3477.
8. *The Canadian Forum*, "Who Pays?" Volume 19, No. 225 (October 1939), pp. 204–5.
9. "Memorandum re. Refund Conditions on 20% Fraction of Excess Profits Tax," p. 2, NAC, RG 19, Volume 3551, File B-01-C. Ironically, about 30 years later, Bryce was appointed to chair a royal commission on "corporate concentration."
10. J.F. Parkinson, "Some Problems of War Finance in Canada," *Canadian Journal of Economics and Political Science* 6, no. 3 (August 1940): 407–8.
11. Higgins, *Canada's Financial System*, pp. 14–18.
12. K.W. Taylor, "Canadian War-Time Price Controls, 1941–6," *Canadian Journal of Economic and Political Science* 13, no. 1 (February 1947): 87. Certain products including fresh fruit and vegetables were exempted from the ceiling due to seasonal variations.
13. House of Commons, *Debates*, 19th Parliament, 2nd Session, 13 November 1940, p. 70.
14. House of Commons, *Debates*, 19th Parliament, 1st Session, 17 June 1940, p. 821.
15. Ibid., 3 July, 1940, p. 1305.
16. House of Commons, *Debates*, 19th Parliament, 3rd Session, 30 June 1942, p. 3803.
17. NAC, RG 19, Volume 3978, File F-1-6.
18. House of Commons, *Debates*, 19th Parliament, 1st Session, 29 May 1940, p. 355.
19. Jack Pickersgill, *The Mackenzie King Record*, Volume I, *1939–1944* (Toronto: University of Toronto Press, 1960), p. 155.
20. House of Commons, *Debates*, 19th Parliament, 1st Session, 29 May 1940, p. 355.
21. House of Commons, *Debates*, 19th Parliament, 2nd Session, 19 February 1941, pp. 841–43 and House of Commons, *Debates*, 19th Parliament, 3rd Session, 26 January 1942, p. 57.
22. Pickersgill, *The Mackenzie King Record*, Volume I, p. 351.
23. House of Commons, *Debates*, 19th Parliament, 4th Session, 12 March 1943, p. 1223; and House of Commons, *Debates*, 19th Parliament, 3rd Session, 3 February 1942, p. 268.
24. Ibid., 16 July 1942, p. 4310.
25. Ibid., 17 July 1942, pp. 4375–76.
26. House of Commons, *Debates*, 19th Parliament, 4th Session, 9 March 1943, p. 1090.
27. Ibid., 1 March 1943, p. 805.
28. House of Commons, *Debates*, 19th Parliament, 2nd Session, 12 November 1940, p. 27.
29. House of Commons, *Debates*, 19th Parliament, 4th Session, 11 March 1943, p. 1183.
30. NAC, RG 19, Volume 4366.
31. House of Commons, *Debates*, 19th Parliament, 5th Session, 12 July 1944, pp. 4759–60.

32. P.C. 2716, 15 September 1939 that promulgated a system of exchange controls that required chartered banks to act as agents of the government.
33. Interview, 1 June 1982.
34. W.A. Mackintosh, "Budget Considerations," 9 May 1940, NAC, RG 19, Volume 3551, p. 4.
35. W.C. Clark to J.L. Ilsley, 5 September 1939, "Re. War Budget and Financial Policy," NAC, RG 19, Volume 3427, pp. 3–4 (emphasis added).
36. Interview, 11 June 1982.
37. W.C. Clark to J.L. Ralston, 18 September 1939, NAC, RG 19, Volume 3978, File F-1-11 (Deputy Minister's Files).
38. S.E. Nixon, Memorandum, "Tap Bonds," 2 January 1942, Bank of Canada Archives, DG 400, "Dominion Government Financing, 1942–1944."
39. 9 May 1940, pp. 6–7, NAC, RG 19, Volume 3551.
40. Towers Memoranda, No. 368, 20 November 1940, "Re. War Loans," Bank of Canada Archives.
41. 24 November 1939, NAC, RG 19, Volume 604, File 155–75, pp. 9, 14.
42. Ibid., p. 14.
43. 2 October 1939, Bank of Canada Archives, DG8–2 "The Deputy Minister of Finance, 1935–1944."
44. Reported in *The Globe and Mail*, "Editorial: A Profitable Conference," 4 August 1942.
45. National War Finance Committee, "The Budget and You—How Your Taxes and Savings Help to Win the War" (Ottawa: August 1942), NAC, RG 19, Volume 3978, File 155–30–2.
46. National War Finance Committee, "Dollars and Sense—How Our Taxes and Savings Help to Win the War" (Ottawa: 1943), NAC, RG 19, Volume 3978, File 155–30–2.
47. CBA President Jaffray to General Manager H.D. Burns, The Bank of Nova Scotia, 12 April 1941, The Bank of Nova Scotia Archives, RG018/01/0007/0000/0176–7, "Victory Loan 1941."
48. National War Finance Committee, "The Role of the Chartered Banks in War Finance," NAC, RG 19, Volume 593, File 155–30–2.
49. A.W. Rogers to General Manager, The Bank of Nova Scotia, 12 December 1941, confidential enclosure, entitled "The National War Finance Committee and the Chartered Banks" dated 9 December 1941, to "Memorandum of a Meeting in Ottawa on Thursday, December 11, 1941 at 1 a.m. in the Office of G.W. Spinney," The Bank of Nova Scotia Archives, RG018/01/0007/0000/0178 (emphasis added).
50. NAC, RG 19, Volume 4366. Hence the claims made by the Social Credit Members of Parliament to the effect that one-third of one percent owned 60 percent of the debt were not as far fetched as they seemed at first blush.
51. Clarence Barber, "Review of Post-War Monetary Policy," in James P. Cairns and H.H. Binhammer, eds., *Canadian Banking and Monetary Policy* (Toronto: McGraw-Hill, 1965), p. 213.

52. "220–25—PostWar Reconstruction and Relief 1944," Bank of Canada Archives (emphasis added).
53. G.F. Towers to J.L. Ilsley, 27 June 1944, Bank of Canada Archives, DG 400, "Dominion Government Financing, 1942–1944."
54. W.C. Clark to Chester Walters, 30 October 1944, NAC, RG 19, Volume 3978, File F-1–11, "Deputy Minister's Files."
55. Interview, 1 June 1982.
56. Towers Memoranda, No. 370, 6 December 1940, "Conversation with Clark, Macfarlane, Johnson, Gordon," Bank of Canada Archives.
57. Towers Memoranda, No. 379, 19 March 1941, "Notes for Speech by Ralston," Bank of Canada Archives.
58. CBA Confidential letter, A.W. Rogers to H.D. Burns, General Manager, The Bank of Nova Scotia, dated 21 July 1942, Enclosure: "Memorandum of Meeting with the Governor of the Bank of Canada on July 20, 1942 prepared by the Public Relations Adviser, Board Room, Bank of Canada, Ottawa, 10:30 a.m.," p. 2, The Bank of Nova Scotia Archives, RG018/01/0007/0000/0160–161.
59. "Summary of Discussions with Governor Towers, 21 July 1942," Enclosure to CBA Confidential Letter, A.W. Rogers to H.D. Burns, General Manager, p. 2, The Bank of Nova Scotia Archives, RG018/01/0007/0000/0160–161.
60. Ibid. (emphasis added).
61. CBA Confidential Letter, A.W. Rogers to H.D. Burns, General Manager, The Bank of Nova Scotia, dated 28 July 1942. Enclosure: "Memorandum of a Meeting of the Members of the Canadian Bankers' Association with the Minister of Finance at his Office, in the House of Commons, Ottawa, at 12 Noon, Monday July 27, 1942," The Bank of Nova Scotia Archives, RG018/01/0007/0000/0160–161.
62. House of Commons, *Debates*, 19th Parliament, 3rd Session, 26 January 1942, pp. 55–56. A similar idea broached a year or so earlier by Keynes was known as a "compulsory savings plan." "Mr. Keynes 'Compulsory Savings Plan'," *The Journal of the Canadian Bankers' Association* 47, no. 3 (April 1940): 256–59.
63. R.B. Bryce, "Notes on 1942–43 Financing and the Conscription of Capital," 1 April 1942, pp. 2–3 (emphasis added).
64. Towers believed that the existing institutional arrangements did not require the creation of separate controllers. Towers Memoranda, No. 430, 1 May 1942, "Remarks on Mr. Bryce's Memorandum of April 1, 1942 entitled 'Notes on 1942–43 Financing and Conscription of Capital'," Bank of Canada Archives.
65. Towers Memoranda, No. 459, 20 December 1943, "Conversation with S.M. Wedd, President of the Canadian Bankers' Association," Bank of Canada Archives.
66. "Summary of Discussions with Governor Towers, 21 July 1942," Enclosure to A.W. Rogers to H.D. Burns, General Manager, p. 8, The Bank of Nova Scotia Archives, RG018/01/0007/0000/0160–161 (emphasis added). On this subject see also Towers Memoranda, No. 574, 1 September 1948, "Memorandum of conversation with Mr. Gillett, Bank of Toronto (acting for CBA)," Bank of

Canada Archives. Loan loss reserves taken by banks for expected loan losses is a method to disguise income if the reserves overstate the anticipated losses.
67. Towers Memorandum, No. 459, 20 December 1943, "Conversation with S.M. Wedd, President of the Canadian Bankers' Association," Bank of Canada Archives.
68. CBA Confidential letter, A.W. Rogers, Secretary to H.D. Burns, General Manager, The Bank of Nova Scotia, dated 17 February 1944. Enclosure: "Memorandum respecting a Meeting of Representatives of Chartered Banks with Governor of the Bank of Canada, Board Room, Canadian Bank of Commerce at 11 a.m., 14 February 1944," The Bank of Nova Scotia Archives, RG018/01/0007/0000/0162–3.
69. Quoted in letter, A.W. Rogers, Secretary, CBA to H.D. Burns, General Manager, The Bank of Nova Scotia, 10 September 1942, The Bank of Nova Scotia Archives, RG018/01/0007/0000/0160–161.
70. Edwin Crockett, Assistant General Manager, The Bank of Nova Scotia, to CBA Secretary [A.W. Rogers], 1 February 1943, The Bank of Nova Scotia Archives, RG018/–1/0007/0000/0158–159.
71. CBA Confidential Letter, A.W. Rogers, Secretary, to H.D. Burns, General Manager, The Bank of Nova Scotia, dated 11 February 1943. Enclosure: "C.B.A. President to G.F. Towers, 9 February 1943," The Bank of Nova Scotia Archives, RG018/01/0007/0000/0160–161.
72. CBA Confidential Letter, A.W. Rogers, Secretary, to H.D. Burns, General Manager, The Bank of Nova Scotia, dated 19 June 1943. Enclosure: "Memorandum of a meeting between the Governor of the Bank of Canada and the General Managers of the Banks at the Mount Royal Club, Montreal on the afternoon of Thursday, June 17, 1943," The Bank of Nova Scotia Archives, RG018/01/0007/0000/0160–161. At a 2 February 1943 meeting, bankers were led to believe that their request for a longer-term, 1.5 percent issue would be forthcoming in July to redeem part of the maturing deposit certificates.
73. G.F. Towers to W.C. Clark, June 1943, NAC, RG 19, Volume 606, File 155–80, Volume 2.
74. Towers Memoranda, No. 574, 1 September 1948, "Memorandum of conversation with Mr. Gillett, Bank of Toronto (acting for CBA)," Bank of Canada Archives.
75. Ibid. This last minute request took place in Abbott's absence.
76. *Minutes of the Proceedings and Evidence of the House of Commons Standing Committee on Banking and Commerce*, 19th Parliament, 5th Session, No. 7, 23 May 1944, p. 203.
77. House of Commons, *Debates*, 19th Parliament, 2nd Session, 29 April 1941, p. 2352. As the minister pointed out this new tax of 15 percent was still lower than the 16.5 percent tax imposed by the United States government.
78. Towers Memoranda, No. 389, 6 May 1941, "Discussions re. application of 15% withholding tax to interest payments in foreign currency," Bank of Canada Archives.
79. Ibid.

80. Towers Memoranda, No. 390, 7 May 1941, "Further Comments on the subject of application of a 15% withholding tax to bonds payable in U.S. dollars," Bank of Canada Archives.
81. Towers memorandum, No. 389, 6 May 1941, "Discussions re. application of 15% withholding tax to interest payments in foreign currency," Bank of Canada Archives.
82. *An Act to amend the Income War Tax Act*, 4–5 George VI, Statutes of Canada, 1941, Chapter 18, Section 22.
83. Towers Memoranda, No. 390, 7 May 1941.

7 ATTEMPTS TO KEEP FAITH WITH BONDHOLDERS, 1946–1952

1. Cited by Victor Quelch, Social Credit M.P. in House of Commons, *Debates*, 20th Parliament, 3rd Session, 10 March 1947, p. 1220 (emphasis added).
2. In January 1945, a Bank of Canada memorandum "For internal guidance" promulgated "a policy which will ensure marketability and stability." Towers Memoranda, No. 480, 8 January 1945, Bank of Canada Archives. This policy was consistent with similar statements issued by U.S. and U.K. authorities.
3. See Robert Bothwell, Ian Drummond, and John English, *Canada Since 1945: Power, Politics, and Provincialism* (Toronto: The University of Toronto Press, 1981), p. 132.
4. See Budget Speech of Finance Minister D.C. Abbott, House of Commons, *Debates*, 20th Parliament, 4th Session, 18 May 1948, p. 4058. Almost one-half of this decline was effected by the Ninth Victory Loan, which raised over $2 billion. Most of these funds were not required and sat as cash in the Consolidated Revenue Fund.
5. D.C. MacGregor, "The Problem of the Price Level in Canada," *Canadian Journal of Economics and Political Science* 13, no. 2 (May 1947): 171–73, and R.C. McIvor, "Canadian Wartime Fiscal Policy, 1939–45," *Canadian Journal of Economics and Political Science* 14, no. 1 (February 1948): 92–93.
6. Irene M. Spry, "The Royal Commission on Prices," *Canadian Journal of Economics and Political Science* 17, no. 1 (February 1951): 79–83; and R. Craig McIvor and John H. Panabaker, "Canadian Post-War Monetary Policy, 1946–1952," *Canadian Journal of Economics and Political Science* 20, no. 2 (May 1954): 212–15.
7. W.A. Mackintosh to W.C. Clark, 21 March 1940, NAC, RG 19, Volume 3581, File N-01.
8. E. Fricker to David Marble, Secretary of the Bank of Canada, 9 January 1942, Bank of Canada Archives, DG 400, "Dominion Government Financing 1942–1944."
9. W.E. Scott for G.F. Towers to S.M. Wedd, President, Canadian Bankers' Association, 17 July 1945, The Bank of Nova Scotia Archives, RG018/01/0007/0000/0185, "Ninth Victory Loan."
10. K.A. Henderson to W.C. Clark, 4 January 1946, NAC, RG 19, Volume 593, File 155-30-4.

11. Towers Memoranda, No. 503, 27 March 1946, "Memorandum of discussion with Clark and Bryce by Henderson and Towers," Bank of Canada Archives.
12. Towers Memoranda, No. 521, 26 June 1946, "Notes re. meeting with General Managers of banks (not including Banque Provinciale), Montreal, June 26th, 1946," Bank of Canada Archives.
13. G.F. Towers to A.W. Rogers, CBA Circular 329-X,19 September 1946, The Bank of Nova Scotia Archives, RG018/01/0007/0000/0168, "Dominion of Canada Savings Bonds."
14. Interview, 1 June 1982.
15. Royal Commission on Banking and Finance, *Report*, p. 459 and Robert V. Roosa, "Integrating Debt Management and Open Market Operations," *American Economic Review* 42, no. 2 (May 1952): 214–35.
16. House of Commons, *Debates*, 20th Parliament, 3rd Session, 24 April 1947, pp. 2357–58.
17. House of Commons, *Debates*, 20th Parliament, 3rd Session, 6 May 1947, pp. 2802–3. Obviously, Macdonnell's vision of what the middle class was is considerably different from the usual conception of the social scientist. Macdonnell's quest for higher rates would have meant that the middle class would have more difficulty financing the purchase of a home.
18. Ibid., 6 June 1947, pp. 3903–4.
20. Hon. D.C. Abbott in House of Commons, *Debates*, 20th Parliament, 4th Session, 25 June 1948, p. 5838.
19. *Annual Report of the Governor of the Bank of Canada and Statement of Accounts, 1948* (Ottawa: Bank of Canada, 11 February 1949), p. 11.
21. Cited in J.W. Pickersgill and D.F. Forster, *The Mackenzie King Record*, Volume 3, *1945–1946* (Toronto: University of Toronto Press, 1970), p. 84. This was at a time when the Dominion was enjoying one of its largest budget surpluses.
22. Towers Memoranda, No. 560, 4 December 1947, "Notes on discussions with banks and others in New York in regard to Canadian financing," Bank of Canada Archives.
23. Ibid.
24. Ibid.
25. House of Commons, *Debates*, 5 December 1947, p. 16.
26. Ibid., 16 December 1947, pp. 331–36.
27. Ibid., p. 337.
28. Ibid., pp. 336–37. These type of bureaucratic controls bothered King considerably. "I asked Council how we would act if we were in Opposition and the Government of the day was given arbitrary powers to decide on anything. I am afraid we may have to back away from a good many of the clauses that have been inserted." Cited in J.W. Pickersgill and D.F. Forster, *The Mackenzie King Record*, Volume 4, *1947–1948* (Toronto: University of Toronto Press, 1970), p. 124.
29. House of Commons, *Debates*, 20th Parliament, 4th Session, 16 December 1947, p. 337.

30. Towers Memoranda, No. 560, 4 December 1947.
31. House of Commons, *Debates*, 20th Parliament, 4th Session, 16 December 1947, p. 337.
32. Towers Memoranda, No. 561, 5 January 1948, "Meeting with Minister of Finance and Dr. Clark, January 3, 1948," Bank of Canada Archives.
33. Ibid.
34. Ibid.
35. In January 1948 Towers told Abbott of "the difficulties in the way of Central Bank control of credit (and) emphasized the need for a conservative fiscal policy and maintenance of Government cash surplus at the highest possible figure." Towers Memoranda, No. 564, 29 January 1948, "Notes on discussions with Mr. Abbott, January 29, 1948," Bank of Canada Archives.
36. Nevil Ford to G.F. Towers, 15 July 1949, Bank of Canada Archives, DG-401–157, "US. Loan. 2 3/4% due 1974."
37. E.P. Neufeld, *Bank of Canada Operations and Policy* (Toronto: University of Toronto Press, 1958), p. 172n.
38. R.H. Cook to G.F. Towers, 12 March 1951, NAC, RG 19, Volume 589, File 155-1-6.
39. Senate, *Debates*, 21st Parliament, 4th Session, 5 June 1951, p. 532.
40. Ibid., 20 June 1951, p. 600.
41. Ibid., 5 June 1951, p. 532.
42. Senate, *Debates*, 21st Parliament, 5th Session, 26 November 1951, p. 138.
43. Towers Memorandum, No. 678, 13 March 1952, "1952–53 Budget," Bank of Canada Archives.
44. The interest adjustments were calclulated first by determining the market premium for bonds in default using a 3.25 percent yield and a maturity date of June 1, 1945. For unmatured bonds the premium was calculated by using a 3.5 percent yield. The premium payment to bondholders totalled $18.7 million. Those with higher original coupon rates received the highest premium. Second, the bondholders were compensated for the difference between the interest paid on both the bonds in default and unmatured for the nine years (1936–1945) and a 3.25 percent rate for bonds in default and 3.5 for unmatured bonds. Those with lower coupon rates received higher interest payments than those with higher premiums. For example a holder of a 4 percent issue in default received 2 percent interest for nine years and was given an extra payment of 1.25 percent (3.25–2.00) for those nine years. This second calculation yielded an additional payment of $9.9 million. As a result, the bondholders received a significant capital gain (not taxable) but only received interest at the June 1936 market long-term rates. In the final outcome, the Province repaid principal in full but symbolically limited interest payments to the June 1936 rates plus a premium. However, interest was never paid on the notional capital gains at the time of the general default and interest reduction (interest on interest) nor did holders of unmatured bonds receive interest at the contracted rate between the default and the date of the reorganization plan.

45. This huge issue was underwritten in Canada by Wood Gundy, Dominion Securities, A.E. Ames, Nesbitt Thomson, Imperial Bank, Royal Bank, Royal Securities, Midland Securities, Carlile and McCarthy, Melody Sellers, and Tanner and Company. The Canadian underwriters collected a fee of 2.20 percent. The U.S. underwriters were The First Boston Company, Harriman, Ripley; Smith, Barney; Halsey, Stuart; and Canadian dealers Wood Gundy, Dominion Securities, A.E. Ames and Mcleod, Young, Weir. The U.S. commission was 2.5 percent.
46. *An Act to provide for the Reorganization of the Funded Indebtedness of the Province*, S.A. Chapter 247. The Act distinguished between "new securities" that were to be issued under the Act and "outstanding securities" or bonds or debentures issued or guaranteed by the province prior to the default on 1 April 1936. The Provincial Treasurer was empowered to make an offer to the holders of outstanding securities in return for the surrender of their securities and release of all claims for principal, interest in respect of those securities in exchange for money or new securities or a combination. In addition the Cabinet was permitted to raise money by way of a loan or sale of securities to repay moneys to outstanding security holders.

8   POLITICS, PUBLIC DEBT AND DEBT MANAGEMENT

1. Emerson P. Schmidt, "Private versus Public Debt," *American Economic Review* 33, no. 1 (March 1943): 121.
2. The "Paris Club" is a forum for rescheduling of debts of nations in default.
3. See Investment Dealers Association, "Capital Market Statistics," 7 April 1996. During 1995 Government of Canada bond trading stood at $2.992 trillion, provincial bond trading at $235.1 billion, corporate bond trading at $24.5 billion and stock exchange trading at $186.3 billion. More recent data on capital markets activities continues to demonstrate the centrality of government of Canada securities trading. The value of stock trading on the Toronto Stock Exchange and the Montreal Exchange in October 1997 totalled $50.2 billion. That month total domestic money market trading totalled $115 billion ($55.4 billion of which were federal treasury bills), bond trading $107 billion ($101 billion of which was Canada bonds) and $496 billion in strip bond trading and sale and repurchase agreements (Repos). (*Bank of Canada Review* (Winter 1997–98): Tables F3, F11, F12, and F14.) One of the ironies in postwar economic development in western economies has been the expansion of credit, both private and public, which during the 1970s and earlier 1980s resulted in rising inflation. It could be argued therefore that in a narrow sense, C.H. Douglas's idea of social credit as a means of eliminating the gap between workers' wages and the production of the economy has been a key method or policy to preserve economic growth and minimize the effect of postwar recessions.
4. See David T. Beers, "Local Currency Ratings Criteria: An Update," Standard and Poor's *Canadian Focus*, July 1995, pp. 8–15.

5. Interview with Stephen Handfield-Jones, Ottawa, 9 June 1982. This view seemed to be more sacred with personnel at the Bank than with the more academic, policy-making officials at Finance.
6. The Canada Mortgage and Housing Corporation and the Export Credit Insurance Corporation (now the Export Development Corporation) are examples of institutional policies premised on government involvement in the financial marketplace.
7. Interview with Stephen Handfield-Jones, 9 June 1982.
8. Pickersgill and Forster, *The Mackenzie King Record*, Volume 3, pp. 165, 168.
9. This conclusion is consistent with studies by Hugh Heclo and Aaron Wildavsky, *The Private Government of Public Money: Community and Policy Inside British Politics* (Berkeley: University of California Press, 1974) and David Good, *The Politics of Anticipation: The Making of Canadian Tax Policy* (Ottawa: Carleton University, School of Public Administration, 1980) that emphasize shared community and cultural values.
10. See for example "Opening Statement by Gordon G. Thiessen, Governor of the Bank of Canada before the House of Commons Standing Committee on Public Accounts, December 12, 1995," on the flight of worried capital.
11. Harold Groves cites one author who found that in 1925, "the United States exercised financial control over more 'backward nations' than any other country. A common practice for governments with weak credit is to pledge a specific revenue source as security for a loan. Thus El Salvador refunded its national debt in 1923 and obtained credit in the United States by pledging as security 70 per cent of its customs receipts. Bolivia pledged the entire receipts of its customs to New York bankers in 1922." *Financing Government*, Fourth Edition (New York: Henry Holt and Company, 1954), p. 543.
12. Towers Memoranda, No. 130, 5 May 1938, "Rowell–Sirois Commission Submission," Bank of Canada Archives. This is very important as Alberta bondholders had no real remedy to get back the full amount of their interest payments in spite of court rulings on their behalf. The bondholders had no lien against any specific revenues or assets.
13. For example the issue of foreign borrowing in an era of volatile floating exchange rates today remains an issue. On November 5, 1991, the Province of Alberta issued $1,000,000,000 U.S. in Europe. The issue was unhedged. At the time of the issue the U.S./Canada exchange rate was between 1.1253 and 1.1193. So proceeds back to the Province would have been approximately $1.125 billion Canadian. The issue matured on November 5, 1998 and with exchange rates of between 1.52 and 1.55, $1.52 billion to $1.55 billion Canadian was required to redeem the issue. The province issued $500 million U.S. in November 1998 to partially refund the maturing issues. (Alberta Treasury Press Release, 28 October 1998.) *Public Accounts of Alberta*, 1997–98, Volume 1, Schedule 10, p. 38 and *Province of Alberta Annual Form 18-K for the fiscal year ended March 31, 1997*, Statement of

Unmatured Debt, p. 34. The Province however deliberately follows a policy of allowing unhedged U.S. borrowing to range between 32 and 35 percent of the direct debt of the province. *Public Accounts of Alberta,* 1997–98, Volume 1, Note 3, p. 29.

Bibliography

Books, Theses, Monographs, Annual Reports

Adams, Henry C. *Public Debts: An Essay in the Science of Finance.* New York: D. Appleton and Company, 1898.

——. *The Science of Finance. An Investigation of Public Expenditures and Public Revenues.* New York: Henry Holt and Company, 1898.

Alberta Bondholders' Committee. Report to Alberta Bondholders' Committee. *A Survey of the Fiscal Problems of the Province of Alberta in Relation to the Economic and Social Conditions Affecting Them.* 17 July 1936. Typescript.

Binhammer, H.H. and James P. Cairns. *Money, Banking and the Canadian Financial System.* Toronto: McGraw-Hill, 1965.

Borchard, Edwin. *State Insolvency and Foreign Bondholders,* Volume 1. New Haven: Yale University Press, 1951.

Bothwell, Robert, Ian Drummond and John English. *Canada Since 1945: Power, Politics, and Provincialism.* Toronto: University of Toronto Press, 1981.

Bothwell, Robert and William Kilbourn. *C.D. Howe: A Biography.* Toronto: McClelland and Stewart, 1979.

Brecher, I. *Monetary and Fiscal Thought and Policy in Canada, 1919–1939.* Toronto: University of Toronto Press, 1957.

Breckenridge, Roeliff Morton. *The History of Banking in Canada.* Washington: Government Printing Office, 1910.

Bryce, Robert B. *Maturing in Hard Times: Canada's Department of Finance through the Great Depression.* Kingston and Montreal: McGill-Queen's University Press, 1986.

Buchanan, James. *Public Principles of Public Debt.* Homewood, Ill: Richard D. Irwin, Inc., 1958.

Buchanan, James M. and Wagner, Richard E. *Public Debt in a Democratic Society.* Washington: American Enterprise Institute for Public Policy, January, 1967.

Buchanan, James M., Richard E. Wagner and John Burton. *The Consequences of Mr. Keynes: An analysis of the misuse of economic theory for political profiteering, with proposals for constitutional disciplines.* London: The Institute of Economic Affairs, 1978.

Buck, A.E. *Financing Canadian Government.* Chicago: Public Administration Service, 1949.

Canadian Bank of Commerce. *Annual Report.* Toronto: various years.

Carr, Jack L., G.F. Mathewson and N.C. Quigley. *Ensuring Failure: Financial System Stability and Deposit Insurance in Canada.* Toronto: C.D. Howe Institute, 1994.

Cole, G.D.H., ed. *What Everyone Wants to Know about Money.* London: Victor Gollancz, Ltd., 1936.

Dennison, Merrill. *Canada's First Bank.* 2 vols. Toronto: McClelland and Stewart, 1967.

Doak, Ervin John. *Financial Intermediation by Government: Theory and Canadian Experience since 1867.* Unpublished Ph.D. dissertation, University of Toronto, Department of Economics, 1970.

Douglas, C.H. *The Control and Distribution of Production.* London: Cecil Palmer, 1922.

——. *The Monopoly of Credit.* London: Chapman & Hall, Ltd., 1933.

——. *Social Credit.* London: Eyre and Spottiswoode, 1934.

——. *The Alberta Experiment: An Interim Survey.* London Eyre and Spottiswoode, 1937.

Finlay, John L. *Social Credit: The English Origins.* Montreal and London: McGill-Queen's University Press, 1972.

Fullerton, Douglas H. *The Bond Market in Canada.* Toronto: The Carswell Company Limited, 1962.

——. *Graham Towers and His Times.* Toronto: McClelland and Stewart, 1986.

Galbraith, J.A. *The Economics of Banking Operations: A Canadian Study.* Montreal: McGill University Press, 1963.

Good, David A. *The Politics of Anticipation: Making Canadian Federal Tax Policy.* Ottawa: Carleton University, School of Public Administration, 1980.

Granatstein, J.L. *Canada's War. The Politics of the Mackenzie King Government, 1939–1945.* Toronto: Oxford University Press, 1975.

——. *The Ottawa Men: The Civil Service Mandarins 1935–1957.* Toronto: Oxford University Press, 1982.

Grayson, Linda M. *The Formation of the Bank of Canada.* Unpublished Ph.D. dissertation, University of Toronto, Department of History, 1974.

Groves, Harold. *Financing Government.* Fourth Edition. New York: Henry Holt and Company, 1954.

——. *Financing Government.* Sixth Edition. New York: Holt, Rinehart & Winston, 1964.

Hackett, W.T.G. *A Background of Banking Theory.* Toronto: The Canadian Bankers' Association, 1945.

Hawtrey, R.G. *Currency and Credit.* London: Longmans, Green and Company, 1950.

Heclo, Hugh and Aaron Wildavsky. *The Private Government of Public Money. Community and Policy Inside British Politics.* Berkeley: University of California Press, 1974.

Higgins, Benjamin H. *Canada's Financial System in War.* Occasional Paper 19. New York: National Bureau of Economic Research, April 1944.

Holladay, James. *The Canadian Banking System.* Boston: Bankers Publishing Company, 1938.

Hooke, Alf. *30 + 5: I Know, I Was There.* Edmonton: Co-op Press, 1970.

Hooke, A.J. *Looking Backward to Go Forward.* Edmonton: A.J. Hooke, 1980.

Hudson, Michael. *Global Fracture: The New International Economic Order.* New York: Harper and Row Publishers, 1977.

Ibbotson, Roger G. and Rex A. Sinquefield. *Stocks, Bonds, Bills, and Inflation: Historical Returns (1926–1978).* New York: The Financial Analysts Research Foundation, 1979.

Imperial Bank of Canada. *Annual Report.* Toronto: various years.

Innis, H.A. In Mary Q. Innis, ed., *Essays in Canadian Economic History.* Toronto: University of Toronto Press, 1973.

Innis, H.A., Plumptre, A.F.W. et al. *The Canadian Economy and its Problems.* Toronto: Canadian Institute of International Affairs, 1934.

Irving, John A. *The Social Credit Movement in Alberta.* Toronto: University of Toronto Press, 1974.

Jamieson, A.P. *Chartered Banking in Canada.* Toronto: Ryerson Press, 1953.

Johnson, Ivan Charles. *Provincial and Municipal Debt in Canada 1946–1966.* Unpublished Ph.D. dissertation, University of Western Ontario, 1971.

Johnson, Joesph French. *The Canadian Banking System.* Washington: Government Printing Office, 1910.

Kennedy, Paul. *The Rise and Fall of the Great Powers since 1500.* New York: Random House, 1986.

Keynes, J.M. *The Economic Consequences of the Peace.* New York: Harcourt, Brace and Howe, 1920.

Lerner, Abba P. *Economics of Employment.* New York: McGraw-Hill Book Company, Inc., 1951.

Lutz, H.L. *Public Finance.* Fourth Edition. New York and London: Appleton-Century Co., Inc., 1947.

Maclaury, Bruce King. *The Canadian Money Market: Its Development and its Impact.* Harvard University Department of Economics, 1961.

Mackintosh, W.A. *The Economic Background of Dominion Provincial Relations.* Toronto: McClelland and Stewart, 1963.

Macpherson, C.B. *Democracy in Alberta.* Second Edition. Toronto: University of Toronto Press, 1974.

Mallory, James. *Social Credit and the Federal Power in Canada.* Toronto: University of Toronto Press, 1976.

Mandel, Ernest. *Marxist Economic Theory.* Trans. Brian Pearce. London: The Merlin Press, 1968.

McIvor, R. Craig. *Canadian Monetary, Banking and Fiscal Development.* Toronto: Macmillan Company of Canada Limited, 1958.

McQuaig, Linda. *Shooting the Hippo: Death by Deficit and other Canadian Myths.* Toronto: Viking, 1995.

Moody's Investor Service. *Municipal and Government Manual.* New York: various years.

Moulton, Harold G. *The New Philosophy of Public Debt.* Washington: The Brookings Institution, 1943.

Naylor, Tom. *The History of Canadian Business.* 2 vols. Toronto: James Lorimer and Company, 1975.

Neatby, H. Blair. *The Politics of Chaos.* Toronto: Macmillan, 1972.

———. *William Lyon Mackenzie King: 1932–1939, The Prism of Unity.* Toronto and Buffalo: University of Toronto Press, 1976.

Neufeld, E.P. *Bank of Canada Operations and Policy.* Toronto: University of Toronto Press, 1958.

———, ed. *Money and Banking in Canada.* Toronto: Macmillan of Canada, 1964.

———. *The Financial System of Canada.* Toronto: Macmillan of Canada, 1972.

O'Connor, James. *The Fiscal Crisis of the State.* New York: St. Martin's Press, 1973.

Parkinson, J.F., ed. *Canadian Investment and Foreign Exchange Problems.* Toronto: University of Toronto Press, 1940.

Perry, J. Harvey. *A Fiscal History of Canada—The Post-war Years.* Toronto: Canadian Tax Foundation, 1989.

Pickersgill, J.W. *The Mackenzie King Record,* Volume 1, *1939–1944.* Toronto: University of Toronto Press, 1960.

Pickersgill, J.W. and D.F. Forster. *The Mackenzie King Record,* Volume 3, *1945–1946.* Toronto: University of Toronto Press, 1970.

———. *The Mackenzie King Record,* Volume 4, *1947–1948.* Toronto: University of Toronto Press, 1970.

Plumptre, A.F.W. *Central Banking in the British Dominions.* Toronto: University of Toronto Press, 1940.

Rees-Moog, Lord and John Dale Davidson. *The Great Reckoning.* New York: Simon and Schuster, 1993.

The Royal Bank of Canada. *Annual Report.* Montreal: various years.

Safarian, A.E. *Canada's Economy in the Great Depression.* Toronto: University of Toronto Press, 1957.

Sarpkaya, S. *The Money Market in Canada.* Second Edition. Toronto: Butterworth, 1980.

Sayers, R.S. *Central Banking after Bagehot.* Oxford: Clarendon Press, 1957.

Shortt, Adam. *The History of Canadian Banking.* Toronto: Canadian Bankers Association, n.d.

Smith, Adam. *An Inquiry into the Nature and Causes of the Wealth of Nations.* New York: The Modern Library, 1937.

———. *An Inquiry into the Nature and Causes of the Wealth of Nations.* Andrew Skinner, ed. Harmondsworth: Penguin Books, 1970.

Stokes, Milton L. *The Bank of Canada: The Development of Central Banking in Canada.* Toronto: Macmillan Company of Canada Limited, 1939.

Wust, Karl Anton. *Debt Management: Canadian Provinces 1954–1965.* Unpublished M.A. Thesis, Carleton University, Department of Economics, 1967.

Wynne, William H. *State Insolvency and Foreign Bondholders Volume II. Selected Case Histories of Governmental Foreign Bond Defaults and Debt Readjustments.* New Haven: Yale University Press, 1951.

Periodical Articles, Speeches

Agger, E.E. "The Money-Management Conflict in the U.S. Banking Family." *The Journal of the Canadian Bankers' Association* 57, no. 2 (Spring 1950): 99–108.

Allely, J.S. "The Central Bank, Bank Reserves and Interest Rates in Canada." *The Journal of the Canadian Bankers' Association* 41, no. 3 (April 1934): 302–18.

———. "The Stock Market and Depression." *The Journal of the Canadian Bankers' Association* 46, no. 2 (January 1939): 157–65.

———. "Some Aspects of Currency Depreciation." *Canadian Journal of Economics and Political Science* 5, no. 3 (August 1939): 387–402.

Anderson, R.V. "Review Article: Policy for Full Employment." *Canadian Journal of Economics and Political Science* 12, no. 2 (May 1946): 192–203.

Ascah, Robert L. "The Deficit Debate: A Survey and an Assessment." A paper presented to the Canadian Political Science Association Annual Meeting, Winnipeg, June 8, 1986.

———. "Testing Theories of Federalism: The Case of the Financial Sector." A paper delivered to the Annual Meeting of the Canadian Political Science Association, Victoria, 27 May 1990.

Bank of Canada, "Cash Reserve Management and Open Market Operations." In James P. Cairns and H.H. Binhammer, eds., *Canadian Banking and Monetary Policy*, pp. 135–47. Toronto: McGraw-Hill, 1965.

Barber, Clarence. "Canada's Post-War Monetary Policy, 1945–54." In James P. Cairns and H.H. Binhammer, eds., *Canadian Banking and Monetary Policy*, pp. 199–214. Toronto: McGraw-Hill, 1965.

Bates, Stewart. "Classifactory Note on the Theory of Public Finance." *Canadian Journal of Economics and Political Science* 3, no. 2 (May 1937): 161–80.

Beattie, J.R. "Some Aspects of the Problem of Full Employment." *Canadian Journal of Economics and Political Science* 10, no. 3 (August 1944): 328–42.

Beckhart, B.H. "Fewer and Larger Banks." In E.P. Neufeld, ed., *Money and Banking in Canada*, pp. 196–205. Toronto: Macmillan, 1964.

Biggar, F.C. "Canadian Bankers and a Central Bank: An address delivered to the Canadian Political Science Association, May 1933."

———. "Monetary Misconceptions." Speech before the Rotary Club of Montreal, Tuesday, 23 June 1936.

———. "I Promise to Pay." Reprinted from *The Financial Times*.

Bloomfield, Arthur. "The Significance of Outstanding Securities in the International Movement of Capital." *Canadian Journal of Economics and Political Science* 6, no. 4 (November 1940): 495–524.

Bradshaw, Thomas. "Maintenance of public credit and its relation to the present financial position of many Ontario municipalities." *Canadian Chartered Accountant* (February 1935): 119–33.

Britnell, G.E. "The Elliott-Walker Report: A Review." *Canadian Journal of Economics and Political Science* 2, no. 4 (November 1936): 524–32.

Brown, E. Carey. "Fiscal Policy in the Thirties: A Reappraisal." *American Economic Review* 46, no. 4 (December 1956): 857–79.

Bryce, R.B. "The Effects on Canada of Industrial Fluctuations in the United States." *Canadian Journal of Economics and Political Science* 5, no. 3 (August 1939): 373–86.
——. "William Clifford Clark, 1889–1952." *Canadian Journal of Economics and Political Science* 19, no. 3 (August 1953): 413–23.
——. "Borrowing and Debt Management." Unpublished manuscript, January 1982.
Bryden, J.T. "The Effects of Movements of Interest Rates." *Canadian Journal of Economics and Political Science* 3, no. 3 (August 1937): 434–39.
Burkhead, Jesse. "The Balanced Budget." *Quarterly Journal of Economics* 68, no. 2 (May 1954): 191–216.
Canadian Bankers' Association. "Bank Investments." In James P. Cairns and H.H. Binhammer, eds., *Canadian Banking and Monetary Policy*, pp. 268–77. Toronto: McGraw-Hill, 1965.
Clark. W.C. "The Flight from the Gold Standard." *Queen's Quarterly* 38, no. 4. (Autumn 1931): 751–63.
——. "Financial Administration in the Government of Canada." *Canadian Journal of Economics and Political Science* 4, no. 3 (August 1938): 391–419.
Coffin, E. Scott. "The Chartered Banks as a Factor in Canada's Welfare." *The Journal of the Canadian Bankers' Association* 46, no. 1 (October 1938): 53–58.
Coe, V.F. "Dated Stamp Scrip in Alberta." *Canadian Journal of Economics and Political Science* 4, no. 1 (February 1938): 60–91.
Cole, G.D.H. "Money." In G.D.H. Cole, ed., *What Everybody Wants to Know About Money*, pp. 21–63. London: Victor Gollancz, Ltd, 1936.
Curtis, C.A. "The Canadian Monetary Situation." *Journal of Political Economy* 40, no. 3 (June 1932), pp. 314–37.
——. "The Bank of Canada." *The Canadian Forum* 14, no. 164 (May 1934): 289–90.
——. "Dominion Legislation of 1935: An Economist's Review." *Canadian Journal of Economics and Political Science* 1, no. 4 (November 1935): 599–608.
——. "The Canadian Banks and War Finance." In E.P. Neufeld, ed. *Money and Banking in Canada*, pp. 206–17. Toronto: McClelland and Stewart, 1964.
——. "The Canadian Monetary Situation." In E.P. Neufeld, ed. *Money and Banking in Canada*, pp. 218–22. Toronto: McClelland and Stewart, 1964.
Deutsch, J.J. "War Finance and the Canadian Economy 1914–1920." *Canadian Journal of Economics and Political Science* 6, no. 4 (November 1940): 525–42
Domar, Eusey D. "The Burden of the Debt and the National Income." *American Economic Review* 34, no. 4 (December 1944): 798–825.
Douglas, Monteath. "Limitations of the Financial Factor in a War Economy." *Canadian Journal of Economics and Political Science* 7, no. 3 (August 1941): 364–85.
Drummond, I.M. "Life Insurance Companies and the Capital Markets 1890–1914." *Canadian Journal of Economics and Political Science* 28, no. 2 (May 1962): 204–24.
Easterbrook, W. T. "Agricultural Debt Adjustment." *Canadian Journal of Economics and Political Science* 2, no. 3 (August 1936): 390–403.
Eastman, H.C. "Recent Canadian Economic Policy: Some Alternatives." *Canadian Journal of Economics and Political Science* 18, no. 2 (May 1952): 135–45.

Eaton, A.K. "A Central Bank for Canada." *Dalhousie Review* 13, no. 1 (January 1934): 435–50.

Elliott, Courtland. "Bank Cash." *Canadian Journal of Economics and Political Science* 4, no. 3 (August 1938): 432–59.

———. "The Importation of Capital into Canada—Its Effects and the Possibilities of Its Control." In H.A. Innis and A.F.W. Plumptre, eds., *The Canadian Economy and Its Problems*, pp. 223–36. Toronto: Canadian Institute of International Affairs, 1934.

Elliott, Courtland and J.A. Walker. "The Elliott-Walker Report: A Rejoinder." *Canadian Journal of Economics and Political Science* 2, no. 2 (1936): 544–49.

Elliott, G.A. "Dominion Monetary Policy, 1929–1934." *Canadian Journal of Economics and Political Science* 7, no. 1 (February 1941): 88–91.

———. "The Significance of the General Theory of Employment, Interest and Money." *Canadian Journal of Economics and Political Science* 13, no. 3 (August 1947): 372–78.

Forsey, Eugene "Inflation in Canada." *The Canadian Forum* 13, no. 147 (December 1932): 88.

———. "Disallowance: A Contrast." *The Canadian Forum* 18, no. 209 (June 1938): 73–74.

———. "The Budget." *The Canadian Forum* 19, no. 221 (June 1939): 76–77.

Fowke, Vernon. "Economic Effects of the War on the Prairie Economy." *Canadian Journal of Economics and Political Science* 11, no. 3 (August 1945): 373–87.

Gardner, B.C. "Bank Credit and Its Relation to Bank Reserves." *The Journal of the Canadian Bankers' Association* 46, no. 4 (July 1939): 464–75.

Gibson, J. Douglas. "The Changing Character of Bank Assets." *The Journal of the Canadian Bankers' Association* 45, no. 2 (January 1938): 145–54.

Goldenberg, H.C. "Money and Depression." *The Canadian Forum* 14, no. 165 (June 1934): 337–38.

Gordon, Donald. "Some Current Problems." *The Journal of the Canadian Bankers' Association* 47, no. 4 (July 1940): 426–37.

Gordon, H.S. "Central Banking and Responsible Government" *Canadian Journal of Economics and Political Science* 27, no. 1 (February 1961): 13–22.

Gordon, H.S. and Read, L.M. "The Political Economics of the Bank of Canada." *Canadian Journal of Economics and Political Science* 24, no. 4 (November 1958): 465–82.

Grayson. L.M. and J.P. Grayson. "Interest Aggregation and Canadian Politics: The case of the Central Bank." *Canadian Public Administration* 16, no. 4 (Winter 1976): 557–71.

Hackett, W.T.G. "Canada's Optional Payment Bonds." *Canadian Journal of Economics and Political Science* 1, no. 2 (May 1935): 161–70.

———. "The Future of Interest Rates." *Canadian Journal of Economics and Political Science* 3, no. 3 (August 1937): 439–48.

———. "Sinking Funds in the Canadian Capital Market." In J.F. Parkinson, ed., *Canadian Investment and Foreign Exchange Problems*, pp. 204–12. Toronto: University of Toronto Press, 1940.

Hanson, E.J. "Public Finance in Alberta since 1935." *Canadian Journal of Economics and Political Science* 18, no. 3 (August 1952): 322–35.

Hargreaves, E.L. "Debt." In G.D.H. Cole, ed., *What Everybody Wants to Know about Money*, pp. 436–76. London: Victor Gollancz, Ltd., 1936.

Irving, J.A. "The Appeal of Social Credit." *Queen's Quarterly* 60, no. 2 (Summer 1950): 146–60.

——. "The Evolution of the Social Credit Movement." *Canadian Journal of Economics and Political Science* 14, no. 3 (August 1948): 321–41.

Jackman, H.R. "Control of Investment and Proposals for Public Works." In H.A. Innis and A.F.W. Plumptre, eds., *The Canadian Economy and its Problems*, pp. 211–16. Toronto: Canadian Institute of International Affairs, 1934.

Knox, F.A. "The Proposals for a Central Bank." *Queen's Quarterly* 40, no. 3 (August 1933): 424–40.

——. "Canadian War Finance and the Balance of Payments, 1914–18." *Canadian Journal of Economics and Political Science* 6, no. 2 (May 1940): 226–57.

——. "Review Article: The International Gold Standard Reinterpreted." *Canadian Journal of Economics and Political Science* 9, no. 4 (November 1943): 502–7.

Lutz, F.A. "Limitations of Monetary Policy." In James P. Cairns and H.H. Binhammer, eds., *Canadian Banking and Monetary Policy*, pp. 25–40. Toronto: McGraw-Hill, 1965.

MacGibbon, D.A. "Inflation and Inflationism." *Canadian Journal of Economics and Political Science* 1, no. 3 (August 1935): 325–36.

——. "Review Article: Fiscal Policy and Business Cycles." *Canadian Journal of Economics and Political Science* 9, no. 1 (February 1943): 77–82.

MacGregor, D.C. "These Insignificant Budgets." *The Canadian Forum* 14, no. 166 (July 1930): 386–89.

——. "The Threat of Financial Crisis." *The Canadian Forum* 13, no. 150 (March 1933): 206–9.

——. "Outline of the Position of Public Finance: Public Debt." In H.A. Innis and A.F.W. Plumptre, eds., *The Canadian Economy and its Problems*, pp. 55–61. Toronto: Canadian Institute of International Affairs, 1934.

——. "The Problem of the Public Debt in Canada." *Canadian Journal of Economics and Political Science* 2, no. 2 (May 1936): 167–94.

——. "Income and Expenditure in Alberta." *Canadian Journal of Economics and Political Science* 2, no. 4 (November 1936): 533–43.

——. "The Problem of the Price Level in Canada." *Canadian Journal of Economics and Political Science* 13, no. 2 (May 1947): 157–96.

McIvor, R.C. "Canadian Wartime Fiscal Policy, 1939–45." *Canadian Journal of Economics and Political Science* 14, no. 1 (February 1948): 62–93.

McIvor, R. Craig and John H. Panabaker. "Canadian Post-War Monetary Policy 1946–1952." *Canadian Journal of Economics and Political Science* 20, no. 2 (May 1954): 207–26.

Mackintosh, W.A. "Government Economic Policy: Scope and Principles." *Canadian Journal of Economics and Political Science* 16, no. 3 (August 1950): 315–26.

———. "William Clifford Clark and Canadian Economic Policy." *Canadian Journal of Economics and Political Science* 19, no. 3 (August 1953): 411–13.

———. "William Clifford Clark: A Personal Memoir." *Queen's Quarterly* 60, no. 1 (Spring 1953): 1–16.

Macpherson, C.B. "The Political Theory of Social Credit." *Canadian Journal of Economics and Political Science* 15, no. 3 (August 1949): 378–93.

Mallory, J.R. "Disallowance and the National Interest: The Alberta Social Credit Legislation of 1937." *Canadian Journal of Economics and Political Science* 14, no. 3 (August 1948): 342–57.

———. "The Lieutenant-Governor as a Dominion Officer: The Reservation of Three Alberta Bills in 1937." *Canadian Journal of Economics and Political Science* 14, no. 4 (November 1948): 502–7.

Marvin, Donald M. "The Bank of Canada." *The Journal of the Canadian Bankers' Association* 45, no. 1 (October 1937): 25–33.

McGoun, A.F. "Social Credit Legislation: A Survey." *Canadian Journal of Economics and Political Science* 2, no. 4 (November 1936): 512–24.

McLeod, J.A., "Presidential Address," *The Journal of the Canadian Bankers' Association* 40, no. 2 (January 1933).

———. "Presidential Address." *The Journal of the Canadian Bankers' Association* 41, no. 2 (January 1934): 192–98.

Michell, H. "Monetary Reconstruction." *Canadian Journal of Economics and Political Science* 7, no. 3 (August 1941): 339–50.

Nixon, S.E. "The Course of Interest Rates 1929–1937." *Canadian Journal of Economics and Political Science* 3, no. 3 (August 1937): 421–34.

Noble, S.R. "The Monetary Experience of Canada During the Depression." *The Journal of the Canadian Bankers' Association* 45, no. 3 (April 1938): 269–77.

Parkinson, J.F. "Some Problems of War Finance in Canada." *Canadian Journal of Economics and Political Science* 6, no. 3 (August 1940): 403–23.

Plumptre, A.F.W. "The Point of View of a Central Bank." *The Canadian Forum* 13, no. 148 (January 1933): 132–33.

———. "Do We Need Inflation?" *The Canadian Forum* 14, no. 160 (January 1934): 129–31.

———. "Central Banking Machinery and Monetary Policy" In H.A. Innis and A.F.W. Plumptre, eds., *The Canadian Economy and Its Problems*, pp. 192–207. Toronto: Canadian Institute of International Affairs, 1934.

———. "The Evidence Presented to the 'Canadian Macmillan Commission'." *Canadian Journal of Economics and Political Science* 2, no. 1 (February 1936): 54–67.

———. "An Approach to War Finance." *Canadian Journal of Economics and Political Science* 7, no. 1 (February 1941): 1–12.

———. "Keynes in Cambridge." *Canadian Journal of Economics and Political Science* 13, no. 3 (August 1947): 366–71.

———. "Currency Management in Canada." In E.P. Neufeld, ed., *Money and Banking in Canada*, pp. 223–33. Toronto: McClelland and Stewart, 1964.

——. "Constitution of the Bank of Canada." In E.P. Neufeld, ed., *Money and Banking in Canada*, pp. 247–52. Toronto: McClelland and Stewart, 1964.

Ratchford, B.U. "The Burden of the Domestic Debt." *American Economic Review* 32, no. 3 (September 1942): 451–67.

Rogers, A.W. "The Bank of Canada." *The Journal of the Canadian Bankers' Association* 42, no. 1 (October 1934): 24–35.

Roosa, Robert V. "Integrating Debt Management and Open Market Operations." *American Economic Review* 42, no. 2 (May 1952): 214–35.

Royal Commission on Banking and Finance. "The Techniques of Debt Management." In James P. Cairns and H.H. Binhammer, eds., *Canadian Banking and Monetary Policy*, pp. 127–34. Toronto: McGraw-Hill Company of Canada Limited, 1965.

Royal Commission on Banking and Finance. "The Status and Organization of the Bank of Canada." In James P. Cairns and H.H. Binhammer, eds., *Canadian Banking and Monetary Policy*, pp. 96–104. Toronto: McGraw-Hill, 1965.

Sarpkaya, S. "Counting Canada's Banks." Reprint from *The Journal of the Canadian Bankers' Association and ICB Review*. October and December 1978.

Schmidt, Emerson P. "Private versus Public Debt." *American Economic Review* 33, no. 1 (March 1943): 119–21.

Spry, Irene M. "The Royal Commission on Prices." *Canadian Journal of Economics and Political Science* 17, no. 1 (February 1951): 76–84.

Stevenson, Garth. "Federalism and the political economy of the Canadian state." In Leo Panitch, ed., *The Canadian State: Political Economy and Political Power*, pp. 71–100. Toronto: University of Toronto Press, 1977.

Taylor, K.W. "Canadian War-Time Price Controls, 1941–6." *Canadian Journal of Economics and Political Science* 13, no. 1 (February 1947): 81–90.

Towers, Graham F. "Functions, Structure, and Operations of the Bank of Canada." In E.P. Neufeld, ed., *Money and Banking in Canada*, pp. 253–58. Toronto: McClelland and Stewart, 1964.

——. "Post-War Monetary Policy." In James P. Cairns and H.H. Binhammer, eds., *Canadian Banking and Monetary Policy*, pp. 190–99. Toronto: McGraw-Hill, 1965.

Urquhart, M.C. "Public Investment in Canada." *Canadian Journal of Economics and Political Science* 11, no. 4 (November 1945): 535–53.

Wagner, Richard E. "Economic Manipulation for Political Profit: Macroeconomic Consequences and Constitutional Implications." *Kyklos* 30 (1977): 395–410.

Waines, W.J. "Federal Public Finance: Canada." *Canadian Journal of Economics and Political Science* 3, no. 2 (May 1937): 181–96.

Walters, John V. "The Limitations of Monetary Management." *The Journal of the Canadian Bankers' Association* 46, no. 3 (April 1939): 339–45.

Watts, George S. "The origins and background of central banking in Canada." *Bank of Canada Review* (May 1972): 15–27.

——. "The legislative birth of the Bank of Canada." *Bank of Canada Review* (August 1972): 13–26.

———. "The first phase of the Bank of Canada's operations: 1935–39." *Bank of Canada Review* (November 1972): 7–21.
———. "The Bank of Canada during the war years." *Bank of Canada Review* (April 1973): 3–17.
Whalen, Hugh. "Social Credit Measures in Alberta." *Canadian Journal of Economics and Political Science* 18, no. 4 (November 1952): 500–517.
Wooldridge, Philip. "Financing activities of provincial governments and their enterprises," *Bank of Canada Review* (Spring 1996): 13–29.
Wright, David McC. "Mr. Ratchford on the Burden of the Debt." *American Economic Review* 33, no. 1 (March 1943): 115–19.

Newspapers Consulted

The Calgary Herald
The Edmonton Bulletin
The Financial Post
The Globe and Mail
The Monetary Times
The Western Producer

Government Documents, Reports, Commissioned Studies

Alberta

Alberta Taxation Inquiry Board. *Report of the Alberta Taxation Inquiry Board on Provincial and Municipal Taxation.* Edmonton: A. Shnitka, King's Printer, 30 November 1935.
Bureau of News and Information. "Democracy Denied." Edmonton: n.d.
Executive Council. *The Case for Alberta.* Edmonton: 1938.
Treasury Department. *Public Accounts of Alberta.* Edmonton: various years.
Viner, Jacob. *The Debt Problem of the Government of the Province of Alberta—A Report submitted to the Provincial Treasurer.* August 1939. (typescript).

Canada

Bank of Canada. *Annual Report of the Governor of the Bank of Canada and Statement of Accounts.* Ottawa: Bank of Canada, various years.
———. *Reports on the Financial Position of the Provinces of Manitoba, Saskatchewan, and Alberta.* Ottawa: Bank of Canada, 7 April 1937.
———. *Submissions by the Bank of Canada to the Royal Commission on Banking and Finance.* Ottawa, 31 May 1962.
———. "Canada Savings Bonds." *Bank of Canada Review* (October 1977): 23–31.
———. "Government of Canada treasury bills," *Bank of Canada Review* (May 1972): 3–13.
———. "Treasury Bills—what they are and how the weekly auction works." Reprinted from the *CBA Bulletin* (April 1980).
"Government of Canada direct marketable bonds." Reprint from *Bank of Canada Review* (March 1980).

Bates, S. *Financial History of Canadian Governments: A Study prepared for the Royal Commission on Dominion-Provincial Relations.* Ottawa: King's Printer, 1939.
Department of Finance. *Public Accounts.* Ottawa: King's Printer, various years.
———. *The Federal Deficit in Perspective.* Ottawa: April 1983.
Dominion Bureau of Statistics. *Canada Year Book.* Ottawa: Dominion Bureau of Statistics, various years.
———. *National Accounts: Income and Expenditures, 1926–1956.* Ottawa: Dominion Bureau of Statistics, 1958.
Hood, William C. *Financing of Economic Activity in Canada.* Royal Commission on Canada's Economic Prospects. Ottawa: Queen's Printer, 1958.
Knox, F.A. *Dominion Monetary Policy 1929–34: A Study prepared for the Royal Commission on Dominion-Provincial Relations.* Ottawa: King's Printer.
MacGregor, D.C., J.B. Rutherford, G.E. Britnell, and J.J. Deutsch. *National Income: A Study prepared for the Royal Commission on Dominion-Provincial Relations.* Ottawa: King's Printer, 1939.
Mackintosh, W.A. *The Economic Background of Dominion-Provincial Relations: A Study prepared for the Royal Commission on Dominion-Provincial Relations.* Ottawa: King's Printer, 1939.
Parliament. House of Commons. *Debates.* 1930–1952.
———. *Minutes of the Proceedings and Evidence of the House of Commons Standing Committee on Banking and Commerce.*
Parliament. Senate. *Debates.* 1930–1952.
Royal Commission on Banking and Currency. *Report.* Ottawa: King's Printer, September 1933.
———. *Proceedings.* August-September, 1933.
Royal Commission on Banking and Finance. *Report.* Ottawa: Queen's Printer, 1964.
———. *Proceedings.* 1962.
Royal Commission on Dominion-Provincial Relations. *Report.* Ottawa: King's Printer, May 1940.
———. *Public Accounts Inquiry. Province of Quebec. Comparative Statistics on Public Finance, 1913, 1921, 1925–1937.* Appendix E.
———. *Public Accounts Inquiry. Province of Saskatchewan. Comparative Statistics on Public Finance, 1913, 1921, 1925–1937.* Appendix H.
———. *Public Accounts Inquiry. Province of Alberta. Comparative Statistics on Public Finance, 1913, 1927, 1925–1937.* Appendix J. Revised.

ARCHIVES

Bank of Canada Archives. Ottawa, Ontario.
The Bank of Nova Scotia Archives. Toronto, Ontario.
Provincial Archives of Alberta. Edmonton, Alberta.
Public Archives of Canada. Ottawa, Ontario.

Background Interviews

Bryce, Robert B. Former Deputy Minister of Finance, Government of Canada. Ottawa.
Garner, John. Former senior official, Department of Finance, Government of Canada. Ottawa.
Gunn, N.H. Former Honorary Chairman, Bell, Gouinlock & Company. Toronto.
Handfield-Jones, Stephen. Former senior official, Department of Finance and Bank of Canada. Ottawa.
Hooke, Alfred J. Former Cabinet Minister, Province of Alberta. Edmonton.
Manning, Senator Ernest C. Former Premier and Provincial Treasurer, Province of Alberta. Edmonton.
McKibbin, Ralph B. Former Deputy Governor, Bank of Canada. Ottawa.
MacLaughlin, W. Earle. Former Chairman, The Royal Bank of Canada. Montreal.
Watts, George S. Former senior official, Bank of Canada. Ottawa.

Index

Aberhart, William, 60–63
Abbott, Hon. D.C., 121, 123–26
Adams, Henry C., 16
Aird, Sir John, 32
Alberta
    Bank of Canada role, 55–56, 58
    debt moratoria legislation, 65, 67, 71–76, 167 n.46
    default, xii, 61–63, 140–42
    economy, 54–55
    loan council, 62–63
    prosperity certificates, 167 n.48
Alberta Bondholders Committee, 67
Alberta's Debt Reorganization. *See* Debt Reorganization, Alberta
Alberta Taxation Inquiry Board, 56
Aldrich, Winthrop, 122–23
allotments, 27, 87–88

Baird, Senator A.B., 128
Bank of Canada, 18–21, 25, 30, 157 n.19, 160 n.24. *See also under* Alberta *and* Canadian Banker's Association
Bank of England, 157 n.21
Bank of Montreal, 20, 26, 61, 90–92
Bank of Nova Scotia, 26, 32, 68, 70, 113
Bank of Toronto, 113–14
banks and banking
    Alberta, 66–76
    Canadian federalism, 70–71
    deposit certificates, 108–14
    nature of, 22–25
    profits, 112
    structure of, 26–27
Bennett, Rt. Hon. Richard B., 5, 34–35, 40–41, 43, 49, 51, 143, 157 n.19
Blackmore, J.H., 98
bonds
    call feature, 3, 58
    gold bonds, 5–7
    optional payment, 37–39, 57–58
    perpetuals, 82–83
    tax-free, 43, 163 n.73
    Victory, 9–10, 105–7, 122, 127, 136
Bracken, John, 66, 123
Bradshaw, Thomas, 58
Bryce, Robert B. (Bob), 66, 111, 120
Budden, W.H., 84–85
Burr, F.G., 68, 74, 169 n.77

Calgary Albertan, 67
Calgary Herald, 67
Campbell, M.N., 36
Canada Savings Bonds, 119–21
Canadian Bankers' Association, 14, 25–26
    Alberta, 71–76
    Bank of Canada, 14, 48, 71–76, 110–14
    loan negotiations, 48, 110–14
Canadian Bank of Commerce, 26, 32
Canadian National Railways, 7, 38, 170 n.90
Casgrain, Senator J.P.B., 157 n.21

Casselman, F.C., 98
Clark, W. Clifford, 136, 157 n.19
   depression, 47–48, 65–66, 79, 82, 85
   post-war, 117, 120
   wartime, 96–97, 102, 108
Cockcroft, Charles, 62–63
Cockeram, A., 121
Coldwell, M.J., 99
commissions, 85–86, 104, 172 n.15
conscription of capital, 99, 111
Coote, G.G., 36
credit rating agencies, xii, 131, 154 n.8
Curtis, C.A., 118

debt management
   constraints, 3–4, 37–39, 51–53, 57–58, 76–80, 89–92, 121–24, 137–40
   defined, 2
   international, 5–6, 49–52, 76–80, 121–25, 139–40, 183 n.13
   objectives, 2–3
   parliamentary debates, 36–42, 98–101, 121–24, 128
   provincial, 37–39, 165 n.14
   refunding, 42–45, 89–92
   wider distribution, 81–94, 99–100, 105–7, 121–24, 128
Debt Reorganization, Alberta, 129–31, 181 n.44, 182 n.45
default
   Alberta, xii, 61–63, 140–42
   general, 34, 160 n.17, 183 n.11
   municipal, 36
deficit finance, xii–xiii
deposit certificates, 108–14
depression, 31–36
disallowance, 72–73, 77–78
Dobson, S.B., 70, 75–76, 110, 112–13
Dodds, Jackson, 48–49, 90–91
Dominion Bureau of Statistics, 33–34
Douglas, Major C.H., 53, 61–62, 182 n.3

Dunning, Hon. Charles, 62–63, 65, 86, 90–91

Edmonton Journal, 67
Euler, Senator E.D., 128
exchange crisis, 121–25, 134
Exchange Fund Account, 83
Eximbank, 123–24

Ferguson, Hon. George, 49–50
finance capital, 16–17, 76–80, 114–16, 137–40
Finance, Department of, 17–18
Financial Post, 151 n.21
Ford, Nevil, 93, 126–27
Fry, Mills, Spence & Company, 86

gold standard, 34–35, 159 n.5
Gordon, Walter, 114
Gouinlock, R.W., 87–88
Gundy, J.H., 42

Haig, Senator John, 128
Hansen, Alvin H., 80
Hanson, R.B., 100
Harrison, G.L., 93
Heaps, A.A., 36
Henderson, K.A., 82, 89–90, 92
Hepburn, Mitchell, 40, 161 n.31, 168 n.69
Hoadley, George, 58, 60–61
Hooke, Alf J., 61
Howe, Hon. C.D., 21
Huckvale, Keith, 129
Hynkla, Anthony, 98

Ilsley, J.L., 101, 110–11
Imperial Bank of Canada, 60–61, 165 n.21
Imperial Conference 1937, 77
inflation, 3, 97–98, 118
Innis, H.A., 1

interest rates, 41–49, 98–100, 102, 104, 125–26, 165 n.14
investment bankers *and/or* dealers, 26–29, 35, 85–89
Irvine, William, 40

Keynes, John Maynard, 1
King, William Lyon Mackenzie, 39, 65, 97, 99, 122, 138, 155 n.13, 180 n.28
Knowles, Vernon, 69

Landeryou, J.C., 41–42
Loan Council, 62–63, 79, 171 n.96, n.97
Low, Solon, 129
Lynch-Staunton, Senator George, 39–40

Macdonnell, J.M., 121
MacGregor, Donald Chalmers, 33–34, 54
Mackintosh, W.A., 103
Magor, R.J., 56, 61, 165 n.23
Mallory, J.R., 63
Mandel, Ernest, 23
Manning, Ernest C., 129, 165 n.23
Manitoba, Province of, 64, 66, 80
Maynard, Lucien, 71
McGeer, Gerry, 39, 168 n.69
McIvor, R. Craig, 32–33
McLeod, D.I., 104
McMeans, Senator L., 41
McMichael, R.C., 68
Midland Securities, 87
Milner, H.R., 67–68, 73
Monetary Times, The, 71, 168 n.8
money market, 14–15, 182 n.3
Moody's Investors Service, xii, 131, 148, 154 n.8
Morgan, Harry, 79, 115
Morgan Stanley, 20, 22, 87, 93–94, 139, 173 n.30

National War Finance Committee, 101–7
Needham, Joseph, 41–42
Nivisons and Company, 50–52, 139

Nixon, Stanley, 102–3
Noble, S.R., 46, 64
Norman, Sir Montagu, 77, 157 n.21

Ontario Hydro, 40, 52, 73, 161 n.31

padding, 27, 85–86
Patterson, H.F., 70
Pearson, Lester B., 77, 122
Percival, J.F., 58–60, 129
Pitfield, Ward C., 35, 87
Province of Ontario Savings Office, 161 n.30
public debt
  distribution of, 2–3, 9–11, 16
  foreign debt, 4–6
  interest on, 7–8
  in relation to war, 95–98
  level of, 6–8

Quelch, Victor, 100–101

repatriation of debt, 4–6,
Rhodes, E.N., 41–44, 46–48, 51
Royal Bank of Canada, 26, 61
Rowe, Swann and Company, 50

Savard, J.E., 86
Saskatchewan, Province of, 64, 66, 72, 80
Sayers, R.S., 14–15
Securities Investment Account, 118, 126–28
Sellar, Watson, 33, 43, 45–46, 136
Shaw, F.D., 100–101
Smith, Adam, 13, 22–23
Social Credit, 41–42, 60–63, 71–76, 98–101
Special Names, 105–7
Spinney, George W., 67, 103–5, 114
stabilization account. *See* Securities Investment Account
St. Amour, J.A., 84
Standard and Poor's, xii

taxation, 51–52, 96–97, 114–15, 163 n.73
Tilley, W.N., 68, 72–73
Towers, Graham Ford, ii, 15, 19–21, 46, 58–61, 64, 66, 70–71, 76, 78–86, 90–92, 99, 103, 107–14, 120, 122–23, 125–29, 181 n.35

underwriting, 21–22, 26–27, 88–89

Walters, Chester, 108, 115
War Savings Committee. *See* National War Finance Committee
Wedd, S.M., 112
Wood, A.R., 115
Wright, P.E., 99–100